Ten Conversations
You Must Have With
Your Son

Ten
Conversations You Must Have With Your Son

Preparing Your Son for
a Happy and Successful Life

Tim Hawkes

A TarcherPerigee Book

tarcherperigee

An imprint of Penguin Random House LLC
375 Hudson Street
New York, New York 10014

First published in Australia and New Zealand by Hachette Australia Pty Ltd, 2014
First published in the United States of America by TarcherPerigee 2016

Most TarcherPerigee books are available at special quantity discounts for bulk purchase for sales
promotions, premiums, fund-raising, and educational needs. Special books or book excerpts also can
be created to fit specific needs. For details, write: SpecialMarkets@penguinrandomhouse.com.

ISBN 9780143109488

Printed in the United States of America
3 5 7 9 10 8 6 4 2

Neither the publisher nor the author is engaged in rendering professional advice or services to the
individual reader. The ideas, procedures, and suggestions contained in this book are not intended as a
substitute for consulting with your physician. All matters regarding your health require medical
supervision. Neither the author nor the publisher shall be liable or responsible for any loss or damage
allegedly arising from any information or suggestion in this book.

While the author has made every effort to provide accurate telephone numbers, Internet addresses,
and other contact information at the time of publication, neither the publisher nor the author assumes
any responsibility for errors or for changes that occur after publication. Further, the publisher does not
have any control over and does not assume any responsibility for author or third-party Web sites or
their content.

This book is dedicated
to my son, Peter,
and his son, William

Contents

Introduction

My motive for writing this book was a growing concern that too many boys seem starved of essential knowledge; the sort of knowledge that can only come from good conversations about good things with good people. The assurance of love, the teaching of life skills, the sharing of wisdom seemed not to happen in the lives of many of the boys I came across as an educator. Small wonder. In an age characterized by frantic pace, incessant obligation and multiple diversions, meaningful conversation between sons and parents is now being measured in seconds a day rather than in minutes.

Making time to talk with a son is one thing; knowing what to talk about is another. In this, parents need not feel discouraged, because each has a compendium of experience that should not be underestimated. Having acknowledged this, teaching a son the skills to enable him to cope with life's many challenges is not always easy. Intergenerational differences and a natural dislike by the younger of advice given by the older means that some ingenuity is needed. This book explores *how* to share with a son as well as *what* to share.

Many people are talking to our sons, but are they the right people and are they giving the right advice? In this book, you will learn what to say to your son about specific matters such as sex, money, health and goals, as well as how to deal with broader, more difficult issues such as character and death. These matters cannot be left to chance. There is a curriculum of life skills, knowledge and wisdom that needs to be passed from one generation to another, and *Ten Conversations You Must Have With Your Son* was written to help with this mission.

My credentials in writing this book are not found in the headship of schools or the authoring of books. They come from being a father whose failure has filled these pages with painful lessons. I have also had the pleasure of witnessing inspirational parenting by others and have listened to conversations that have stimulated and transformed a boy. These stories I share, as I do ancient wisdom and modern thinking on what must be said to our sons.

Tim Hawkes

Why?

To suggest the sorts of conversations a parent should have with their son is not much short of arrogant. Each son, each parent and each family is unique in what it is they need to talk about, so providing a formulaic list of required conversation is as presumptuous as it is unhelpful.

Then there is the matter of the number of conversations. *Ten—you must be joking!* You should be having thousands, even tens of thousands of conversations with your son, with each discourse delicately nuanced so that it is uniquely relevant to the situation.

The only plea I can enter to both of these charges is: *guilty.*

However, I maintain my direction and purpose. Why? Because of a wearying amount of evidence that too many of our sons are starting adulthood with insufficient mentoring. An unacceptable number appear to be unable to cope well with their growing independence. Some progress through the decades after childhood in a state of perpetual adolescence, unwilling to commit, unwilling to assume responsibility and unwilling to grow up. Addicted to the trivial, preoccupied with pleasure and suffering domestic dyslexia, several are making a mess of their relationships and a mess of their lives.

In nearly a quarter of a century as a headmaster, I have seen too many parents frustrated by their inability to connect with their sons, and too many sons hobbled by a lack of communication with their parents. The generation gap has long been recognized as the culprit in preventing good conversation. Many parents are not always comfortable communicating with their teenage "twitterati" using contemporary means. It is not just because they have no idea what "lol" means. It is because they have limited opportunity to talk and such opportunity they do have is often rushed and inadequate. Playgroups, preschools and primary schools steal their children away from them. Then televisions, computer games and social-networking sites abduct their offspring. Thereafter, the parent must line up behind the secondary school teacher, football coach, best friend and girlfriend to speak to their son.

The information blackout between generations is not assisted by the growth of independent living in the home. Some parents escape the noisy chatter of offspring by bunkering down in a parents' retreat, shutting themselves in a study or hiding behind a newspaper. Many sons are no better. They protect themselves from the verbal intrusion of their parents by ensuring their bedroom is equipped with enough electronic self-sufficiency to free them from the obligation to speak to anyone except the cat.

In addition, any possible place of conversation in the home is often rendered sterile. The dining table is used only when guests arrive. Chairs are aimed at the TV instead of each other. Ensuite bathrooms cater for independence. Backyards are shrunk to a size that frustrates most opportunities for a chat with Dad while playing a game of catch.

The time has come for parents and sons to recover the value of regular conversation with each other. Failure to do so will impoverish both, and hinder the transfer of wisdom and experience from one generation to the next.

*

I have three reasons to claim that my credentials in writing on this topic are strong. They come from my failure as a father, my betrayal as a headmaster and my inadequacy as a son.

Failure as a father

As a father, I have sought for too much significance outside the home and not enough significance within it. I take little comfort from the fact that I may not be the only father who has erred in this way. The trouble is that many of us dads become so consumed by the task of collecting twigs for the nest we rarely find time to sit in it. Some of us are not content with producing 2.3 children. We must also produce 1.5 cars and 1.3 houses. The effort required to do this can lead to us being marginalized in our own home. Just when we realize the error of our ways and seek to increase our significance in our son's life, the chick has grown up. The father then becomes an embarrassment or, even worse, irrelevant.

I recall a scene with my son, Peter, some 20 or so years ago when he was ten. In the afternoon, Peter had come into my study wearing a baggy green cricket cap that swamped his tousled locks. He was lugging his cricket bag. The impudence of dragging the trivial into a room made serious by my shelves of learning irritated me.

Would I like to play some cricket?

Stupid question. Did the boy not have eyes in his head?

"I'm sorry, Pete, I have to finish this work. Perhaps later."

His words said it didn't matter, but his body language said that it did. He crumpled into resigned acceptance and turned to leave, but retreat was blocked by his mother.

"I'm sure that if we give Dad two minutes to come to a convenient stop, he'll come out and play." It was not a suggestion—it was a command. Her level eyes were a mixture of accusation and judgment that hinted at the possibility of an unpleasant sentence if compliance was not forthcoming. They were angry eyes; eyes that asked how I could forego my responsibilities to my family in my quest to fulfill my responsibilities as a head of a school.

Did they not know that playing happy games was not an act that was going to give me joyful release from my labors? My work would not go away if I did not do it. It would sit there and wait for me to return. When I did get back, it would have increased and the time available to complete it would have decreased. *Damn*.

"Okay—let's do it, Pete," I said with barely concealed ill grace. But the gods were listening. Painful judgment and a guilty redemption were to follow.

"I hit Dad in the nuts," proclaimed Peter triumphantly at dinner that night.

An inability to understand the pain associated with this event left Peter's two younger sisters unmoved.

"It hurt," advised my ten-year-old son, in an effort to explain the significance.

Too right it had hurt! When he bowled his first ball at me, it had looped into the air, bit into the ground and kicked up. I had expected a rubbish delivery but had been given a gem of a ball. As I crumpled to the dirt, my son danced with delight. I had been conquered.

"Did you have a good time?" asked my elder daughter helpfully.

Peter looked at Alicia with some confusion before grinning and saying, "Yeah . . . Dad groaned a lot."

Reflecting on the dinner conversation a little later, I thought of a number of things. The first was that my son was growing up at a pace of which I was not aware. The second was that I should wear a protective cup next time I played cricket with him. The third was that I had loved playing cricket with my son and, despite very few words being spoken, we'd had a long conversation in the nets.

The deliveries I bowled at my son were questions. "How are you going?" Each ball probed and tested. A short, sharp delivery on his leg stump, always a hard shot to play, rapped him hard on his pads. A wry smile said, "I can take it, Dad." A confident stroke played by Peter to mid-wicket said, "I'm growing up, Dad." A dream of a ball that snuck its way through my defenses and hit me in the balls said, "You don't know me as well as you should, Dad."

Tucking Peter into bed that night, I ruffled his hair and said, "Goodnight." Peter said much more. He said, "Dad, thanks for spending time with me today. I know you had other things to do and I know that you really wanted to get on with your work, but I loved it when you were prepared to put your work on hold and play cricket with me. I hope you are proud of me. I hope you like me. I hope you think I am growing up." Of course, Peter did not actually say these words. He put things far more concisely. He said, "Thanks, Dad."

Why had I not done this sort of thing more often?

Betrayal as a headmaster

My betrayal as a headmaster was realized several years ago after reading an observation made by a philosopher who operated some 400 years BC. When Aristippus of Cyrene was asked what sons should be taught, he replied, "Those things which they will use when men."

What, then, were the things I needed to teach the boys in my school? What were the certainties in life that they would face as men and how well was I, as an educator, preparing them for these certainties?

Of course, the certainties in life are well known. They are death and taxes!

I reflected on the recent death of my parents and concluded that my boys, when confronted with the death of a loved one, would, like me, probably end up in an emotionally fragile state and not be able to contribute meaningfully to the logistics of the funeral or any associated tasks. Like me, they would probably not know what probate was and whom they had to notify about the death. Like me, they were unlikely to know the duties of an executor and may not be able to cope well with their own grief.

Then there was the issue of taxes—a topic that can be expanded to financial literacy. I looked at my students and saw that far too many of them were becoming financial victims. In their use of credit cards, in their management of debt, in deciding which phone plan to use, too many were making poor choices. Even though money is supposed to make the world go round, I wasn't teaching the majority of my boys anything about it. I was not teaching them to budget, to save or to escape from a perpetual fiscal reliance on their parents.

How *was* I actually preparing my boys for the real world? They were leaving school blessed with a command of quadratic equations, knowledge of the split infinitive and a capacity to list the major exports of Botswana. As worthy as these things are, it appeared to me that I was at risk of losing sight of those things that a boy would need as an adult. Aristippus would not have been pleased with me.

I sought solace in the fact that I was hamstrung in what I taught by a state examination system that was generally designed to assist with selection into tertiary education. Warming to the task of self-defense, I also noted that there had been a surge in accountability reporting—school league tables, and so on—which required me to concentrate on the examinable curriculum. In short, I had to play the game.

But, in my heart, I knew I was betraying my students.

This led me to think of those things that a boy might need to know when he grew up. Conclusions to this question varied, but the following ten topics tended to stay on my list longer than most:

1. The ability to give and receive love.
2. The ability to know yourself and what you believe.
3. The ability to choose an appropriate moral code.
4. The ability to accept responsibility.
5. The ability to live in a community.
6. The ability to achieve a worthwhile goal.
7. The ability to handle intimacy and sex.
8. The ability to manage financial matters.
9. The ability to stay well.
10. The ability to be resilient.

Other topics came and went on this list. A whole swag of life skills could be added, such as how to cook, clean, iron, mend, garden and maintain a car. I also thought that teaching the art of communication was important. But even my ten-point list began to illustrate something of the chasm between what a boy at my school needed to know and what he was usually being taught. In my educational offering, I was failing my students.

With this in mind, I began to look at ways and means to drip-feed more life skills into the school curriculum. This needed to be done carefully. Things could be taken too far. I did not want my boys to become like Byron's Don Juan:

> He learned the arts of riding, fencing, gunnery,
> And how to scale a fortress—or a nunnery.

There was limited virtue in training boys to scale nunnery walls. However, there were other, more important life skills that could be taught. As a headmaster, I had the power to craft a curriculum that prepared a boy not just for an exam but also for life . . . and, perhaps, even death.

Inadequacy as a son

My inadequacy as a son rested in the fact that I was not immune to the toxic touch of testosterone, and this, of course, meant the temporary loss of speech in my teen years. By any stretch of the imagination, I could hardly have been described as one who had contributed richly to dialogue with my parents. Such utterances I did share were little more than Neanderthal grunts.

Other sons have shared this problem. When I was the principal of a coeducational school, I would look out of my study window at lunchtime. Most boys were on the football field or playing handball in the quadrangle. Those boys not in packs grunting at each other were in isolation, chatting to a voiceless avatar on their computer.

By contrast, the girls were seated in small circles. They were talking to each other. A lot. Their conversation was rich and healing. Sometimes, one of the girls would cry. There would be hugs, advice and comfort given before the group returned to their classes having exercised their verbal skills and been restored by its healing power. The boys would follow some time later, odorous and mute. When I was a boy, I had been no different.

Overvaluing words

What might be said to a boy to encourage him to improve his communication skills? In asking this, we need to recognize that eloquence is hardly necessary when playing a game of "murder ball." We must also note that, when a ball is thrown, other social connections are formed that should not be trivialized. The arc of its passage can be a powerful conversation—as can a cricket ball bowled in the nets. There is a place for banter and primeval noises. It is not always necessary for a conversation between a parent and a son to be on matters of great consequence.

Neither is it necessary to speak like a typewriter. Remember those? There are some whose auditory assault on their sons can only be tolerated by their sons engaging in a noise-abatement program or "zoning out." This tactic has the happy effect of reducing unwanted dialogue to the ambient hum of an air conditioner. As parents, we need to be careful not to overstate the value of words. There is a time for silence and there is truth in the saying that there are times we need to say less in order to be heard more.

That said, there is also truth in the observation that sometimes we need to say more to our sons, and our sons need to speak more to their parents.

*

I was only in the restaurant because someone else was paying. It was the sort of place you would go to if you had a gold mine, a 50th birthday to celebrate or someone you wanted to impress. In this case, it was the latter. A parent wanted to persuade me of the better virtues of his son—who was in some serious trouble at my school—hence the heavily crystalled table, linen napkins and regimented cutlery.

I was distracted from the menu (no prices) by the arrival of food at a nearby table. The plates were massive, but no amount of colored sauce artfully drizzled on the plate could disguise the fact that their portions were minute. Seated and sullen were two teenage boys and their parents. The boys were not long in clearing their plates. They then fidgeted. Neither attempted to voice an opinion about the food—or anything else, for that matter. Both slumped silently into their chairs. The shadow of their caps could not conceal their boredom, so it was not long before one built walls using sugar cubes and the other began to massage his cell phone.

The parents were equally mute. He conducted an imaginary symphony with a salt spoon (I did say it was an expensive place). She smiled an *isn't-it-nice* smile. Except it wasn't. The lack of conversation had resulted in a dismal evening for her that could not be improved by a $250-per-head meal.

They left shortly after a Bombe Alaska was disarmed. One boy returned a minute later to pick up some forgotten earphones. "Fuck," he said. It was the first word I had heard him utter all evening.

*

A lack of good conversation is not limited to the starchy environment of a high-priced restaurant. The local pub, where a good feed can be had for $25 per head, can disappoint. They can be places where patrons go to watch. They watch in groups of one as the poker machine tumbles their fortune. They watch the game on the big-screen TV. They join the lucky draw for the meat tray before inoculating their loneliness with another drink and going home to a sleeping household.

Perhaps, this is all that is needed—to hear noise and to watch others. Noise suggests a connection with life. The beauty of noise is that it offers engagement without demand. You can listen without contributing, until it is your turn for a round of drinks. If pressed for a verbal confirmation, then "Damn right" usually suffices. If it doesn't, then "Hell no" will often serve. No—the problem is not the place. It's the people. It's us.

*

Inadequate conversation is not just to be found outside the home; it can be found within the home too. The mid-week meal can be a silent affair, with the TV providing the only commentary. Even the weekend dinner party can be a limited place of colloquy.

The table is set, the napkins folded and the cutlery laid out with regimental precision. Attention is also paid to mood. The surround-sound system is programmed to create the canvas of noise on which to paint the evening's conversation.

Then there is the choice of wine. Each bottle is selected with care. The labels of the better bottles face the guests. Those that are cheaper face the wall. In disgrace.

The central agenda is, of course, the meal. Menu options are considered and rejected. Try something brave and new or stick with the tried and tested? Possibilities are tested on the family. The "yuck" monitor is employed and a careful scrutiny made of the residue on plates.

Then follows the shopping, the unpacking, unwrapping, uncertainty, preparation and presentation.

Such care. Such devotion. But a key ingredient to the success of such evenings is often neglected—the conversation. We can treat the palate of our guests with reverence but their intellect with disdain. No wonder our sons sit silent and sullen at the meal table. Their bovine behavior is entirely understandable if parents have allowed the dining table to become nothing more than a feed lot.

AN IDEA

Invite conversation to dinner

Although breakfasts can be frantic and lunches often consumed in different locations, it is often possible for a family to dine together in the evening. These meals should be seen as precious times. To this end, I share the following tips to encourage good conversation at the dinner table:

- Dine together at the same time and in the same place.
- Turn off the TV.
- Ban cell phones, electronic games and all social-networking devices from the dining table.
- Switch phones to silent during meal times.
- Make the dining table attractive. Candles and simple table decorations can help.
- Choose a seating arrangement that allows family members to face each other.
- Distribute tasks so one person (usually Mom) is not always the one leaving the table to serve and clear away.
- Encourage each family member to share something about their day.
- Be prepared to discuss things such as what has been in the news.
- Establish the meal time as a "putdown-free zone" where teasing, freeze-outs and general displays of antisocial behavior are not tolerated.
- Don't rush the meal. Slow food can be more satisfying than fast food.

Making conversation

Having assembled the clan at the dinner table, what do you then talk about? To help a son improve his conversation skills, a parent can encourage him to think of a topic. The acronym TOPIC—**T**hem **O**ccasion **P**eople **I**nterest **C**ompliment—is a way of remembering how a boy might avoid becoming an utter bore when conversing with others.

Them

Center on THEM. Curiously, people find conversation enormously improved when it is centered on *them* and rather less compelling when it is centered on *you*. Ask questions, invite opinion, encourage reflection. You may find that this has the happy effect of improving your reputation as a conversationalist.

Occasion

Offer thoughts that relate to the OCCASION. If turning 16 has brought people together, say something about turning 16. If a farewell to Year 12 has brought people together, say something about the Year 12 group. If it is lunch in the playground, exercise your negotiation skills by swapping the less appealing bits of your lunch for the more appealing bits of another's.

People

Fuel can be added to a flagging conversation by talking about PEOPLE. It need not be a fascinating yarn or some delicious gossip. It can be as simple as inquiring, "Which player is going to have the greatest impact on the Grand Final?" or as complex as, "I note His Honor, Justice Powderwig, is present at our gathering. I understand he is currently hearing a case of Internet extortion by a bunch of 16-year-old hackers." PEOPLE are interesting.

Interest

Go on . . . you can do it! There *is* something of INTEREST you can talk about. Have another think—what has caught your eye in the news? What event in your life do you feel others might find interesting? Everyone has a story. Everyone has been wowed by something. Everyone has a "this makes me mad" topic or a "chuckling moment" hidden away somewhere. However, be sensitive. An earnest interjection on the importance of winning the next game of interschool football, when conversation has been meandering pleasantly on the merits of planting hydrangeas over azaleas in the garden, can come across as a bit forced.

Compliment

Paying a person a COMPLIMENT is a great trick to building a reputation as being exceedingly good company. It need not be obsequious and it must not be forced. It is worth choosing the topic of your compliment carefully. It may be a great toupee, but . . . The compliment can target the generosity of the host, the flavor of the sausages or the dress that is being worn. If all else fails, comment on the beautiful weather. (Check first that it is not raining.)

*

Finally, remember that great conversation needs good eye contact, good posture, good concentration and a good number of nods and smiles. It also requires a judicious amount of listening. Those who listen more than they speak are often considered very fine company.

SUMMARY

Parents need to have conversations with their sons because:

- Time spent talking can reaffirm love and connection.
- Too many sons are entering adulthood without some vital life skills.
- Sons need adult mentors who can pass on wisdom and knowledge.
- Sons need to take part in conversations within the home to balance the conversations they hear outside the home.
- Sons need to learn to converse and articulate their feelings.
- Society, in so many ways, rewards those who are good at conversation—and conversation skills *can* be taught.

What?

THE WORD "CONVERSATION" comes from the Latin *conversari*, meaning "to associate with." The term suggests an oral exchange of views, feelings and ideas. It implies communion, the getting together with at least one other in order to share sentiments. Herein lies the essential prerequisite of conversation: that it involve another. Getting a son to engage in a conversation can be problematic. It is even more difficult if he is addicted to his computer and would prefer to have his meals sent up to his bedroom so he dines only with avatars. Don't do it! Let hunger drive him to associate with real people in the communal dining room.

This book seeks to advance an idea expressed rather beautifully in the Quran: "A good word is like a good tree whose root is firmly fixed and whose top is in the sky."

This hints at good conversation coming from a source that is nourishing and dependable. It also hints at information being transferred to a new place, where it flourishes and produces a thing of worth. This might be somewhat idealistic, but it is important to remember that conversations can either be good or bad . . . but to be either, they must actually happen.

When the constellations are aligned to the extent that conversation is possible between a parent and a son, it is as well to know what to chat about. This will depend on many things, not least being the issue of the moment. A boy fishing for a piece of toast in the electric toaster armed with nothing but a knife and a dangerous amount of ignorance will, doubtless, elicit a shrill command to stop, followed by some explanation, followed by a request that the boy put on some calming music involving whales and surf.

Developmental psychologists have recognized that certain issues arise and particular questions are asked by a boy at different periods of his life. Erik Erikson, one of the most influential writers in this field, suggests that a boy seeks answers to eight questions throughout his life. Helping him to answer these questions can form the substance of many conversations over the years—but not all of them. Sometimes, a parent will need to talk about toasters and knives.

Eight key questions a boy will ask from infancy to adulthood[1]

	AGE	KEY QUESTION
1.	Newborn to 18 months	Who can I trust?
2.	18 months to 3 years	Is it all right to be me?
3.	3–6 years	What is it okay for me to do?
4.	6–12 years	Can I make it in the world?
5.	12–19 years	Who am I and what can I become?
6.	19–40 years	Can I love and be loved?
7.	40–65 years	Does what I do count for anything?
8.	65+ years	Have I done all right in my life?

These questions reflect a boy's gradual transition from egoism (It's all about me) to mutualism (It's all about us). They also reveal a boy's fundamental need for some sort of identity, some sort of acceptance and some sort of purpose.

Erikson's list of questions points out that the necessary conversations to be had with a son will be dependent on many things—not least of which is his age and level of maturation. For this reason, it is important for parents to know something of the developmental stages of their son's life and the issues associated with these stages.

Developmental stages of a boy

There are four areas of development required of the growing boy:

1. Physical development
2. Intellectual development
3. Social and emotional development
4. Spiritual and moral development

Parents need to have some idea of the issues being faced by their son as he matures in these four areas. This understanding can help frame the way they mentor him as he grows. All too often, adults can visit upon their offspring expectations that may be blindingly obvious to them without recognizing that it is not nearly so obvious to someone who has a quarter the number of candles on their birthday cake.

What parents need to practice is mindfulness—an understanding of where their son is at. This mindfulness will enrich their conversation with greater relevance and understanding.

PHYSICAL DEVELOPMENT

PREADOLESCENCE 9–11 YEARS	Physically obvious sex differences can emerge more clearly. Boys may begin to develop enlarged genitalia and the capacity to procreate. Physical maturity is generally greater in girls than boys. Both sexes may be somewhat awkward as muscle development may not match the growth of longer arms and legs. Coordination and dexterity may be a little limited. A very active lifestyle means a good night's sleep is needed.
EARLY ADOLESCENCE 12–14 YEARS	This is generally a period of significant physical sex differentiation. The upsurge of testosterone in boys leads to voices breaking, greater muscle bulk, more aggression, body hair and a sexual awakening. Many boys become self-conscious about their bodies. This can be a period of some anxiety as the early adolescent wants to "own" a body that is less sexually neutral. Acne can begin to be a problem. Much reassurance is needed as there can be some insecurity in boys at this age.
LATE ADOLESCENCE 15–18 YEARS	Greater strength and size can give the appearance of a maturity that may not be matched by intellectual, social and emotional development. This can lead to frustration, for the visual clues to maturity in a boy are not always matched by reality. Physical sex differentiation nears complete development. There is a continued interest in personal appearance along with proof one has acquired the features of a desired gender. Muscle development approaches that of an adult, as does dexterity and coordination. Skill development at sports can reach a peak at this time.

INTELLECTUAL DEVELOPMENT

PREADOLESCENCE 9–11 YEARS	Boys need to explore, experiment and question as they become actively engaged in assimilating new learning experiences and accommodating more information. Much guidance is needed but learning tasks need not be too complex or abstract. There is generally a strong element of trust and taking things at face value. At this age, many boys feel more secure with routines and completing shorter "closed tasks." The capacity for extended periods of concentration may not be great. Much variation in learning tasks is needed.
EARLY ADOLESCENCE 12–14 YEARS	The early adolescent years can witness the greatest difference in academic standards between boys and girls, with girls often being well in advance of boys, particularly in literacy-based tasks. Boys may be stronger in spatial tasks and in physical activities, such as sports. There is an emergence of an ability to engage in more abstract thinking, to cope with symbolism, inferences, reasoning and the teasing out of relationships. Boys at this age can question things more and challenge both facts and opinions.
LATE ADOLESCENCE 15–18 YEARS	The continuum seen in the early adolescent years advances further so that complex concepts can now be handled together with higher-order thinking skills, such as the synthesis of information and the solving of more difficult problems. Critical- and creative-thinking skills are more developed at this age. Boys are usually able to concentrate for longer periods and engage in extended learning tasks. The capacity for self-directed study can be greater, although some boys can become disengaged from the learning situation and deliberately underperform to remain accepted by their peers.

SOCIAL AND EMOTIONAL DEVELOPMENT

PREADOLESCENCE **9–11 YEARS**	Socially and emotionally, boys are still very dependent on the family, although this will diminish over the years. Boys now begin to orient themselves more toward their father. Play tends to be in same-sex groups. The capacity to keep emotions and feelings hidden is not yet strong but is getting stronger. Boys are somewhat biddable although there may be growing defiance and autonomy. Some fallibility is beginning to be noticed in parents and other authority figures. The desire to please parents and teachers is strong but can weaken throughout this stage.
EARLY ADOLESCENCE **12–14 YEARS**	These can be the insecure years both socially and emotionally. The worries of changing from primary to secondary school combine with a growing sexual tension and an acute awareness of one's acceptance or otherwise by peers, to make these years difficult. Doubts and lack of confidence can lead to problems such as homophobia and bullying. Anxiety may stem from a transfer of allegiance from family to friends. Parents and teachers are often challenged and their rules tested. The generation gap becomes more apparent. Sexual exploration and experimentation can begin and the later years of this stage can witness the development of romantic relationships. Early adolescents are generally in a hurry to grow up.
LATE ADOLESCENCE **15–18 YEARS**	Characteristically, there is a strong orientation to friends. The family, as a major social and emotional reference point, can be replaced by peers. Growing autonomy from the family can be assisted by the growth of romances. Many of these relationships are not long-lasting and can often be more platonic and experimental than truly amorous. Nonetheless, "crushes" can occur, as can falling in love, which can bring some intensely rewarding as well as hurtful experiences. Emotional feelings can usually be controlled better at this age than when younger.

SPIRITUAL AND MORAL DEVELOPMENT

PREADOLESCENCE 9–11 YEARS	Boys are generally moving from a period of a literal acceptance of the great religious stories to engaging with the more symbolic and abstract understanding of faith.
	During this preadolescent phase, a boy's faith begins to be influenced by peers and the media. However, faith tends to remain conventional.
	Morally, there is a strong dependence on the ethics of others, such as parents, which are then adopted as their own moral principles.
EARLY ADOLESCENCE 12–14 YEARS	The influence of the family on faith and beliefs diminishes and the influence of other forces increases, particularly the prevailing culture, peers and the media. Faith development begins to show greater individuality. There is less reliance on an inherited faith stance.
	Morally, there is a greater capacity to decide ethical matters for oneself, although the desire for acceptance by peers might be so strong that one's innate moral code can be made subservient to the morals of the group.
	Rebellion against authority figures can be evident, and moral and spiritual conventions can be tested.
LATE ADOLESCENCE 15–18 YEARS	In late adolescence, there can be a consolidation of one's beliefs and a preparedness to demonstrate one's faith even if it should not accord with that of family or friends. This is a period of questioning and searching for answers.
	Morally, there is significant ownership of one's actions, although this may not stop the use of excuses for inappropriate behaviors.
	Experimentation with new moral and spiritual codes may occur.

Don't always be age-appropriate

Okay—the sensible stuff has been shared. Parents must ensure that any conversation with their son is age-appropriate. Now for some heresy.

It is sometimes good to chat about adult things with young people. Most boys can deal with grown-up topics if they are presented well. Failure to speak of things that stretch a boy's understanding is to condemn him to perpetual immaturity.

We can sometimes fail to extend our students. We can inadvertently stifle progress so that every child conforms to the average. Developmental targets in schools often seem overly concerned with what a typical child can cope with, rather than ask what a child could cope with if taught the proper way.

It is the same with conversations between parents and sons. Most topics can be chatted about, provided it is done sensitively and with illustrations and imagery that a boy can relate to. Think dinosaurs. Think sports. Think . . .

Why the ten conversations were chosen

Pain has played a significant part in my selection of the ten conversations in this book. Sometimes, the pain came from my own upbringing. At other times, it has been the pain witnessed in others. On occasions, it has been both.

When I look at my record book of boys suspended or expelled, I am saddened. Some boys never stood a chance. Their parents failed them. Their friends failed them. Even their headmaster failed them.

Yes—boys must learn to accept responsibility and take ownership of their decisions. But, they are young and the product of varying circumstances, some of which may result in a reduced ability to make good choices. Boys need good mentors. I suspect that, had some of those boys been given sound advice, a number of my empty desks might still be filled.

It is even more painful when death takes one of my boys. More than once, I have seen a coffin slide behind a curtain to be cremated and wondered if I could have done more to have kept the boy alive.

The following ten conversations are the ones that, as a father and as a teacher, I wish I had shared with my sons—all 1,531 of them.

The content of these conversations has generally been oriented to the needs of a boy in his teen years. I've had to do this to prevent this book from becoming an unmanageable tome. However, an astute parent should be able to take the topics described in *Ten Conversations You Must Have With Your Son* and deal with them in an age-appropriate manner if their son is not in their teen years.

1.   Telling a son that he is loved

The world is not always an encouraging place. There are many who lack kindness and who can make a boy feel unloved.

Tragically, there exist some parents who do not love their sons. Some will *say* that they do, but there is no link between word and deed. Fortunately, most parents *do* love their sons, and demonstrate this love faithfully even when that love is seriously tested by bovine behavior.

Boys get their identity, security and nurture from a group—usually made up of family and friends. Without this connection, a boy is vulnerable. However, it is not just company that is needed; it is love.

Love is desiring the best for another, but it is more than this. It is also affection. Some parents manage the first requirement but not the second. They describe themselves as *loving* their sons but not *liking* them. This is not enough—even though the latter might be justified by a son playing up like a second-hand lawnmower.

Some parents, particularly fathers, will present evidence of faithful provision as proof of their love. This is also not enough. A son needs to enjoy his father's company, to feel his father's touch and to hear his father's words. Meaningful conversation between fathers and sons can be pitifully infrequent. Fathers will often defend their absence from their son's life by claiming their duties as a provider. But, a father's provision must not be limited to hunting mammoths. It must include giving guidance.

With one marriage in three disintegrating in the western world, there are a lot of sons who have suffered reduced or total loss of access to a parent. Some are lucky and find a wonderful stepparent to lessen their sense of bereavement. Others are not so lucky—either because there is no one stepping in, or because those stepping in are not able to replace the love of a parent lost.

A son needs at least one adult who adores him—preferably two. A son needs to know that he is a priority in someone's life. A son needs to be loved and he also needs to know he is loved.

2. Encouraging a son to know himself

Too many boys do not know who they are. They have little idea of their own ability. As a result, their unique talents remain undiscovered and their life is blighted by potential never being realized.

The teen years are years of searching for an identity that is their own—an identity that is independent of family, and possibly even of friends. Too many boys are accidental in the formation of their faith, conviction and politics. Others are worse—they haven't formed ideas about anything and seem content to drift through life unlabeled (often seen as a good thing) and uninformed (often seen as a bad thing).

It is important for a boy to know his history and inheritance. While recognizing that there can be understandable sensitivities in some family circumstances, such as with an adopted son or a stepson, a boy needs to know something about the genes he has inherited. What were his ancestors like? What are the character traits of his real or adopted family? What are the lessons to be learned from his past and what does this suggest for his future?

A son must develop an understanding of self. He will have worked out that his biological assignment is male, but he may not have worked out the implications of this. A boy needs to understand his body, mind, heart and soul as well as his chemistry, his hardwiring, his character.

3. Helping a son to choose an appropriate moral code

A boy requires guidance in selecting appropriate behaviors, for within the dark corners of society a moral blindness can stop the recognition of that which is right. Within this shadowy world, ethics can writhe into convenient distortions of the truth. Values often melt and slump to a level that allows a boy to excuse the inexcusable.

What will be the reference points for a boy's behavior? What will be the navigational markers he will use to travel the world? There are many competing philosophies that will beckon alluringly to him. By which ones should he be guided? There are many choices, including the secular philosophies associated with humanism, existentialism, utilitarianism, consequentialism and a lot of other "isms." There are also divine directives to consider. Examples include the Noble Eightfold Path of Buddhism, the Ten Commandments of Judaism and Christianity, and the Quran of Islam.

In the end, character is demonstrated by choices. There can be a temptation for parents to leave many of these choices to their son. More than one parent has told me, with a virtuous glow, that they are leaving the issue of values for their son to work through. This might be admirable if it were not for the fact that the son is then given no information to help him make his choice. The results of these uninformed choices can be tragic.

4. Assisting a son to accept responsibility

Many students like to watch. Watching is safe: you bear no responsibility; you accept no accountability. Today's teenagers have been described as "screenagers." They look, comment and criticize from the comfort of their couch. The child then grows into an adult who finds it difficult to do much more than spectate. Our sons need to be taught to take ownership of their behaviors. They need to learn how to be leaders and how to be servants. They need to be encouraged to take ownership of their lives.

There is a hunger for authentic leadership today. There are too many who cannot lead themselves let alone anyone else. There are parents who cannot lead a family and there are many in business who confuse management with leadership.

A boy hell-bent on acquiring the heady joys of increased freedom with age must be introduced to the reality of increased responsibility and the even less alluring reality of increased accountability.

5. Instructing a son how to live within a community

Although some boys remain active and involved with society, there are a number who are lazy blobs. Entertained by a range of expensive electronic equipment, many sons limit their social interaction to a number of e-relationships, which are often short term, disposable and shallow.

The exercise of social skills strengthens a community. If neglected, a boy can become self-centered. In short, he can become a social liability in a group larger than one. Boys require guidance in how to live within a community. They need to learn the skills of living with people who are different from them. This will enable them to operate in a world of the icon and the idiot. A boy must learn that the inept and indifferent cannot always be removed by the press of a delete button.

Living within a community requires an ability to manage mood and impulse. Our prisons are full of sons who would not be there if they had mastered the art of counting to ten before acting. Impulsive behavior is born of the reptilian part of the brain being exercised. Other parts of the brain need to be activated if our sons wish to avoid gaining a zebra tan in prison.

The "fight or flight" behaviors exercised by boys are genetically useful when hunting saber-toothed tigers or defending a cave from intruders. But they are slightly less useful in contemporary community; except, perhaps, in sports or when running to catch the school bus.

Living within a community requires people to adopt behaviors that others find pleasant. For example, it is probably all right for a boy to eat like a pig, but he must know he is eating like a pig and be able to cease eating like a pig when the situation demands it. There are other social behaviors that, if not learned, can result in a boy being disadvantaged. The simple act of sending a thank-you message for a present, shaking hands in an appropriate manner, knowing which cutlery to use, addressing a letter correctly and understanding what "formal" means are just some of the skills that need to be learned by a boy if he is not aspiring to a career as a cast-away on a deserted island.

6. Helping a son to optimize performance

Most of our sons want to do well in life. They are usually assisted in this quest by parents, and schools also partner in this pursuit. Schools usually boast they "help the child realize their full potential." Mine certainly does. However, some schools can often do the opposite.

Contemporary society is hobbled by a "mean, median, mode" mantra that is designed to ensure a person is "normal." There is a gravitational pull to the center of the spectrum of performance. Boys are often complicit in this because there is comfort in not being labeled either a "geek" or "dumb."

Very little in this world is attained without the price of hard work. Unfortunately, in this add-water-and-mix age of instant gratification, the ability to work long hours toward a deferred reward is fast evaporating. We complain when we are parked for two minutes to wait for our cheeseburger. We petition for faster broadband access to the net. We fume over our glacial promotion up the company hierarchy.

Many of our sons would be advantaged to know something of the tricks that can be employed to achieve success in life. One of the best tricks is to get lucky—but this cannot always be relied upon. This leaves the rather depressing alternative of having to work for our success.

7. Mentoring a son in the area of sex and intimacy

The western world generally does a poor job of preparing its sons to be intimate. There are always exceptions, but in general a boy is required to navigate his way through the sexual swamp with minimal direction. Such signposts that are given to him can be vague and contradictory. The parents say this and the school says that, but the porn site says something completely different. Where adult direction falters, peer direction takes over. The "leader of the sack" can, in boastful voice, suggest the path to the forbidden fruit in a manner that is not always helpful.

The proper people to educate a boy about sex are his parents. Some parents are wonderful at giving their children guidelines on sex, whereas others are not. The range of excuses is extensive: "It's not my job . . . the school will deal with it." "I'm too busy." "It's the sort of thing you have to learn for yourself." "They probably know more about it than I do." "I'm not quite sure what to tell them." There are plenty of excuses to choose from. Other parents teach their children an attitude toward sex that is unworthy of a civilized society. They model abusive and angry relationships, unfaithful relationships, degrading relationships. The son watches it all, memorizes it all and repeats it all.

Schools can also fail their students. Classes will teach boys to do penciled drawings of reproductive organs and become experts on how babies grow in the womb. They will be introduced to the horrors of sexually transmitted diseases in a theoretical way. Some of the luckier ones may get to roll a condom onto a banana and giggle their way through a lecture on dating. The mind is fed but not the heart. The questions a son wants to ask, he is not allowed to ask, for it is not in the syllabus. So, answers must be looked for on the net, in magazines and on the back of toilet doors.

We must do a better job of teaching our sons about sex and intimacy. They have little need to hear more about the biology of sex, for this is generally done well in schools. Nor do they need to hear about the morality of sex from adults who are no longer excited by sex and who have no connection to the virility of a teenager. They want to know what they can, where they can, why they can, when they can, how they can, if they can. They no longer need to know how they measure up inside an environment of unconditional love. They need to know how they measure up outside, in the real world, where love, like and lust churn dangerously.

It is not just smut and titillation that boys want, for they can get these sorts of things quite easily these days. What they want is something that is more elusive, something that is rare. They want guidance on how to be a man.

8. Assisting a son to manage financial matters

The level of ignorance in young people about financial matters can be frightening. This is revealed in the number who get into financial trouble through an inability to budget, a failure to understand the traps associated with credit cards and an incapacity to retire debt. Too many are persistently living beyond their means, over-relying on parental assistance and making unwise choices when selecting hire-purchase options, cell-phone plans and car-leasing arrangements.

The science of wealth generation and wealth management also needs to be taught. Advice on saving and the traps to avoid when borrowing or when getting involved in get-rich-quick schemes needs to be shared with sons if we are ever going to expect them to manage their financial affairs appropriately and look after us in our dotage.

9. Encouraging a son to stay healthy

Too many of our sons die prematurely. Some die because of accidents—accidents are the major cause of death for those aged under 45 in many developed countries. For others, death is not an accident; it is embraced. In much of the developed world, 20 percent of teen male deaths are due to suicide.

These are horrifying statistics, as is the fact that one of the quickest growing medical problems in teenagers is depression.

Too many sons squander the possibility of longevity. Alcohol, cigarettes and a range of illegal drugs are used with little to no understanding of their long-term health cost. Stir into the mix a range of sexually transmitted diseases and the dangers associated with a tricked-up V8, and the chances of a son ending up in a morgue become painfully real.

To this depressing litany must be added the health issues associated with "secret men's business." Our sons need to be aware of matters such as prostate cancer, testicular cancer, erectile dysfunction and infertility. This is not to frighten them. It is to inform them and to encourage them to never take their health for granted.

Finally, there are the usual grim reapers of cardiovascular and coronary disease and a range of cancers that, statistically, are the main reasons we read obituaries. However, a boy can be taught to adjust his behaviors so that his eulogy need not be written for a long time.

10. Helping a son to deal with grief and loss

Life cannot be expected to provide a constant stream of fun, praise and success. If a boy is going to crumple because he does not get his hourly fix of praise, he may stay crumpled. Self-esteem needs to be built up but never to a stage that ordinary performance is exalted as extraordinary. "Warm fuzzies" are good but so too are words of correction if they are shared with wisdom and understanding.

Sons should not depend on a diet of constant praise. Disappointment happens, discouragement happens, distress happens. It might be as well to remind some sons that resilience is needed against life's misfortunes.

The gods play with all and cause us to laugh and cry. Therefore, some emotional and physical courage is required. As it is said, we are all born naked, wet and hungry and things then get worse. Fortunately, things also get better, because life, for most people, is a constant journey through high points and low points.

Other areas

There are many other topics that should be the subject of conversations between parents and their sons. One of these is the art of effective communication. The grunt might work well on the football field but not in the workplace or home. In addition to speaking well, there is the need to be able to write well. A boy needs to recognize that content governs less than 10 percent of the impact of speech. The remaining impact is controlled by the appearance and sound of the speaker. The science of voice projection, articulation, accent, pitch and pace needs to be taught, together with posture, grooming and appearance. Sons also need to be taught to read body language, to sense mood, to interpret the unspoken feelings of another. They need to improve their ability to send and receive unspoken messages, other than raising the middle finger.

Another topic that should be added to the list of essential skills is that of being able to drive and maintain a car. Given the carnage on our roads and the large number of sons being mined for body parts, it is a wonder schools allow any student to graduate without teaching them how to drive safely. A boy should also be taught how to look after a car, how to change a wheel, and how to undertake a basic car service.

There are also matters of the soul that need to be explored. The symptoms of this failure are revealed in shallowness, loss of meaning and a failure to recognize the sacredness of ordinary things. Irrespective of the family's faith position, all parents should require their sons to keep their soul healthy by a diet of noble actions, moving experiences and the opportunity to reflect on life and, perhaps, death.

SUMMARY

When engaging in important conversations with your son, keep the following points in mind:

- Answer the questions your son is asking.
- Be developmentally appropriate, but do not underestimate his powers of comprehension.
- Cover elements of your son's physical development, intellectual development, social and emotional development, and his spiritual and moral development.
- Affirm that he is loved.

How?

THIS BOOK CONCENTRATES on conversations between parents and sons that are designed to encourage growth. These conversations are about teaching, guiding and mentoring. This is not to say that other forms of conversation are not important. Banter is essential. So is silence. Time spent listening and in small talk is seldom wasted. The foundational base of the trivial is necessary for the significant conversation to take place. The significant must build on the trivial—hours of it. Therefore, wheeling out Dad to give the finger-waving lecture, when his conversation with his son for the rest of the week has been limited to a request for a beer uttered from behind a newspaper, is unlikely to be effective.

The expectation that a boy will even listen to a parent, let alone be influenced by what the parent has to say, is not always realistic. Boys have a variety of ways of relating to adults and a variety of ways of responding to adults who want to talk to them.

SOME WAYS BOYS RELATE TO ADULTS[1]

The Resistor:	Resists the influence of adults. Prefers to relate to peers. Often has a rather immature outlook on life. *You suck.*
The Column of Smoke:	Apathetic toward adults. Generally passive about any influence adults seek to exert. *So what?*
The Seeker:	Prepared to interact with adults but does not accept everything they say. *Maybe you're right . . .*
The Dutiful:	Accepts everything an adult says without question and imports their values from adults. *Okay, Mom.*
The Head Boy:	Accepts external influence from adults but mixes it with internal convictions to arrive at their own opinion. *Weighing up what I've heard . . .*

Blocks to effective conversation

If a son is proving resistant to a parent's influence, it might indicate a need to build a stronger relationship before embarking on a quest to get him to share anything of consequence. Initial conversations may need to be little else than bridge-building exercises—shared activities that both parent and son enjoy. This may start with sharing humor and the chances of Manchester United winning the Premiership.

Effective communication can be diminished if that which is shared is inappropriate. I've found this out when interviewing boys for scholarship. Exasperated by carefully rehearsed answers drilled into applicants by cram schools, I decided to try to find out the true qualities of the applicants by giving them a series of unexpected tasks.

The game of indoor soccer succeeded in ranking their teamwork skills in exactly the reverse order of their academic ability.

The dissection of the rat was enjoyed by those with strength in the humanities but loathed by those with high scores in science.

The challenge to speak on an unrehearsed topic was a similar disaster. I asked one boy to speak for five minutes on drugs in sports.

He blinked owlishly at me through bottle-lens glasses before proceeding to take a piece of paper from his pocket and read:

> *I am the academic dux of my school and came tenth in the State in this year's spelling bee. I have been given a Premier's Award for Mathematics and hope one day to be a doctor. My other achievements include . . .*

Other things can derail communication. Lectures and monologues used to elicit improvement in a son are at grave risk of not being received well and even less so if the volume is turned up—in fact, especially if the volume is turned up. Volume does little other than cause anger levels to rise to the extent that the target of the high-decibel assault no longer listens. All a son is likely to hear is his blood boil. All he is likely to think is, *Get me the hell out of here*. All he is likely to do is play defense and "zone out," or play offense and mentally craft a cruel response.

That is if his brain is working at all. Anger does not tend to activate that part of the brain that contributes to thoughtful analysis. Adrenalin levels can be such that the only part of the brain that is activated is the "fight or flight" section. Any higher brain function—typically associated with the cerebral cortex—may have been anesthetized by his anger.

Parents can render the conversation ineffective if they don't reinforce what they say by what they do. Actions speak louder than words. A son needs to watch a lifestyle rather than listen to a sermon. Profound learning requires significant reinforcement.

For some key concepts to be understood, they may need to be repeated verbally. Herein lies a problem. Repetition can lead to boredom. In other words, nagging seldom works. The brain pays attention when it is interested. It will allow itself to be influenced if an idea is presented in a way that is new and stimulating. The neural pathways will only fire up when they are aroused, not when they are stupefied by boredom. An idea is imprinted more by reinforcement than repetition. This is the essence behind the words found in the old scriptures:

> *Keep these directions in your hearts.*
> *Impress them upon your children.*
> *If you are at home, talk about them.*
> *When walking along the road, discuss them.*
> *Whether lying down or standing up, consider them.*
> *Remember the commands in what you do and what you think.*
> *Let them be acknowledged on the inside of your house as well as on*
> *the outside.*
>
> (Deuteronomy 6:6–9)

These words are an essay on learning. Here is modern pedagogy captured by ancient wisdom. It is all there—informing, imprinting and impacting. Deuteronomy describes not only a conversation; it describes a lifestyle. Some lifestyles detract from the integrity of a conversation. Other lifestyles add to it.

I remember having to talk to a father about his son who had been caught plagiarizing in an exam. They were both in my study. The son was sullen, the father was angry and the headmaster was exasperated. After my predictable finger waving, an exchange took place between father and son that went something like this:

FATHER: "You are an idiot, boy! And a bloody disappointment. I don't know where you are picking up these values—probably from school." (He then looked accusingly at me.)

This comment was a mistake. It made the boy and me allies. We were united in anger. My mind began a mental response that fulminated along the lines of:

I don't think it is either fair or appropriate for you to start blaming the
school. By the time your son entered our school gate, he had spent the

*formative years under your influence . . . and a fat lot of good that
appears to have done him. Even now, when he is supposedly "at
school," he is under our tutelage only seven hours a day for 184 days
of the year. This, you bone-headed twit, amounts to a third of a day
for little over half a year. Your boy is probably spending more time
computer gaming and social networking than he is in my classrooms.
Are you exercising any control in your boy's life in these areas? Probably not, from the look of things. He is spending significantly more
time under your roof than he is mine. Besides, all this blame shifting
gets us nowhere, you choleric clown.*

Instead, I said: "Possibly." However, the boy had more courage.

BOY: "I learned all about cheating when you started screwing around,
Dad."
FATHER: (Gasps and turns red.)
HEADMASTER: (Cuts in quickly, reduces the boy's intended suspen-
sion period by half and his punitive essay to only 1,000 instead of
2,000 words.)

*

Many parents are pure gold and have an excellent rapport with their
sons. A few do not. Most are of varying effectiveness in communicating with their sons. Success often depends on mood, weariness
and whether the parent had a good day at work.

Having a place within the home that is conducive to conversation can also help build rapport between parent and son.

AN IDEA

Establish a Tummy-Tickling Place in the Home

"Some people use Facebook, but I talk to the dog," said a friend
of mine when he learned I was writing a book about conversations.

This caused me to go home and strike up an earnest conversation with Mollydog—a black-and-tan Cavalier Spaniel. It's a miracle dog. No brain. Which is why it stared stupidly at me as I regaled it with the virtues of good conversation. It then nuzzled my hand, flopped on its back and demanded its stomach be tickled.

All households need a tummy-tickling place—a place where the expression of absent-minded affection might occur, and, perhaps, even conversation. This is one of the reasons we need city malls, town halls and village greens.

We also need kitchens. Most households have a kitchen whose allure as a place of gathering is enhanced by the fridge, the pantry and the smell of something delicious being prepared for dinner. These natural places of congregation can be improved by a few kitchen stools and a bench bearing a small quantity of sinful confectionery. With not a lot of effort, most kitchens can be converted into a place that beckons. With family members tempted to solitary existence by well-equipped bedrooms, every effort is needed to create a place where a family might gather.

Communities have their pubs, and homes have their kitchens in which inhabitants might rest, refuel and reflect in the company of others. For this reason, it can be a good idea for a household to do an audit of their house to ensure there is a natural place of gathering. If there isn't one, create one. Design a space where a boy might flop in the company of his parents. Let it not be contaminated by electronic distraction. This kills conversation as do TV screens in pubs.

Types of communication

There is a hierarchy of communication, which, if not understood by parents, can make conversation with a son a bleak and unproductive experience.

Consider Figure 1. It shows a range of communication styles that parents might use with their son. The scale runs from showing and sharing to telling and yelling.

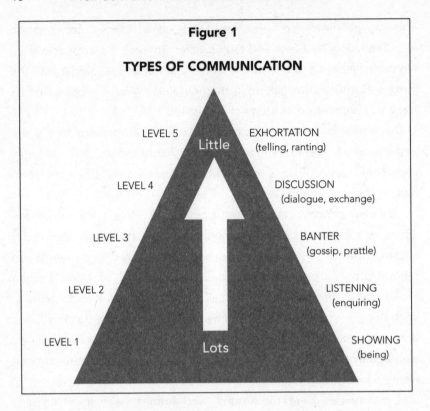

Figure 1

TYPES OF COMMUNICATION

LEVEL 5 — Little — EXHORTATION (telling, ranting)

LEVEL 4 — DISCUSSION (dialogue, exchange)

LEVEL 3 — BANTER (gossip, prattle)

LEVEL 2 — LISTENING (enquiring)

LEVEL 1 — Lots — SHOWING (being)

Figure 1 suggests that the effectiveness of each level of communication will only be realized if underpinned by the exercise of the communication styles under it. As parents, we are unlikely to be effective in communicating with our sons using an ear-blistering rant, however satisfying we might find it. As parents, we must win the right to be listened to by modeling what we say—and this can sometimes be done in silence.

On top of the obligation for words to match actions is a parent's ability to be silent. We must be prepared to listen. When conversing, many think they are listening when they are not. They are mentally refining their own point of view, preparing a rejoinder and wondering whether the cat has been fed. Active listening requires deliberate mental engagement with what is being said and the demonstration of this with appropriate questions, nods and grunts. Little is more flattering than to feel one has been forensically listened to.

It can also help if there is a sense of enjoyment when chatting.

The best formula is relaxed banter, with a smattering of juicy gossip topped off by lighthearted humor. Discussing something "heavy" with a son should only be done if there has been sufficient practice in discussing something "light." A boy will quickly back off if he thinks that every time a parent opens their mouth he is going to receive a joyless sermon—however well-intentioned it may be.

However, there *is* a place for serious conversation . . . but its frequency should be limited to when it really matters. Just what these heavier sorts of conversations might be is the theme of this book.

Getting the timing right

On a few occasions, a son can be given a verbal broadside. However, the impact of a rant of this nature will probably be in inverse proportion to its frequency. I've found this out through the frequent castigation of our Year 9 boys. (Why is it always Year 9?) Those who are yellers-and-tellers will find the effectiveness of these exchanges limited over time. However, there can be the odd occasion when a comprehensive bawling out can be given to good effect.

If the frequency of modeling-a-point exceeds yelling-the-point, then a wide and stable base to the communication pyramid is created. On the other hand, if the communication pyramid is made top heavy with too much ranting, attempts at effective communication with our sons (and with Year 9) will fall over.

AN IDEA

Work Out Your Average Point of Communication

As parents, we might benefit from asking ourselves where our average point of communication is. (See Figure 2.) If this is a scary task for parents, then have some sympathy for headmasters. My average point is probably in a fairly northerly place!

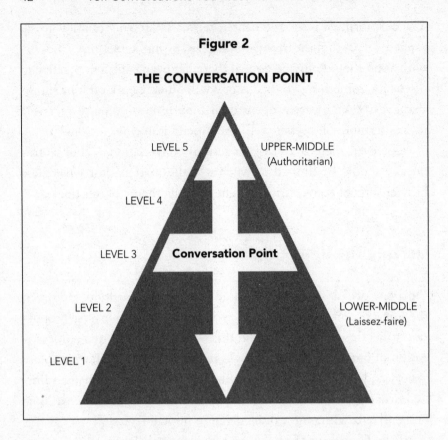

Figure 2

THE CONVERSATION POINT

LEVEL 5   UPPER-MIDDLE
                (Authoritarian)

LEVEL 4

LEVEL 3   **Conversation Point**

LEVEL 2   LOWER-MIDDLE
                (Laissez-faire)

LEVEL 1

Most parents will probably say that their average conversation point is somewhere in the middle. However, I'm going to press the matter further. Exactly *where* in the middle? Upper-middle, middle-middle or lower-middle?

If an analysis puts us in the upper-middle of the conversation-point continuum, then a more authoritarian style of conversation is likely to characterize our parent/son interaction.

If an analysis puts us in the lower-middle of the conversation-point continuum, then a more laissez-faire, or relaxed, conversation style is likely to characterize our parent/son interaction.

Both conversation styles have their place, but the sort of conversation that is encouraged in this book is that which is found in the exact *center* of the communication pyramid. A bit like the baseball bat, this is the sweet spot that can have the greatest impact on propelling a boy in the desired direction.

The wordless conversation

Having a meaningful conversation with a son need not require the formalities of Socratic debate or the skilled oratory of a practiced interlocutor. A conversation can be wordless. It can be in a smile that says, "I love you." It can be a handshake that says, "I'm proud of you." It can be raised eyebrows that ask, "Are you okay?"

A son sitting with a father at a football game will often be a wordless experience other than some gratuitous advice shouted at the referee. Nonetheless, the conversation is real. The companionship, if not the words, eloquently tells of the affection that compels the one to be with the other. At other times, a few words can be useful. But, they needn't be many words.

*

They were delightful parents whose older son was at my school. Their younger son was at a school for students with special needs.

Countless insensitivities and cruelties mean that a boy with Down syndrome sometimes doesn't smile. He didn't smile. Instead, he studied me with unnerving seriousness. Then, recalling what he must do next, he called his mother. The man coming for dinner was here.

Mother came. After greetings and the transfer of flowers to her, the boy was shepherded forward. Mother then said, "This is my son."

The boy was transformed by this proud introduction. His uncertainty dissolved and was replaced by a smile so authentic I was entranced. "Look how lucky I am," he said wordlessly.

He was right. He had heard only four words from his mother, but they were magical words. He belonged. He was loved. He was her son.

Conversation-killing dads

Some dads are not so good at the conversation thing. There are probably a few moms who are not doing a crash-hot job in this area but, from my experience, it is more often the dad who can ruin a promising conversation. Talk to a man about his mother and most will smile at cherished memories. Talk to a man about his father and many will wince at painful memories.

That said, some dads are brilliant in conversing with their sons. Most of us are somewhere in between.

Many things conspire to make meaningful dialogue between sons and fathers problematic, chief of which is a natural inclination in dads to engage in one, or a number, of the following behaviors:

- Dad restricting his conversation to reforming, reorganizing and even redeeming his son. This is the "blue-pencil dad," editing his son's behavior so that it complies with approved guidelines. Love is expressed in a desire to better his son.
- Dad being alienating and antagonistic. This dad exhibits a low-level animus toward his son. It can owe its genesis to the quality of fathering experienced by the father. It can also be the product of bitterness caused by family break-up, poor health or a failure in professional life.
- Dad being cold and distant. This dad sees communion with his son as an obligation and regards parenting as a duty rather than a pleasure. This can result in minimal connection between father and son and conversation that is dull, mechanical and functional.

Some fathers need to reconnect with their sons. Frank Pittman writes:

> For a couple of hundred years now, each generation of fathers has passed on less and less to his sons—not just less power but less wisdom. And less love.[2]

Steve Biddulph, author of *Raising Boys*, suggests that there is a "father hunger" in many sons.[3] Biddulph and Pittman warn that some fathers can be reluctant to anoint their sons as men.[4]

A father's duty

After helping to produce a child, a father has a duty to nurture a child. There is the temptation to think that, in the initial years, an infant boy must bond predominantly with his mother. Wrong. In the initial years, an infant should bond with *both* his parents. It is true that the biological advantages of the mother combine with social expectations in deciding who must leave the nest to collect the worms, resulting in a baby spending most of its time with the mother. Yet these conventions must not be allowed to marginalize the father in a baby boy's life.

Even in the early years, a baby must hear the baritone voice, must feel the love of the father as well as the strength of the father so that the infant learns that strength need not be disassociated from gentleness; that men need not be disassociated from emotion; that males need not be disassociated from tenderness.

Much has been written about the importance of the father being on hand when the preteen boy begins a search for his male identity. This advice is flawed. A boy searches for his identity the day he is born. Therefore, fathers should be encouraged to become involved with their infant son and model maleness in the early years of the baby's life. A son's conversations with a father need to begin when he lies wet and messy in his father's arms in the delivery room.

Fathers can be particularly effective in teaching a son the rules of life. These rules are better modeled than lectured. A father who tells off a son for bad behavior, and then enters into a high-decibel confrontation with his wife that is concluded by a slammed door and several hours of injured isolation, is sending mixed messages about appropriate behavior.

Accounts of fathering can involve tales of neglect and abuse of power. There is more than one son who suffers a profound sadness born out of a lack of real connection with his father. Society needs fathers who love their sons, not by controlling or criticizing them, but by being a positive example of what it means to be a father, a husband and a man.

Positive parenting

A wonderful example of positive fathering is provided by Dick Hoyt. The www.teamhoyt.com website gives directions as to how the full story can be accessed, but, in short, it started when Dick Hoyt's son, Rick, was born with brain damage due to his umbilical cord wrapping itself around his neck *in utero*. He was condemned to a vegetative state. Then, one day, Dick noticed his son's eyes. They followed him about the room. It was the only thing that could. But, it was enough.

A visit to Tufts University for ideas on how to communicate with his son was frustrated until the academics heard Rick laugh at a joke they told. They were amazed and inspired to develop a touch-activated, computer communication device. This allowed Rick to converse with his dad using head movements. Although this was a great advance, the adventure was not over.

Conversation was now possible but Rick's life still needed purpose. He needed something to talk about. This was solved by Dick responding to his son's desire to enter a five-mile charity run to raise money for a paralyzed classmate. So they ran, with the father pushing the son in a special buggy. This experience led to many others. Over several years, both father and son participated in the Boston Marathon and more than 200 triathlons. Their most grueling challenges have been several Iron Man competitions. To see Dick push his son on the runs, carry his son on the bicycle and pull his son when swimming left many crowds in tears when father and son eventually crossed the finish line.

Although this is an extraordinary story about extraordinary people in extraordinary circumstances, it is not beyond the ability of most fathers to share a hobby or to engage in some activity that causes a son to feel that, with his mom and dad, he is part of an awesome team.

AN IDEA

Talk to Your Son About Fathering

The theme of fathering is, itself, a great conversation to have with your son. As a topic, it is unlikely to be raised in the natural course of events. Help is provided by some excellent literature such as:

- *The Last Lecture* by Randy Pausch
- *Keeping Faith* by John and Frank Schaeffer
- *Night* by Elie Wiesel

There are also films to watch such as:

- *Big Fish*
- *Field of Dreams*
- *Road to Perdition*
- *The Pursuit of Happyness*
- *Finding Nemo*

One of the most moving films on the topic of fathering is *My Life*, in which Michael Keaton plays a man who has terminal cancer. He leaves advice for his unborn son on several matters, including simple life skills such as how to shake hands.

Care is needed to choose films and books that are age-appropriate.

AN IDEA

Learn to Share When Talking to Your Son

When talking to your son, it can be helpful to SHARE. This stands for **S**implicity **H**umor **A**ctivity **R**einforcement **E**lectronic.

SIMPLICITY

A parent can get so excited when they talk to their son that they embark on a verbal assault born of a burdened silence on a whole host of matters that they have been itching to talk about. Whoa, there! You might drive your son back to the shrug-and-grunt stage. Choose one topic and one topic only. Avoid the "... and another thing ..." syndrome.

HUMOR

This does not require a parent to be a stand-up comedian. Even a smile will do, as will a parent sharing something strange, interesting or unusual they have witnessed during the day. A parent's laughter is often a siren call to a son to join the conversation. The emailing of jokes and images siphoned from the net can also help the parent whose funny bone has gone missing. After all, laughter and humor are difficult to resist.

ACTIVITY

Shared activities are a fertile means to encourage connection between a parent and a son. Okay, so you are no good at football. Take your son to a football game and watch those who *are* good at football. Such experiences linger and can fuel reminiscences about shared activity later on. "Do you remember when we ..."

REINFORCEMENT

No—this is not an invitation to nag. It is an invitation to give thought to how an issue, already discussed, might be reinforced without rehashing that which has already been shared. A chat about sex might be followed up by a relevant DVD or book. A discussion on bullying might be followed by a YouTube link to an appropriate video.

ELECTRONIC

Very few sons can resist the allure of contemporary technology. The "Netolescents" love the cyber world. So, use it. Text your son and join him—even if tentatively—in Cyberia. It's still a conversation.

SUMMARY

Just how a parent converses with a son will depend on many things, but the following should be kept in mind:

- A foundational base of the trivial is necessary for the significant conversation to take place.
- The blocks to effective conversation—including speaking when angry and saying one thing but doing another—must be removed before talking to a son.
- The effectiveness of mentoring is improved by reinforcement, but not by nagging.
- Design a conversation-friendly part of the home that is in popular use by the family.
- Effective conversation should be done with enough gentleness to be accepted, and with enough authority to be effective. Exhortation and ranting should be used sparingly, and listening should be done generously.
- Some of the most effective messages, such as "I love you," can be

given by actions as well as words. A message is more likely to be imprinted if a son witnesses the truth of it within his family.

- Fathers can be particularly vulnerable to inadequate conversation with their sons, but they can take steps to improve.
- When talking to their sons, parents can be more effective in conveying a message if they keep it simple, use humor, exchange thoughts when sharing in an activity and reinforce the message using different approaches including electronic and other contemporary means of communication.

CONVERSATION ONE

You are loved

A HEADMASTER'S STUDY is not always a place a boy wants to go.
True, it can be an occasional source of affirmation, congratulation
and recognition, but rather too often it is a place where a boy is sent
when he is in trouble. If his parents are also there, he is in really big
trouble.

I remember one boy slumped in a chair glowering with anger at
the indignity of being called to explain his habit of stealing from
fellow students within the boarding house. He did not appear to be
angry with himself. He didn't even seem to be angry with me. It
almost seemed as if he wanted to get caught. But, he *was* angry with
his parents and here he now was, in my office, daring his parents to
hate him.

"But why?" wailed the mother. "We've given you everything."

The boy remained sullen as his mother leaned forward to stroke
her son's arm. He shrugged it off as if her fingers were the legs of a
spider. The mother's fingers crawled on his arm again, but he twisted
away in disgust.

"I've done everything for you," the mother cried, and looked at
him with watered eyes. Indeed she had. Her natural inclination had
been to fuss and cosset, but, after her divorce, she had stepped up the
attention, particularly during the war for more-favored-parent sta-

tus. Her ex had the worrying (for her) habit of taking the boy out for excursions that resulted in her son returning with a (for her) depressing glow of excitement. So, she baked his favorite treats, gave him permission to drive her car and allowed him a license on the weekend that made him the envy of his Year at school. She was right—she had given a lot to her son.

"Answer your mother," snapped the stepfather, bristling with I'll-sort-this-out purpose. I could hear the man's thoughts. *Am I not the one now paying the bloody fees? And a fat lot of good that appears to have done. The idiot of a boy is now facing the possibility of expulsion. I've never got on well with the boy—and this spate of thefts confirms why. The boy is an unpleasant piece of work. Can't his mother see that he needs whipping into line?*

"Is this all you can say after the love we've shown?" shouted the man.

A son needs to know he is loved

A son needs to know he is loved. This is unlikely to happen if he is not loved. Furthermore, a boy will need to be reminded that he is loved with sufficient regularity to counter any evidence that he is not, and also to show him that, regardless of the frequency with which he might do things that test the patience of his parents, he still deserves to be loved.

Too many sons believe parental love to be conditional. Tragically, some of them are right. They have heard the snarl, they have suffered the rebuke, they have seen the look of disgust to the extent they doubt whether they are loved at all.

Some sons are loved but run close to the wind of not being liked. Truculent and demanding, they are quick to hurl the accusation at a non-complying parent that the parent is mean, unreasonable and unloving. Repeated often enough, this behavior can begin to fulfill their taunt.

The cruelty inflicted by some children on their parents can be frightening. Intuitively, children know how to cause pain. The cruelest thing they can say is that they hate their parents, and that their parents hate them. A few parents deserve this barb. Most don't. In the parental rush to refute these claims, a momentary advantage is given to the child, who uses it to demand proof of affection—with the only acceptable evidence being the double choc ice-cream complete with sprinkles, or a surround-sound system for the bedroom.

A conversation that causes a son to understand that he is loved is an important one to have. This conversation need not be a constant bombardment by saccharine words. Love can be tough and uncompromising, it can be insistent on certain behaviors, it can even be angry.

*

On frequent occasions, I see parents unfold themselves out of four-wheel drives after a bone-wearying journey from the country to visit their son at school. The diesel engine shudders to silence, squealing doors are pushed open and cramped legs stretch gratefully to the ground.

Red dust has caked the number-plate, but the son recognizes the car. He has been looking out for it. Despite the car windows being obscured by an entomological graveyard, he sees the occupants through the half-mooned smears. The boy tries to disguise his smile as he ambles from his friends and toward the car with forced nonchalance.

The mother "Oh darling"s her boy and the father hugs him. These gestures, while welcome, even by a self-conscious boy, are not necessary for him to know that he is loved. The evidence is in the lateritic dust, the dead locusts and the $150 diesel bill.

They are here to watch him play his game of soccer. But that is not why they are really here. Yes, there will be some entertainment promised by the Under 14C soccer team, but the real reason they are here is because of their love . . . and, deep down, the son knows that.

He knows he's not that good a player.

Loneliness

One of the greatest burdens that an unloved son must bear is that of loneliness. If a boy is not accepted and is isolated from the herd, he can feel an outcast.

Tragically, the boy who is a bit different can sometimes be expelled from the group. A boy can be made to feel a pariah for having limited sporting skills or for being from a particular racial or ethnic group. There are many reasons why some boys do not speak to others. They have often learned these reasons from adults.

Modern technology can also spread loneliness. It can substitute reality with virtual reality; it can substitute social discourse with electronic isolation. Although opening communication to an unimaginable host, computers can also trap a boy into a virtual existence instead of a real one.

Dysfunctional families can spread loneliness, for when the place of belonging becomes a place of hurt, when the safest refuge in the world fails you, there can be a crushing loneliness born of broken trust. The lonely must then wrap their arms around themselves and rock. There are no other arms to hold them and there is no one else to rock them.

Institutions can spread loneliness. Their hierarchies and rules can isolate. Schools can be some of the most hierarchical institutions around. Seniority can be energetically protected by quarantining students into Year groups. This starves the young from the enrichment that can come from cross-age mentoring. Even within a Year group, there can be problems. Sympathy and understanding cannot always be relied upon because of the presence of competition within a Year group and a propensity to gossip.

Loneliness is one of the greatest threats to our quality of life. As we move into the twenty-first century, our major battles may be to deal with the unloved, the disconnected and the lonely.

Loving too much and too little

On the other hand, there are boys who are loved too much. Some can be suffocated by the attention given by a parent. They are adored to the point that ordinary behavior is exalted as extraordinary and ordinary achievement is accorded a recognition that employs most superlatives.

And there are boys who are loved too little. The boy is an inconvenience. Even worse, he is a drain on parental money, parental time and parental freedom. The problem is exacerbated if the son should be developmentally delayed in some way, as some boys are. *Oh, why can't he be like our daughter!*

Parenting: too much and too little

The term "helicopter parenting" is currently in vogue. It describes those parents who are up in the air, constantly hovering above their child and affording them little independence. Some of these parents are content to use commercial helicopters. Others use military gunships from which they rain down withering bursts of fire on any real or imagined threat that might endanger their offspring.

Such parents are so protective they will speak for their son, they will act for their son, they will think for their son. The result can be a frightening lack of resilience and a loss of identity in the son. Through the expression of their love, these parents are harming their children. Parents who are "up in the air" are unlikely to be able to enter a genuine conversation with their son. Any conversation that occurs is likely to be reduced to a parental lecture that gives the boy answers to issues that have their origin in a parent's fear rather than in a son's needs.

There are other parents who are all at sea. Tragically, this condition describes many fathers who disappear over the horizon to earn money for the family. After months at work, the parental "mariner" reenters the son's life to sort everything out. Months of inactivity are exchanged for frenzied action and catching up on the just-wait-until-your-father-returns issues.

Frustrating the parent who has been away "at sea" can be the son's unwillingness to enter immediately into deep dialogue with them. The extended absence needs to be repaired by an extended presence before most sons will open up.

If something "heavy" needs to be taken over the waters from parent to son, a strong relationship bridge is needed. If only light conversation is being transported, then a flimsy bridge will do. The trouble is that some parents sometimes expect to talk about heavy things using light bridges, with the result that there is a collapse of any meaningful communication. Building strong bridges takes time.

Finally, there are parents who have both feet on the ground. They are neither up in the air nor at sea. They are sufficiently engaged with their son's life for conversation to come naturally, be it trivial or meaningful.

These are the parents who commune at the dining table rather than in front of the television. These are the parents who text their sons and leave notes in their lunch box. These are the parents who ask their sons how their day has been with sufficient interest to show that their inquiry is genuine.

Types of love

The Ancient Greeks had many different names for love. Following are the three that are particularly relevant to sons:

- *Agape*: An ideal form of love that creates goodness. It is generative, selfless and unconditional.
- *Philia*: A desire to be with. It is based on a delight with being in the presence of another. It is the enjoyment of a person because of who they are.

- *Storge*: The love born of nature and nurture. It is the love that expresses itself in the relationship between a parent and child.

A great definition of love was given by a tentmaker originally called Saul nearly 2,000 years ago and it is still relevant today. He wrote to people in Corinth that:

> Love was patient, love was kind. Love didn't envy, it didn't boast and it wasn't proud. Love didn't put others down, it wasn't self-promoting, was not angered easily and kept no record of things done that were wrong. Love didn't enjoy anything that was evil, but enjoyed things that were good. Love was protective. Love was trusting. Love was positive . . .
>
> (1 Corinthians 13:4–8)

Ways of showing love

A parent has at least four ways of showing love: through words, through deeds, by being present and by providing.

Words

Even if words do not come easily to a parent, most should be able to manage "I love you, son." Four simple words. Four important words. Four endangered words. A son dispatched to school with the reminder that he is loved is a son equipped to withstand the emotional and social attrition wrought by a world given to withering putdowns. Okay, so you missed saying it this morning. Make amends with the cell phone. Email or send a text. Text something like: *thinking of u. just wanted u to know that I love u. have a gr8 day :)*

Words are powerful because they are windows into our heart. When a son bumps into a parent, what spills out of the parental heart? If the parent's heart is full of anger, an angry retort will spill out. If the parent's heart is full of worry, concern will spill out. If the parent's heart is full of love, love will be evident in the words that are spoken. What is spilling out of our mouths when our sons bump into us?

Deeds

Typically, boys are visual learners. They like to watch. For a parent to communicate with their son, there needs to be a congruency between that which is heard and that which is seen. A boy would rather see a truth than have it described to him. A parent who says they love their son but does not make their son a priority in their life will not be believed.

*

My son, Peter, decided to turn 18 on a most inconvenient day. I was booked to go to Tasmania to attend a very important conference for heads of schools. "I'm so sorry to miss your party, Pete, but know that I will be thinking of you." Then I flew away.

At the conference, I was morose and unsettled. My paternal glands were agitated to the extent that I could not enjoy the easy camaraderie of fellow heads. I found the excellent speakers to be dull and irrelevant. It was not their fault. It was mine. A quiet stroll around Hobart's harbor and its delightful collection of Huon pine boats finally put me in touch with the source of my discomfort: I should not have been there. I booked a flight back to Melbourne and arrived, on our front doorstep, just as Peter's party was starting.

"Dad," said Peter as he answered the door and hugged me. "I wasn't expecting you."

How tragic was that?

Presence

For millennia, the job of the father was to go out, kill something and bring it back to be eaten. Now, the job of the father is to go out and earn money, which is brought back to be spent. Over thousands of years, our task as fathers has not changed. *We go out.*

In going out, we became separated from our family, our children, our sons. Prior to the Industrial Revolution, the separation from our sons was not for long. Very soon, a son was indentured into the task of helping his father hunt or farm. There was a reconnection with the father as soon as a boy could prove useful. Then the Industrial Revolution stopped things. Sons seldom worked with their fathers. Maleness became a mystery and fathers became strangers. The situation did not improve in the post-industrial age.[1]

Not surprisingly, a whole raft of social and emotional disorders then appeared in our sons. These included ignorance about fathering and ignorance about being a man. Generations of under-fathered boys were created who went on to perpetuate the problem in their own sons.

A son needs to be shown love by a father choosing to be a presence in his life. Effective parenting is about good choices. Does a father choose to play catch with his son or work in his study?

In a time-poor society that is given to showing love through the gift of material possessions, the greatest demonstration of love a parent can give is to offer their son the gift of time.

Providing

Let's not be too dismissive about the things that money can buy. The material needs of a son must be met. But there is a difference between need and greed.

When one thinks of provision, one thinks of the basic things in Maslow's hierarchy of needs (see Figure 3)—things such as food, shelter and protection. Most parents are pretty good at making these things a priority. But Maslow—perhaps the best-known authority on human needs—points to the other needs a parent must meet and other ways a parent may demonstrate love for their son.

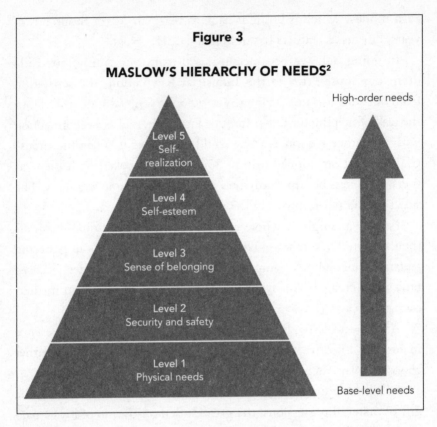

Figure 3

MASLOW'S HIERARCHY OF NEEDS[2]

High-order needs

Level 5
Self-
realization

Level 4
Self-esteem

Level 3
Sense of belonging

Level 2
Security and safety

Level 1
Physical needs

Base-level needs

A parent needs to ask not just whether they are meeting the basic needs of their son, but whether they are meeting his higher-order needs as well. A son may be well fed and sheltered, but is he being encouraged to consider his destiny, his faith and his purpose? A parent's love is shown by giving attention to all these areas.

AN IDEA

Work Out How You Show Love

Consider the different ways we can show love. The options I have just discussed are: through words, through deeds, by being present and by providing for your son.

It can be a useful exercise to give yourself a score out of ten against each of these four different ways of showing love.

If the score is low in WORDS, then you might consider building in more conversation time in the following ways:

- Share conversation during meals.
- Ban cell phones and individual entertainment devices in the car in favor of conversation.
- Regularly discuss issues in the news.
- Become a Facebook friend with your son.
- Send regular text messages and emails to your son.
- Share with your son the issues you are wrestling with. The likelihood of a son then sharing the issues in his life will increase.
- Write a letter and post it to your son.
- Establish a network of mentors for your son.
- Develop a good relationship with your son's friends.

If the score is low in deeds, then a similar list of action points can be drawn up. Likewise with being a presence and being a provider.

Love languages

Having acknowledged that parents have a variety of ways to express their love to their son, we also need to recognize that all parents have legitimate strengths in some areas of showing love and legitimate weaknesses in other areas. Parents should not berate themselves for not being stellar in all the ways of showing love.

This concept was explored by Gary Chapman in his pioneering work on "Love languages." Chapman argued that, although everyone is able to express their love in different ways, a person will have a natural preference for expressing love in one particular way. Chapman's options were:

- Giving words of affirmation.
- Spending quality time with someone.
- Giving and receiving gifts.
- Giving acts of service.
- Physically (hugs, cuddles and kisses, et cetera)[3]

Parents cannot love too much, but they can *express* it too much. In the exercise of their love, some parents can smother, cosset and bubble-wrap their sons. Such expressions of love, however well meaning, can be disastrous and result in a son being fearful, paranoid and unable to cope with the bumps and bruises of everyday living.

True love will endure short-term unpopularity to achieve long-term good. True love will be tough on behaviors that are not worthy of a son. True love can mean saying "no."

Tough love

The concept of tough love has been around for some time. It was probably first used by Bill Milliken in his 1968 book *Tough Love*.[4] Essentially, the book encourages parents to exercise stern and un-compromising "authoritative parenting" in order to build appropri-ate behaviors in their children. It is suggested that failure to do so can result in a child being spoiled and lacking in resilience.

Others are less enthusiastic about the concept of tough love. They do not support the idea of sending recalcitrant sons to military-style boot camps in the middle of wilderness areas where they have to start cooking fires using nothing but two sticks and a bit of tum-bleweed.

Tough love, however, need not be limited to such extremes. And it is important that authoritarian parents do not leap upon the notion of tough love in order to justify their snarling. Tough love is not about disciplining. It is about loving.

It can be about a parent saying "yes" at the right time and "no" at the right time. It can be about a parent saying, for example, "In this family and under this roof, there will be *no* acceptance of illegal drugs." It can be about a parent allowing their son to learn by failing.

A great phrase used to sell Irish ale and music is "Strong words, softly spoken." This is not a bad description of tough love. In the end, tough love is about putting principles before popularity. And this can be just as tough on a parent as on a son!

Love is not a weak concept. Love can mean saying goodbye to a son and pushing him out of the nest when he is 36 years old, employed in a good job and addicted to his mother's cooking.

The letter

Not all conversations need be verbal. One of the most effective ways of getting a message to a son is to write. Sandra Carey-Boggans knew she was dying of breast cancer. Initially, her doctors thought they had halted the disease—but they were wrong. Despite a mastectomy, chemotherapy and radiation, the cancer spread to her bones and her stomach. Sandra died at St. Barnabas Hospice in Worthing, England, at the age of 44.

Before she died, Sandra made personalized gift boxes for her two sons, Jacob, 13, and Lewis, 10. These boxes were only to be opened after she died. In them, she placed photos, a CD she had recorded called "My Journey," some of her perfume (so that her sons could remember her smell) and some letters. In the letters, she told her sons how much she loved them. Sandra also encouraged them not to complain if things went wrong, to not be afraid of making mistakes and to always think of others.[5]

This moving story has been played out in many other families. A Bangladeshi mother, Nargis Sultana, left a similar note to her only son, Upaul, when she knew she was dying. Nargis advised him to be honest and kind, but not to let others exploit him. She warned him to be careful because there are wicked people in the world as well as nice ones. Nargis went on to advise her son about his diet (he had allergies), what to do during empty holidays and what to do if his father died prematurely (a distinct possibility in her country). She finished by encouraging Upaul to have a wonderful life and to visit her grave sometimes with flowers. Her final advice was to marry while young, to have more than one child and to fill his house with laughter.[6]

A message from a parent to a son that is thoughtfully written and raw with honesty is a letter that a son is likely to treasure for the rest of his life.

AN IDEA

Write a Letter to Your Son

Not every parent is possessed of the poetic skills of a Nobel laureate such as Kipling, but they *are* able to write a letter.

Why not write a letter to your son? Imagine you had only one letter to write to your son: what would you say? Why not say it now and give him the assurances of love and the words of wisdom you want to be certain he hears?

Some parents leave the writing of such a letter to the eleventh hour, only to be separated from their son in the tenth hour.

SUMMARY

The most important things to keep in mind during this conversation are:

- A son needs to know that he is loved and needs to be reminded of this love regularly.
- A balance needs to be struck between expressing too much parental love and too little.

- There are different ways parents can show love toward their son: through words, through deeds, by being present and by providing for him, as well as through seeking to meet not only their son's physical needs but also his need for security and safety, a sense of belonging, self-esteem and self-realization.
- There are different "love languages" parents can use: words of affirmation, quality time, gifts and acts of service.
- At times, parents will have to exercise tough love—this is about putting principles before popularity.
- A well-written letter can be a good reminder of a parent's love for their son.

Identity

IT IS IMPORTANT for a boy to know who he is. He needs to know what he is capable of physically, intellectually, socially, emotionally and spiritually. A boy must also work out who he wants to become. In short, he has to take ownership of his own identity.

One of the more important things a boy can be told is that, as a person, he is special. This statement is true even if the son is playing up to the extent that a parent would cheerfully trade him in for a concrete garden gnome. Every son needs to know that he is a biological wonder and a miracle of creation.

A son has about 70 trillion cells and a brain infinitely more powerful than the world's biggest computer. He has some 650 muscles to buff up and about 30,000 miles of nerves to soothe. Defying belief is a boy's capacity to detect 10,000 different smells—which, although a little less than his mother's ability, is still impressive. Yes—our sons are a biological wonder.

*

Some sons have no idea who they are or what they believe. If a boy does know what he believes, it may be only because he has inherited his opinion, rather than arriving at it himself. A son must eventually "own" what he believes in. This can take some effort because his preference might be to mimic a political opinion from friends, a faith from a parent and a cause from a teacher. While entirely understandable, particularly in the younger child, eventually a son must find his own voice.

The religious reformer Martin Luther (1483–1546) once stood before his critics and said, "Here I stand, I can do no other." Our sons need to know where they stand. An alarming number, however, appear happy to progress through life without cause, creed or conviction.

They do not know themselves. They have no understanding of their unique gifts. They have no idea of who they are or what they want to become.

AN IDEA

Show how others have found their identity

There are many stories about men in search of their identity. These stories can be useful as a catalyst to talk to your son about *his* identity.

For example, if your son is in his late teens, you might draw him into a conversation about identity after he experiences the musical *Les Misérables*. Within the musical, one of the characters is Jean Valjean. He is a fugitive from the Bagne of Toulon, a Toulon prison. Valjean is hunted by the police inspector Javert, who mistakenly arrests a man called Champmathieu, thinking him to be Valjean. A tormented Valjean, although severely tempted not to, steps forward and proclaims loudly that an error has been made and that *he* is the fugitive. He is Jean Valjean. He is prisoner 24601.

It is a powerful scene and one that works on many levels. The scene is not just about one man stopping another (innocent) man from going to prison. It is about a man choosing who he wants to be—a prisoner, yes, but also a man of integrity.

If your teenage son is not interested in musicals, then a good film can also be a great way to start a conversation about identity. In the film *Gladiator*, Russell Crowe plays the role of Maximus, a much-loved Spanish general who is to take over as Emperor from Marcus Aurelius. However, the son of Marcus Aurelius, the evil Commodus, murders his father, crucifies Maximus's wife and son and sells Maximus as a gladiator. Maximus survives and eventually finds his way to the fighting arena of the Colosseum in Rome. On winning, Maximus is congratulated by Commodus. The scene is an epic.

Commodus, anxious to share and even usurp the adulation of the crowd, asks Maximus to reveal himself and his real name. Maximus tells Commodus that his name is Gladiator. Then he turns and walks away. Commodus is incensed at this calculated insult and demands that the slave remove his helmet and tell him his name. Maximus turns slowly and faces his enemy. With the crowd entranced, the gladiator removes his helmet. In strong and measured words, he states boldly that his name is Maximus Decimus Meridius.

Lest Commodus be in any doubt of the gladiator's identity, Maximus goes further and states that he is Commander of the Armies of the North and General of the Felix Legions, a loyal servant of the *true* Emperor, Marcus Aurelius, father of a murdered son, and husband of a murdered wife.

Everyone—particularly Commodus—is stunned at the revelation of identity and at the audacity of the gladiator, who concludes his speech with the chilling threat that he will have his vengeance on Commodus in this life or the next.

There was a man who knew who he was.

Maximus knew he was not just a slave. He was a loyal General and a loving father. Our sons need to know that they are not just a boy with limited vocabulary, uncoordinated limbs and an odor issue. They are a unique assemblage of gifts and abilities. They are a wonder of creation and they have a reason to be on this planet.

Standing out

Many of our sons do not like to be in the center of an arena. They like to be in the crowd, the same as their peers, watching and commenting from the safety of the stands. Parents need to talk to their sons about the romance of the lone individual versus the comfort of the herd. When is it right to stand out and when is it right to blend in?

When is it right for a son to be silent and when is it right for a son to speak out? What they speak, how they speak and when they speak are revelations of who they are. There is a time when silence does not enrich or edify. Silence can be a terrible thing. Silence is not always golden; it can be yellow, the yellow of cowardice that stops us from speaking when we should. When we see a bully at work causing physical, social or emotional harm and we do not speak, we are cowards; when we hear a cry for help and remain deaf within a silent cone of indifference, we are heartless.

There is a time when our sons need to speak, particularly when their voice can bring justice, take away pain or right a wrong. There is a time for a boy to declare who he is and what he stands for in the arena of life. A parent needs to discuss with their son the difference between good silence and bad silence.

*

We knew that something wasn't right, but the final thing that brought him into my study was a series of dark drawings in his art portfolio. The agonized faces in his sketches hinted at an inner torment. What was wrong?

His parents were sensible, meat-and-three-vegetable types. They now sat around my coffee table. He was white with worry. Her eyes were red with tears and she twisted her handkerchief around her wrist like a tourniquet.

The boy was unresponsive to my gentle probing about his well-being. He remained unresponsive to the more direct questions about his well-being. The inquiry was not going well. A pastoral session was fast becoming a disciplinary one, for the boy matched my growing exasperation with growing belligerence.

The parents were horrified at the growing truculence of their son. He seemed to be on a journey of self-destruction. The in-your-face responses, in front of his headmaster, suggested he no longer cared what anyone thought of him. The atmosphere grew tense—very tense.

Then it happened. Like an exploding champagne bottle, the boy leaped to his feet and shouted, "I'm gay!"

Hyperventilating and wild of eye, he stood flexing his arms as if for a fight. Then he waited for the inevitable outpouring of shock and disgust.

No one moved, so the boy shouted once more, "I'm bloody-well gay!"

The silence that followed this reaffirmation was eventually broken by the mother, who said, "Yes, dear. We've suspected this for some time. Your father and I just want to know what the matter is."

Identity formation

Neither a son nor his parents usually have much say in his sexual orientation. However, other aspects of his identity, beliefs and values are influenced by those who nurture him. The chief influence, in this regard, is usually his family. However, over time, the family influence is modified by other sources. The boy puts his nose over the backyard fence and smells different things. He watches television and surfs the net and sees different things. He goes to school and hears different things. The boy has discovered that there is a big world out there, an exciting world with conflicting beliefs and values, a dangerous world where acceptance is conditional, a beguiling world that provides alternative points of view. The boy begins to work out that it is ultimately the world in which he must live and that it is ultimately the world that will define him. So, it is to the world he must begin to turn for his identity.

Les Parrott, a professor of clinical psychology for Seattle Pacific University, suggests that teens struggle with identity formation in five different ways:

1. Through having the right possessions—clothes, phone, DVDs, et cetera.
2. Through mimicking adult behavior, particularly in relation to sex, alcohol, smoking, other drugs and the use of the car.
3. Through rebellion and taking deliberate steps to differentiate themselves from their parents.
4. Through the adoption of heroes and an alliance with attractive role models.
5. Through inclusion and exclusion. This involves association with certain groups and communion with certain cliques. (Consider the time spent by many boys on social-networking sites.)[1]

To this list of Parrott's, a sixth way can be added. It is a way that is particularly pertinent to a boy:

6. Through trials, challenges and tests.

This can be done in many ways, including wrestling with Dad, doing a science exam or going on a camp in a wilderness setting.

"He's not going"

This was Groundhog Day. For the past three years, the mother had given me a doctor's certificate that excused her son from having to go on the Year 7 camp, the Year 8 camp and then the Year 9 camp. He was now in Year 10.

The boy was quite bright, especially in math and science. He could have been even more accomplished, except he was addicted to computer games and social-networking sites. Socially, he had limited interpersonal skills. Physically, he was a pudding. Morally, he seemed compliant except for the discovery of some hard-core porn in his locker six months earlier. If anyone needed to go to Cadet Camp, it was this boy, and I told his mother so.

But his mother was adamant. "He's not going."

I'd been in this frustrating position before, not just with camps but also with annual cross-country runs in which the whole school participated—theoretically. Bad back, death of a relative and a severe cold had frustrated this boy's ability to run thus far into his school career.

As the only son of a doting family, the boy had become a manipulative headache. He was also becoming more disconnected from his peers. The shared experiences at school had unified his peers, but the boy had not been a part of these adventures and, as a result, he was finding it difficult to be accepted.

"He's not going," the mother repeated.

I said that it was most unfortunate and that I hoped he would soon recover from what the doctor had described as sore tendons.

What I wanted to say was, *When a boy goes through the terrifying experience of having to rappel down a cliff, he learns a little more about conquering fear. When he treks to exhaustion, he learns a little more about overcoming fragility. When he shares a tent with others, he learns a little more about community living. He not only learns about map reading, camp craft and how to treat a blister, he learns about himself—his strengths and his weaknesses. Furthermore, he learns that he can use that which he is good at to help others and use others to help him with what he is bad at.*

"He's not going."

And he didn't. Not long after, the boy was withdrawn to go to an academically selective school that had no sporting or co-curricular expectations.

"He's going to a better school," his mother explained.

AN IDEA

Get your son to write his CV

A task that might be useful in order to choreograph reflection on identity is for your son to write his curriculum vitae. The exercise can cause him to reflect on who he is—his strengths and weaknesses, his salable assets and even his liabilities.

ADVICE ON WRITING A CV

There are no hard and fast rules. A good CV is one that works to get an interview and job. Those requiring CVs differ so much in what they like and do not like, it is difficult to give firm guidelines as to how to write one. You should also remember that there are different styles of CV needed for different types of jobs.

Having noted the above, the following guidelines are shared as a starting point:

- Make the CV no longer than four pages.
- Ensure that the CV is easy to read, does not look cramped, has well-spaced text and uses short paragraphs.
- Use bullet points to summarize a lot of information in an economical fashion.
- Use good-quality white or cream paper. It can have a subtle fleck in it but nothing obvious.
- Print the CV with clear ink so it is easy to read. Do not hand-write the CV.
- If other binding techniques are used, choose a method that allows each page to be turned easily so that it can be photocopied without difficulty.
- Number the pages and put a footer or header that states something like: *Page 2 of 4 Curriculum Vitae for John E. Hopeful.*

- Use a font that is easy to read such as **Times New Roman** (if you prefer a serif font) or **Helvetica** (if you prefer a sans serif font) in either 12 point or 14 point.
- Limit underlining. Use **bold** instead.
- Justify against the left margin. Justifying against both left and right margins is also fine.
- When listing employment history, education and so on, do so in reverse chronological order—i.e., with your most recent activity or achievement listed first.
- Have a slightly bigger margin at the bottom of the page than the top of the page, particularly if you are using a footer.
- Avoid long lists. They are difficult to read and digest.
- Be economical with words, and what words you do use should be chosen for their engagement and accuracy.

When your son has checked his CV for errors, get him to do it again. When he has double-checked, suggest he give the CV to a capable person who can also check it.

THE ORDER OF MATERIAL

There are no absolute rules about the order of presenting material in a CV. However, the following order works well for a school graduate.

1. Name, address and contact details.
2. A brief personal overview that is designed to capture the interest of the reader.
3. Educational history and record of academic achievements.
4. Personal interests and achievements.
5. Other relevant personal details, such as whether you have a driver's license, etc.
6. Contact details of references and copies of letters of commendation and/or written references.

When preparing a CV, it is best to write in the past tense, which gives the indication that something has been achieved. It is also best to use active verbs rather than low-impact or passive verbs. For example:

■ "I helped with social events at school" sounds a bit lame when you can write "I negotiated with suppliers to ensure school dances made a profit."

■ "I helped a group of junior students" is weak when it is just as accurate to write "I counseled a Year 7 tutor group and advised them on pastoral matters."

■ "I set up a cafeteria group" can be put as "I initiated a product advisory committee for the school's cafeteria."

Starting each point with a powerful verb such as "negotiated," "counseled," "constructed" or "initiated" can make a CV very effective.

SPICING UP THE CV

It is vital that whatever is written is the truth and nothing but the truth. Improving the presentation is one thing. Improving the facts is an entirely different thing. There is nothing wrong with the former, but the latter is unethical. However, while not straying from the bounds of factual accuracy, it is entirely possible to take a very tame CV and make it far more interesting, as in the following examples:

■ "I like watching TV" could be accurate but it will probably be a turn-off for the reader, who could be tempted to condemn you as a couch potato with little energy, imagination or wit. It would be much better to say "I enjoy courtroom dramas."

■ "I like reading" is very tame when one can write "I am interested in maritime novels set in the eighteenth and nineteenth centuries."

■ Even the listing of subjects studied at school can be enriched. "Geography" could be changed to "Physical Geography with a particular emphasis on coastal landforms," and "Economic

Geography including studies into the retail habits of London shoppers."

RELEVANCE

Information must not become long-winded or irrelevant. Not all employers will be impressed by studies into the retail habits of London shoppers. Then again, someone considering an applicant as an employee in a shoe shop may be very interested. Boys need to give information about themselves that is relevant to the position for which they are applying.

A CV should be handled with care, with a good balance between understatement and overstatement. There needs to be enough "wow factor" to turn a reader on, but not so much that it turns a reader off.

For example, the following is probably a little too strong:

I am incredible at seeing through people and am able to sense what is troubling them. I am able to mix in fantastically well with others and lead them socially for I am particularly skilled in sensing how others are feeling. People always tell me that they want me as their friend because I am so caring. This means I am wonderful at customer relations, and have the extraordinary ability to make others feel good.

This might be more appropriate:

My particular strengths are in working with people. I have demonstrated that I have the interpersonal skills necessary to be an effective counselor. Volunteer work with the school's helpline has exercised and extended my abilities in this regard.

TELLING IT LIKE IT IS

A CV, even one written with integrity, tends to dwell on the better attributes of the subject. This is entirely understandable, but danger comes when one believes one's own publicity. The desire to be thought well of, annexed with wishful thinking, can lead a boy to give himself a CV that is unrealistically rosy.

Schools can also be guilty of "gilding the lily," which does not help a boy understand what others truly think of him. It is far easier to write a good report card than a poor report card.

More than once, I have been tempted to write a reference on a boy along these lines.

HEADMASTER'S REFERENCE

Academically, Doofus is a passenger in class who gives little back other than a mediocre effort that has done little to extend him. He rouses himself from average performance in those few subjects that interest him, but he requires such high maintenance from his teachers to get him to produce anything like the work he is capable of that they get tired and discouraged. This results in Doofus blaming them for his ordinary performance.

In the co-curricular life of the school, Doofus has remained largely indifferent to the many plays and musical events, and takes little pleasure in the visual and performing arts. He has engaged in music classes but this is no great achievement given that it is a compulsory activity. Like most boys, Doofus enjoys sports. Like most boys, he is moderately good at it but not as good as he thinks he is.

In terms of character, Doofus enjoys his friends but thereafter his interest in the well-being of others is limited. He develops a nasty whine when confronted by critics and is prone to immature sulks if he does not get his own way. Doofus is a low-level racist, with his body language and occasional snide remarks revealing a real discomfort when he is with boys of backgrounds different to his own. Possessed of a critical spirit, Doofus is quick with a verbal taunt but is even quicker to avoid the blame.

On spiritual and ethical matters, Doofus remains two-dimensional and lacks substance. His religious activities are driven more by social convention than spiritual conviction, and his current attitude toward all things spiritual can be described as "passive resistance." Doofus is an occasional smoker and he has been suspected of the theft of an iPad.

I cannot really commend Doofus to you with any pleasure. In time, he might improve, but I rather suspect his character traits are set for life.

Yours with unaccustomed sincerity, et cetera.

But, in the end, I don't write this sort of thing. The result is that the boy remains ignorant of his real qualities. And, I'm part of the reason why.

The need for care

Helping a boy find his true identity is all well and good when that identity is a good-news story, but when that identity is of questionable value, the experience—as shown above—can be crushing. Therefore, care is needed when helping a son along a journey of self-discovery.

It has been suggested that it takes three positive comments to counter one negative comment. Barbara Fredrickson and Marcial Losada reckon that the tipping point between flourishing and languishing is a person hearing 2.9 positive comments to every negative one. Other researchers suggest even more positive comments are needed to neutralize a negative one.[2]

Parents, and even headmasters, can struggle to deliver the requisite number of positive comments. We show our care by trying to improve those in our charge. Our zeal for betterment expresses itself in a constant stream of correction. Even worse, we can engage in shaming our sons:

You ought to be ashamed of yourself. Don't you know what your behavior is doing to your mother? In my day . . .

But be warned: shaming a son hardly ever works.

Giving feedback

Some time ago, I was invited to stay at a farm in the Hunter Valley region, a few hours' drive north of Sydney. The farmer was a parent of one of my boarders and I was extended the warmth and generosity that is the hallmark of so many who work the land. They were gentle folk, but they were also folk who would think nothing of killing a steer if they needed meat. As farmers, they exercised an authority over their farm that was uncompromising, yet they had compassionate and sensitive hearts. Hardness when it mattered. Gentleness most of the time. No wonder their son was a gem. He had experienced authoritative parenting.

This same authority could be seen in the way the father rode his horse. The bond between horse and rider could not be doubted. The horse was quick to trot over and nuzzle his master when entering the dressage arena; it then had its nose stroked and its flanks patted. The two were close. I was treated to an extraordinary demonstration of horsemanship with the horse being put through the most intricate and complex of maneuvers with nothing more than nudges from the rider's knees.

When parents give their son small nudges, he will go in the right direction throughout life without the need for harsh control. If the boy is untrained, he will need reins. Nothing other than a violent pull on the bit in the mouth and a painful dig in the sides will get him to turn in the right direction.

Regular, authoritative feedback that is given lovingly will direct a son in a way that months of silence, interrupted by violent confrontation, will not.

A boy needs feedback to understand himself and who he is, and also to know how people view him. A natural time to give feedback is when writing a son a birthday card. *To John, With love from Mom and Dad*, can be improved. Try something like, *Dear John, You continue to bring a great deal of joy into our lives. Thank you for being you. I have particularly loved the way you have grown in the area of . . .* And away the parent goes with their letter of affirmation.

However, the other 364 days of the year also need to be employed to give feedback to a son. Notes on pillows, emails, words of encouragement and other methods of affirmation can all be used to encourage appropriate identity formation in a son.

AN IDEA

Arrange a positive postal program

In the 1970s, a program emerged called The Emmaus Walk. It was an initiative that grew out of the Christian church, but has also been enjoyed by a multi-faith community. Essentially, it involves a three-day retreat that encourages a person to reflect on who they are and what they want to become. As part of this program, the person receives letters—designed to affirm and encourage—written by friends, colleagues and other acquaintances.

It is possible to arrange a similar program of positive feedback for your son. This could coincide with a special event such as a birthday or going to a new school. Friends and relatives can be asked to write or email a personal reflection.

It can be helpful to guide this reflection by giving some headings such as the following:

- What I admire about you (e.g., kindness, helpfulness, independence, team skills, resilience, cheerfulness, wisdom, thoughtfulness, talents, ability).
- What I hope for you (e.g., potential, possibilities for the future).
- What I suggest for you (e.g., academically, socially, physically, emotionally, morally, spiritually).

You could collect these letters and give them to your son at the appropriate time, such as a birthday dinner.

Give specific feedback

"Good puzzling."

What a curious thing to hear. The praise had come from my daughter-in-law and had been directed to one of her children. Sometime later, I heard, "Good sweeping."

Intrigued, I asked her why she was using these novel terms of encouragement with my grandchildren. Her answer was that it was a result of some reading she had done and some observations she had made about the risks associated with giving over-generous and un-qualified praise.

I sat somewhat chastened (I am a doting grandfather) as she ex-plained that saying things such as "You're wonderful" and "You're clever" was often not helpful because a child would begin to believe they were wonderful, when they had done little to deserve it, and that they were clever in everything—when they were not.

Needless to say, this saying has now become a virus in our house-hold. "Good waiting." "Good phoning." "Good . . ." You get the idea.

I think it works.

Exploring a son's history

A boy is fashioned by his history. This history is a complex interac-tion of nature and nurture, both of which impact to forge his char-acter. It is surprising how many boys have little or no idea of their history, and no idea of their ancestry. Sometimes, there are good reasons for this. Adopted and fostered children may be happier not to know about their bloodline. Sometimes, there are bad reasons for this. Some sons have not been curious enough and some parents have not been open enough about their past.

There needs to be some sensitivity about this initiative because some families have histories that should be quarantined from inquiry. However, despite there being the odd black sheep spotted within the family flock, family histories generally can be shared to great advantage. Few families have not been touched by scandal or shame, but most have things in their past that deserve to be acknowledged and celebrated.

Knowing something of the family past can be rewarding not only in terms of interest but also in terms of lessons learned. Some of these lessons can be lifesaving. Is there a history of diabetes in the family? Is there a history of prostate cancer in the family? Is there a history of high cholesterol?

Most family histories have great stories that should be told. Despite me having my grandfather's Military Cross for a decade, I've only just found out why it was awarded.

A case study of discovered family history

Lieutenant Thomas Andrew Lawrie was taken off to the battlefields of the First World War at an average speed of 25.92 kilometers an hour. The single-funneled *Clan MacGillivray* had been leased by the Commonwealth Government from its Glasgow owners to serve as one of His Majesty's Australian Transports. Thomas Lawrie was in demand. He was part of the February 1917 reinforcements—and reinforcements were continually needed in the grim squalor of the European battlefields. Even though Australia was in a different hemisphere to the main theater of war, its men enrolled in droves. In the First World War, 61,000 men of the fledgling nation were killed, a larger proportion than almost any other nation. Seventy-five percent died in France and Belgium—which was where Thomas was heading.

Thomas was a "Magnificent Bastard"—a nickname given to those who served in the 7th Field Company Engineers. He was a combat engineer whose job was to provide support for the Allied infantry and tanks chasing the Germans out of France. Unfortunately, the Germans were proving hard to dislodge. They had built themselves a well-designed series of defensive trenches, concrete ma-

chine-gun emplacements and artillery positions along what was
called the Hindenburg Line.

The habit of herding infantry against well-positioned German
machine guns had been modified after the senseless carnage of previous battles such as the Somme, where the British Expeditionary
Force suffered 58,000 casualties in one day. The use of tanks to support the infantry had been shown to work well by Sir John Monash,
the Australian commander who orchestrated the first full breach of
the Hindenburg Line in late September 1918. However, in the days
following this initial success, things got difficult. Further penetration
of the Hindenburg Line was frustrated by a lack of certainty about
where the Americans were positioned. This closed down artillery
support for fear of hitting the American troops. Progress was also
halted by stout German resistance from their line of defenses—the
Beaurevoir Line.

After heroic action, the British 46th and 32nd Divisions, together
with the Australian 2nd Division and their Magnificent Bastards, finally overran the Beaurevoir Line. The action involved the use of
artillery and tanks to support face-to-face fighting undertaken using
Lewis guns and grenades. The victory heralded the beginning of the
end of the First World War. Armistice Day was declared a month
later on the eleventh hour of the eleventh day of the eleventh month.
It was in these final battles that Thomas won his Military Cross.

The citation speaks of conspicuous gallantry during an attack
near Beaurevoir on October 3, 1918. The engineer had followed the
attack and, despite heavy machine-gun fire, high-explosive shells
and gas, had crawled forward to reconnoiter the newly captured
ground. As an enemy battery pounded the area, Thomas crept forward and made a "recce" along an 880-meter stretch. He secured
valuable information about road positions and enemy soldiers mass-
ing for a counterattack. Under what was described as "a perfect hail
of bullets," Thomas made his way back to his lines and advised the
artillery of the situation; measures were then taken to neutralize the
threat.

I have my grandfather's Military Cross. It was an award created for commissioned officers of Captain or below, and for Warrant Officers. It is awarded for acts of exemplary gallantry against the enemy while fighting on land. I now know why he won it. So does my son.

*

Not everyone will have stories like this they can share with their son, but they have other stories, many of them even more absorbing. We must tell them. Australian Aboriginal people often gather their sons and tell them the great Dreamtime stories of their heritage and cultural beliefs. By so doing, they transmit identity and belonging. In the western world, we tend not to do this. We let our sons congregate in front of the computer and we leave the storytelling to Hollywood. We shouldn't always do this. Our stories are often better.

AN IDEA

Hold a family history evening

There is value in holding a family dinner, with as many relatives present as possible, in order to talk about the family's history. You might want to go further and formally research your family history. However, a few anecdotes and a couple of yellowed photos might be all that is needed to have a successful family history evening.

Not all the stories shared need to be about winning a Military Cross. Stories of family failure can be just as important for a boy to hear. (Thomas Lawrie went on to virtually abandon his wife and children in order to pursue a career as an engineer. He eventually died of heart failure while still quite young.)

Boys love stories and boys love heroes. A son who hears heroic stories about his family can feel inspired and uplifted. Even if there are no heroes to celebrate, tales from the past can cause a boy to recognize that he has a unique history, that he belongs, that he has a story.

Secret men's business

Secret men's business can profitably be included in the social agenda of a growing boy. These are times when male family members and male friends gather to enjoy activities typically appreciated by males (sports, fishing, playing pool, camping, tinkering with a car). The importance of these times, however, lies not only in the fun but also in the male mentoring a son can receive.

A boy needs to know how to handle his maleness. He needs to know why his penis is erect in the morning, why he has wet dreams, why he wants to masturbate. He will need to understand the importance of using his strength wisely. He will need to understand how to handle the "fight or flight" impulses that have been imprinted into his mind by thousands of years of hunting and fighting. He needs to understand the physics of his body. He also needs to understand its chemistry.

A boy will get his first significant injection of testosterone at about age six. This will cause him to migrate a little from a mother's apron strings and journey toward his dad's overalls. However, the main surge in testosterone comes when a boy is about 12. Testosterone levels in boys can soar to 20 times the level in girls. This anabolic steroid helps beef up the body and assists it to repair and grow through the capacity of testosterone to facilitate the storage of phosphorous, calcium and other elements.

A parent needs to remind his son that, while accounting for slightly less than 50 percent of the population, males perpetrate most of the physical violence and a good proportion of the emotional violence throughout the land. Scientists have sought to find out why. By the simple expedient of subtracting testes from a number of once-proud animal subjects, it was found that levels of aggression could be reduced. Thus, a major culprit for the querulous nature in males was found to be testosterone. A prize Brahman bull positively radiant in testosterone does not make for a docile family pet.

A boy needs to know why it is that at the age of about 11 he wakes up one morning with an attack of the grumps that lasts for several years and only begins to diminish when he is about 18. His voice drops an octave and language regression happens, with communication limited to a few hostile grunts. Bodily hair and muscle definition occurs, together with a belligerent slouch. The once-perfect skin can take on the cratered appearance of the moon, and confrontation occurs about bed times, clothes, money, hair, homework, manners, hygiene and cell-phone bills, with the result that parents face serious temptations to sell the son on eBay.

A father, or a father figure, needs to talk to their son about what it means to be a male. This should not be limited to an awkward birds-and-bees talk. It needs to be a constant conversation in which a son is guided in his understanding of his body and how to look after it.

AN IDEA

Hold a ceremony to induct your son into manhood

There is benefit in formally inducting a son into manhood. All too often, a boy is left wondering whether he has reached manhood and whether he has the qualities necessary to be considered a man. Families in developing countries often affirm their sons have reached manhood better than those in the developed world. An initiation ceremony that involves a touch of body scarring, a night or two of dancing and a period of enforced isolation on "walkabout" is apt to make an impression on a boy and leave him in no doubt that he has been admitted to the ranks of manhood.

It might be unwise to replicate some of these induction ceremonies, but there might be wisdom in taking the principles of initiation and translating them into a culturally relevant setting. For example, it might be possible to spend a weekend celebrating your son's transition to manhood when he is somewhere between the ages of 14 and 18. This should not just be another party, or a case of merely throwing car keys at him. It needs to be an occasion that reminds him what the qualities of a man are and affirms that he has these qualities. Furthermore, this judgment needs to be made by those whose opinions he respects.

Those of the Jewish faith will know of the coming-of-age ceremonies given for a boy who has turned 13. It is a time when a boy is judged as being accountable for his actions and able to understand and live by the Torah. Festivities sometimes include a *seudat mitzvah*, or celebratory meal with friends and relatives. It is a practice that has much to commend it.

Standing for something

There is an aphorism that suggests "If you stand for nothing, you will fall for anything."

Although it is not unknown for the young to have strong opinions, whether they are *informed* opinions is another thing entirely. Personal conviction in the young can sometimes be hard to find. Apathy, cynicism and downright laziness conspire to persuade many sons not to believe in anything.

When young men find themselves of an age to go to the ballot box, the experience can leave some feeling overwhelmed. Small wonder. Many have not thought through their political convictions. Some will be drawn to fashionable political stances. There is more than a little attraction to vote for a political party that pledges to save the world from human despoliation. Indeed, a growing concern for the environment is one of the more encouraging characteristics of the young. However, politics is about more than a single issue. For this reason, it is important for a boy to know things about their party other than its policy on bulldozers and carbon emission. What is their education policy? What is their foreign policy? What is their tax policy?

The habit many teens have of seeing issues in black and white also needs to be dealt with. Shades of gray must be entertained, presumptions tested and options properly considered. A boy also needs to learn some of the political realities of life, including the fact that most politicians have a persona that is for display purposes only.

AN IDEA

Explain the meaning of some key political ideologies

It is good to teach a son the differences between left-wing and right-wing ideology and the basic tenets of some of the major political orientations. It is important to give this information in an unbiased way so that your son can have ownership of his convictions rather than inheriting a political disposition from you.

The sort of "neutral" information about politics you could share with your son includes the following.

SOCIALISM

- Left wing in political orientation.
- Sometimes linked to communism, which seeks a classless society in which everyone is equal.
- Promotes the control of production by an elected government that runs it for the benefit of everyone on an equal-share basis.
- Tends to be strong on social-welfare issues.
- Distrusts the corporate world and capitalism.

CAPITALISM

- Right wing in political orientation.
- Economy is driven by a profit motive and characterized by private ownership rather than ownership by the government for the people.
- Usually related to free enterprise and individual effort: if you work hard, you earn more; if you are successful, you earn more.
- Linked to liberalism and a free-market economy in which the strong thrive and the weak "go to the wall."

In order for your son to find his political voice, you might have a chat about where he stands on the following continuums.

LEFT WING	RIGHT WING
Generally like change	Generally like status quo
Attracted to democracy	Attracted to rule by the strongest
Attracted to a classless society and equal wealth	Attracted to free enterprise and reward for effort
Attracted to production being run by the government	Attracted to production being run by private organizations
Attracted to socialism	Attracted to capitalism
Support the idea of the government providing help	Support the idea of self-help
Believe there should be more freedom	Believe there should be some limitations
Usually believe many traditions and customs are dated	Usually enjoy traditions and maintaining past customs

*

The intention of this exercise is to illustrate that, with a little thought, parents can do a great deal to help their son find his identity. This can be done in many domains other than politics. Character, personality, faith, preferred learning style, aptitude, and a plethora of other dimensions can also be explored.

Just how it is done is open to debate. That it should be done is not. Our sons need to know who they are.

SUMMARY

The most important things to keep in mind during this conversation are:

- A son must know that he is special, that he has unique gifts and is a biological wonder.
- A son must know who he is physically, intellectually, socially, emotionally and spiritually, and he must eventually take ownership of his own identity.
- Maturity in our sons comes from knowing when to blend in and when to stand out, and when to speak and when to be silent.

- Teenage boys find their identity in many ways, and in order for them to develop an accurate understanding of self they must receive honest and regular feedback from their parents.
- Our sons must be encouraged to find out what they believe and to stand for something.

CONVERSATION THREE

Values

A VISIT TO PARKLEA CORRECTIONAL CENTER in Sydney's outer west is a confronting experience. My visit was made necessary by a godson being incarcerated in the maximum-security prison because of a variety of offenses related to alcohol and drug addiction.

After parking in the prison car park, I didn't know where to go, so I trailed two people who were huge, tattooed and angry. Following their swear words, I journeyed past the chirruping of voices from a childcare center established for the families of visitors—a touch of soft innocence in a hard and guilty place. Then we lined up to get into prison. It would have been quicker to throw a brick through a window.

They needed to know the prisoner's number. I don't know why they wanted this information; I had already provided it when applying for permission to visit some two weeks earlier. I stood next to a young mother with a baby who needed assistance to write her details—she had difficulty shaping her words. So did I. It was that sort of a place.

We went inside and waited in a room where people were used to waiting. As I shrank into a plastic chair, Asian groups chattered, Middle Eastern gangs whispered and Anglo wives swore.

No, you can't see your old man.

Why the fuck not?

He's been a naughty boy.
What's he fucking well been up to?
He's been using stuff inside that he shouldn't.

The warning signs were a distraction. They told me that displays of affection were to be limited to a kiss on arrival and on departure, that my dress had to be modest and that nothing was to be taken into the prison other than baby food. I took comfort in the knowledge that my godson did not like baby food and I was wearing slacks. And the only thing my godson was getting from me was a hug.

Photographed and fingerprinted, I was allowed into the prison. However, it took two attempts. After being searched and passing through a what-are-you-hiding machine, I was caught. In disgrace, I was sent to put the errant piece of paper—on which I had written my godson's prison number—into a locker.

I was pushed toward a heavy iron door. No one told me what to do. It clicked, so I pushed. It didn't move. So I pulled. It moved. I stepped in. Unbidden, the door closed behind me and I faced a second iron door. I felt trapped and longed to be anywhere but here. Eventually, the door clicked. I pushed. It moved. I then stepped into a space that looked like an indoor basketball court. To my right was a big desk filled with big guards. To my left was a cage full of angels.

Except they were not. They were inmates laced into white, pocket-less boiler suits. The word VISIT had been stamped blackly on their backs. A name was called. My godson was released from the cage and hugged me. I cried.

Consequences

The consequences of moral failure can result in toilets without lids. They can result in being locked in a twin cell from 3 p.m. to 9 a.m. They can result in having no rights to property until you have earned the money to buy it, including a kettle, sweatpants and extra coffee. Prison is not a happy place.

My godson comes from a middle-class home. His parents are my close friends. His sister is happily married. He wants to be, but various addictions and some personality issues are making it difficult.

Where did it all go wrong? I am frightened—because I do not know.

At a school assembly the following day, I looked out over the sea of faces. I could not tell them a guaranteed way to keep out of prison. My conversations with a godson had not worked.

What are morals?

Morals relate to that which is right and wrong. The degree to which we live in a "right" way is an indication of our morality. "*Morality*" comes from the Latin *moralitas*, which means behavior and manners that are thought to be proper. Socrates defined the term as "how we ought to live." It implies adhering to required standards.

There is more than a touch of the headmaster about the term "morality," so I wouldn't use it when chatting to a boy. Lest a son switch off when confronted by a rampant parent wanting to talk about the morals associated with chucking the cat into the fish pond, we need another term. Using the word "ethics" is not much lower on the crabbiness scale, and it really doesn't get us anywhere because ethics is merely the branch of philosophy that looks at morals. So, we're back to where we started.

The concept that is probably best to use when chatting to a son about what is good to build into their character is values.

Values are those things we believe to be important. They are an indication of the priority we attach to those things. They are a chosen code to live by. They are what might be recorded on our epitaphs.

A necessary conversation

Whereas the previous chapter looked at who a boy is, this chapter looks at who he should be. A son needs to hear, with sufficient regularity to stop the cat from being traumatized, the code of behavior a family chooses to live by. I say "family" because, even in this age of children's rights, this decision should not be given to a son, particularly to a young son.

A dangerous conversation

Talking to a son about values is both difficult and dangerous. It is difficult because the conversation can so easily degenerate into a sermon, which can so easily morph into a lecture, which can so easily end in a fight. It is dangerous because the exchange can so easily result in a strained relationship and a desire by the son to be anywhere other than within the audible range of the parent's voice.

Being difficult and dangerous does not necessarily disqualify a task. That said, values are best taught by wordless examples. If a parent does not pay for a parking space that relies on an honesty system, they give their son a definition of honesty. If a parent has demonstrated that they are a promise-breaker, their capacity to be taken seriously as a moral mentor is undermined. If a parent does not match their words with actions, they surrender the right to any high ground when talking to a son about being good. That said, it is also important to acknowledge that no one is perfect.

We are all dishonest. We tell tales of the Easter Bunny to explain the eggs, thank Santa for the presents and suggest the Tooth Fairy is a major carrier of loose change. We smile when we want to cry. We say, "Fine, thank you," when we're not. "Good to see you," when it isn't.

Some of our models of honesty have disgraced themselves. Politicians have been shown to lie, police to succumb to corruption, televangelists to sin, parents to abuse.

We mustn't grope to remove the speck in our son's eyes when there is a log in our own. It is as well to remind ourselves that most have fiddled, falsified, fabricated, fibbed, forged, faked or feigned, and that's just using the letter "f." We could go on. Let's try "d' . . . doctored, distorted, deceived, duped . . . The very existence of so many words describing a lack of honesty under almost any letter of the alphabet bears testimony to the frequent nature of dishonesty in our lives.

How many of us have won the right to accuse others of being dishonest? Who among us has never done one or more of the following?

- Fabricated an excuse to avoid an obligation.
- Cried crocodile tears over the misfortune of another.
- Borrowed something and never given it back.
- Argued a correct decision by an umpire or referee.
- Taken something that does not belong to us.

Are we the sort of parent who would always:

- Return money to the police if it were found on the footpath?
- Report damage we had accidentally caused?
- Fill in a tax return honestly?
- Pay a parking fee if it relied upon an honesty system?

So—we are all at risk of being crossed off Santa's list. However, this does not disqualify a parent from being a moral guide. Indeed, it can even strengthen their credentials. A parent's regret can be a powerful story to share with their son.

A difficult conversation

Chats to a son about morality and values usually arise because of a specific situation. Perhaps a son has exhibited some ordinary behavior that has resulted in a neighbor wanting to know why a cat has just dripped water throughout her house and is now shivering under a blanket in the spare room. Occasionally, and with regrettably less frequency, the conversation will be elicited by a son exercising good moral choices. It is worth celebrating these times. It is worth trying to balance the compliment/complaint ledger. It is worth reinforcing those times when a son's behavior causes a parent to smile.

Look for an excuse to give praise.

*

"Who says so?" the boy snarled.

It was not a question; it was an attack.

The mother, white with fatigue, was loading bags of shopping from a badly behaved shopping cart that seemed to want to deliver its contents to the car in the next parking bay. With a foot wedged under a cart wheel and straining under the weight of bags filled with orange juice and bottled water, the mother said, "God said so."

I was loading my own shopping into my car. Sensing my surprise, she looked at me and shrugged.

Choosing a code of behavior

"Who says so?" is not a bad question—if it is a question and not a get-stuffed-you've-no-right-to-tell-me-what-to-do statement. Whose standards does a family choose? Which values and what moral code are the right ones to pass on to a son? The recourse to "God" is very attractive because the trouble of working out what is right and what is wrong is hand-balled to a divine being.

Unfortunately, divine directive seems to be open to some alarmingly different interpretations. When is it right for the Christian to be loving and turn the other cheek, and when is it right for the Christian to turn over the tables of money changers at the temple? When is it right for the Muslim to kill the infidel, and when is it right to welcome him into the home?

Confusion in this area has resulted in God's name being used as an excuse to commit the most horrendous of crimes, at which God must weep. "God wants us to . . ." becomes easily confused with "I want you to. . . ." Introduce the human factor and pretty quickly that which is compassionate and loving becomes divisive and judgmental.

Things are not much easier in the secular world. What is deemed right and what is deemed wrong is blighted by an interpretative element that does not always distinguish neatly between these options. It merely advances what the dominant culture *considers* right and wrong. This is fine providing one feels at home with the dominant culture.

Any study of morality throughout the ages will show that it has been heavily influenced by the need to survive. It classes as "right" those behaviors that help a group survive and flourish, and it classes as "wrong" those behaviors that cause harm. This results in societal pressure to restrict individualism when it threatens the well-being of the broader community, and the cat.

So, in choosing the code of behavior to pass on to their son, parents have choices. Some will adopt a religious code that will align with divine imperatives. And why not? Many of these directives are rather good. Whatever faith stance a family has, it is difficult to improve on "Do to others what you want them to do to you," and "Love your neighbor as yourself."

There are also secular options. Some of these are also fairly attractive.

Celia Green, a British philosopher and psychologist, talks of there being:

- A Tribal Morality—which imposes behavioral norms on a son that are heavily influenced by the pervading culture in which his family lives. In other words: *This is how we do things here!*
- A Territorial Morality—which forbids behaviors by a son that are dangerous to property or people. Thereafter, anything goes. In other words: *If it doesn't hurt anyone, do it!*[1]

Unfortunately, it is not always that simple. What is accepted in one place may not be accepted in another. What doesn't hurt some people will hurt others. For example, saying "shit" in front of Aunt

Agatha may not be quite as acceptable as saying it when a 280-pound gorilla stamps on your foot in a football brawl.

All sorts of other things can influence the values and moral code of a family—even geo-historical factors. The close, homogeneous communities of rural areas are typically more conservative, whereas the loose, diverse communities of the cities are typically more liberal. Big cities and interior trading centers have usually been influenced by the arrival of many different people, many different faiths and many different morals. Small settlements are usually more unified in their outlook. They reinforce each other in those attitudes that are theirs. They talk it in the pub, they marry it in the church, they reinforce it in the home.[2]

The Buddhists have ten rules by which they try to live:

1. I will not kill any living creature.
2. I will not steal.
3. I will refrain from sexual misconduct.
4. I will not lie, gossip or speak ill of anyone.
5. I will not consume intoxicating drinks or drugs that impair the function of the body or mind.
6. I will not indulge myself with food.
7. I will not indulge in activities such as dancing, singing, music or any worldly act that debases me or others.
8. I will not seek to beautify myself with clothes and jewels but with good thoughts and deeds.
9. I will not seek luxury or rest until I have gained enlightenment or while others do not enjoy such comforts.
10. I will not seek wealth but will seek to conquer greed.

Many in the western world would be more familiar with the Ten Commandments written in Chapter 20 of the *Book of Exodus*.

1. You shall have no other gods but Me.
2. You shall not make or worship idols.

3. You shall not use God's name in vain.
4. You will remember the Sabbath day and keep it holy.
5. You will respect your father and mother.
6. You will not commit murder.
7. You will not commit adultery.
8. You will not steal.
9. You will not be untruthful.
10. You will not long to have things owned by other people.

AN IDEA

Develop a household code

Even though your family might already have a strong allegiance to an existing religious code, there is value in writing a family code as well, and doing so with input from all family members. Such an exercise can draw your family into supporting a mutually agreed values system. As an activity, the journey is as important as the destination. Deciding what the household code should be is, in itself, a useful exercise to undertake. Here is an example.

OUR HOUSEHOLD COMMANDMENTS

In this household, you are required to do the following:

1. Respect all people. (This includes the cat.)
2. Be kind.
3. Tell the truth.
4. Be generous.
5. Encourage each other. (The home will be a "putdown-free zone.")
6. Pull your weight with household chores.
7. Be safety-conscious.
8. Be resilient and handle setbacks well.

9. Share your thoughts with each other.
10. Demonstrate your love for each other.

In the film *Gladiator*, the gladiators encouraged each other with the words "Strength and honor." Families can develop their own phrases of encouragement, phrases that become part of the family tradition, phrases that encourage members as they go to fight their own battles each day.

Encourage your son to "get a grip"

You need to get a grip on yourself, boy! In my arsenal of headmasterly rebukes, I have used this phrase more than once.

In trying to unpick what I actually want this command to mean, I have come up with the following play on the word GRIP: **G**ood **R**ight **I**mproving **P**roper.

Good

We should encourage behaviors that are excellent, that have merit, that are noble, honorable and distinguished.

Right

We should encourage behaviors that are proper, just, truthful and fair.

Improving

We should encourage behaviors that are positive, generative and effective in progressing a matter.

Proper

We should encourage behaviors that the majority of society sees as fitting and appropriate.

By "Get a GRIP," I mean to encourage a boy to behave in a way that is good, that is right, that improves a situation and that is proper. Expanded further, it means the following.

Good

Intuitively, most of our sons know what is good. This, however, does not necessarily stop them from doing things that are bad. Luke Skywalker was not the only one to be tempted to join the dark side. Our sons continuously veer between the forces of good and evil.

A story is told of a much-troubled Indian brave who was tormented by this battle between good and evil. So, he went to his chief and said, "It is as though there are two dogs at war with each other in my head. One dog is black and, when he is winning the fight, I am badly behaved. I snarl and steal and hurt people. At other times, the white dog is winning the fight. I know this because I am well behaved. I am companionable, loyal and useful. Tell me, Great Chief, which of these two dogs will eventually gain control of my life?"

The old chief looked kindly on the young brave and, after a few moments' thought, replied, "The dog that will win will be the dog that you feed."

How true.

A boy who feeds his mind with violent computer games is often a boy who becomes desensitized to violence. A boy who feeds his mind with porn is often a boy who becomes desensitized to intimacy. A boy who feeds his mind with muck is often a boy who produces muck.

Rubbish in. Rubbish out.

For this reason, it is important for parents to ask who is mentoring their son. Is it the parents, or is it the adult-movie world? Is it the school teacher, or is it the computer world?

A 15-minute sermon from a parent each week is no match for 15 hours of instruction in sex and violence on the computer. Count up the hours good people are mentoring our sons and compare it with the hours bad people are mentoring our sons—and be scared.

Be even more scared if you cannot answer the question. Not knowing how a son spends his time should frighten a parent. There are usually reasons a son does not want his parents to know.

According to the developmental psychologist Thomas Lickona, a son should be required to know the good, desire the good and do the good.

Lickona suggests that in our conversations with sons we need to encourage them to know what is good. We then have to encourage them to want to behave in a way that is good. Finally, we need to allow them to exercise themselves in doing good.[3]

Great advice.

Right

An understanding of what is right, of what is proper and principled, is not as clear in many of our households as it once was. Culprits could be a decline in the fear of divine retribution and an increase in the power of self. It could be because of the hypocrisy seen in those who tell boys what is right . . . such as headmasters!

The failure to do the right thing threatens to create a new set of laws in our society, laws that are dangerous and not worthy of us. These new laws suggest it is:

- Reasonable to be dishonest, because everyone else is.
- Okay to take someone else's, if yours is missing.
- Fine to lie, providing you're not found out.
- Okay to keep something you have found, even if it does not belong to you.

- Okay to steal if you are in difficulty.
- Acceptable to cheat if it's the taxpayer who is robbed.
- Permitted to misbehave if you're drunk.
- Allowable to do wrong if it is a "brain snap."

Parents must state and restate clearly what the rules are for their household. Curiously enough, our sons can find comfort in such rules.

Some time ago, I was told of a new school that was built close to a busy road. A temporary fence was placed to protect the children from the traffic. However, it was only a three-strand wire fence, with the result the children were fearful and played well away from the fence. When the temporary fence was replaced by a strong, six-foot-high fence, the children immediately felt comfortable playing right up to the fence.

Our sons generally feel more secure if they are surrounded by well-defined behavioral boundaries.

Improving

Some years ago, I taught at a school that just about sat on a railway station in northern Sydney. This is why it didn't take me long to be told that one of my students had been run over by a train.

I dashed to the station to find an injured boy lying on the platform. I could not see how serious the injuries were due to the crowd around the boy—doing nothing. In their ghoulish curiosity, they were threatening to hinder my administration of first aid. In addition, their audible gasps of shock and horror were inflaming the panic of the semi-conscious boy.

On parting the crowd, I was pleased to see that the boy was not cut in two and still had his arms and legs. However, he was badly injured. The handle of his school bag had caught a handle on the train and it had pulled him under and rolled him between the train and the edge of the platform. It was later divined that several of his internal organs were significantly damaged.

I tried to bend over the boy to comfort him but was prevented by the tut-tutting crowd. Incensed by the unhelpfulness of this group who showed a marked reluctance to step back and stop their negative prattling, a few of my students pushed them away and, together, we did what we could until the paramedics arrived.

The boy's physical pain was dulled by oxygen and painkillers but his mental anguish remained significant, so I traveled with him in the ambulance. It moved unnervingly slowly. They did not want to jolt the boy. Sensing the unnatural pace of the ambulance, the boy gripped my hand and asked, "Will I die?"

"Of course not," I said.

I was wrong. He "died" three times that night and each time had to be brought back to life.

Some people's actions can detract. Others can enrich. Some people's comments can be unhelpful. Others can bring comfort. The sort of behavior we want to encourage in our sons is not that of the bystander. It is that of the contributor. It is that which is positive, even if the help offered is limited to a word of assurance.

Proper

Ancient wisdom reminds us that, although many things are lawful, not everything is helpful.

It is entirely reasonable to expect a son to engage in behavior that is proper. It can, however, be difficult to know what is proper these days. We must also acknowledge that it has only been through challenging what is "proper" that the world has been gifted some of its greatest developments in art and science.

I am not advocating conservatism but rather mindfulness of what is appropriate. We don't want our sons to be John Cleese characters who entertain Second World War widows by doing Hitler impersonations. Great as comedy. Crass at any other time.

Doing that which is proper implies sensitivity to, and understanding of, a situation.

One of my past parents had regular sessions with a counselor in order to empower himself in a hard and competitive world. Emboldened by this initiative, he invited me out on his motorboat to do some fishing. Once out on the water, and without a baited line in sight, he began to share his feelings about the failings of the school. I felt trapped. At the end of a crushing monologue, he said, glowing with justification, "It's so important that you say what you feel." It was the start of a very long day.

When I returned home, I replayed in my mind what he had said. With the clairvoyance that only comes when you missed saying something at the proper time, I recognized that it was not always proper to share what you feel. Indeed, if I were to share what I really felt about some of the parents I have had to deal with, I would probably no longer be employed as a headmaster.

This is not a bad lesson for any parent chatting with their son. Wanting to tell him that the nose-ring looks awful might be understandable, but it may not be helpful if the parent wants to maintain a close connection with him. What is more important? A relationship or a nose-ring?

Our sons also need to understand that telling someone how you feel is not always a virtue. We must teach them to be sensitive to what is appropriate not just for themselves but for others too.

This applies not only to conversations but also to behavior. A few years ago, one of my Year 12 boys hit another Year 12 boy at a party. It was ugly. The injury to the victim prevented him from completing some very important exams. Alcohol was the trigger—but a bad relationship was the cause.

I hooked the assailant into my office together with his father. Neither was prepared to talk about the matter in any great detail. "It would be improper to say anything—there could be legal ramifications," the father said primly.

That was when I lost it.

"Improper!" I roared. "Improper is *assaulting a boy!*"

When examining the behavior of a son, there can be value in getting him to reflect on whether he had a GRIP on the situation. Was his behavior:

- GOOD for the situation?
- Was it RIGHT for the situation?
- Did the behavior IMPROVE the situation?
- Was it PROPER for the situation?

If not, then he might profit from being told to adjust his GRIP.

Some secret parents' business

There may be some parents who would like a bit more "meaty stuff" about morality and values. Here it is, but it is limited because the genre of this book is not one that is going to see it gracing the philosophy section of most university libraries. Nonetheless, it can be useful to enrich a debate with a heavily opinionated son when you are losing an argument about why he should not be allowed to have his 18th-birthday party in the red-light zone of the city. So, the following information might be useful for the parent who wishes to infuse a touch of Philosophy 101 into their conversation, or when "*Because I told you so!*" is no longer accepted by a son.

Consequentialism

Although it sounds frightening, the concept is quite simple. The clue to its meaning lies in the word "consequence." If the consequence of an action is an overall increase in happiness, then it might be the right moral course to take. This is known as "the greatest happiness principle," and was supported by great thinkers such as Jeremy Bentham and John Stuart Mill. "John, playing the drums at midnight might be improving your skills, but it's stopping your mother and me from sleeping and the cat has run away!"

Existentialism

This approach is often associated with people such as Søren Kierke-gaard, Friedrich Nietzsche and Jean-Paul Sartre. It is a moral code that centers on the individual. Each person has the responsibility for determining what is moral. Existentialists believe that there are no good or bad morals. Before a son gets too excited by this philosophy, the right action considered by existentialists is the one that past experience has shown to be the best. "I don't care what you think! You can't use the air rifle. Last time you used it, you shot the cat."

Humanism

If a son is going to reject an imperative to behave that is based on religious beliefs, he does not necessarily escape the obligation to treat the cat properly. Although humanists do not give God a look-in and do not agree that behavioral codes are dictated by supernatural be-ings, they still believe in morality, except that it is a morality that is decided by people. This is done by thinking through what is best for the well-being of all. "Stealing the neighbor's cat won't send you to hell, but it will upset the neighbors. If we all go around stealing things, it will cost a fortune in extra locks and it will turn our happy community into a sad one. So, we don't steal—and we haven't got any cat food."

Analytic philosophy

The name says it all. People such as Bertrand Russell suggested that our morals should be influenced by analysis, logic and by a reference to the natural sciences. Morals are worked out by testing and careful observation. "Although it is said that a cat has nine lives, experience has shown this is not always accurate. Therefore, you will not throw the cat in the fish pond."

Free thought

The pansy flower is the symbol for the free-thought movement. The word "pansy" comes from the French word *pensée*, which means "thought." Pansy flowers nod forward in summer, as if deep in thought. Morals are decided by thought. They are decided by reason and are not influenced by the past. "I know normally we should try to find the owner of this cat, but given that it has no collar and seems unkempt, I don't think it belongs to the neighbors—therefore, we'll keep it."

Anarchism

This is a term that can excite a boy. However, it doesn't mean going around and blowing things up. Anarchists do not like imposed rules and favor voluntary codes of behavior. The word comes from *anarchos*, which means "without rules." "I don't care what the authorities say about vaccinating the cat. I'm not doing it. It's not going to catch rabies in this neighborhood."

*

That's enough of that! Although some sons may be interested in philosophical standpoints, most would prefer to hear a rollicking good yarn.

AN IDEA

Tell stories about heroes and heroines

Typically, boys love stories. Selecting an age-appropriate book about heroes and heroines can provide excellent material for a conversation about morals.

However, all this can have a touch of *The Waltons* about it. Do it if you can, but it might be better to get your son to read about moral issues independently. There is plenty of reading material to choose from, both in print form and online. Newspapers are full of moral questions.

When it is age-appropriate, your son should be encouraged to read the newspaper and develop an informed opinion about what is going on. For this reason, giving him an app for the daily newspaper, or making sure the newspaper is not whisked away for the exclusive use of his father, is important. Even watching the news on television can provide fruitful material for the discussion of what is right and wrong. Allow your son to become an armchair judge, but require him to justify his sentences.

There are also many good movies and books that deal with moral issues. Films can provide excellent material for a "Secret Men's Business" evening with your son. Boys like to watch, so try the following: *The Lion King*, *Star Wars*, the *Shrek* films, *The Lord of the Rings* and the *Harry Potter* series. For older boys, try: *Jurassic Park*, *Gladiator*, *Braveheart*, *The Shawshank Redemption*, the Michael Moore films such as *Bowling for Columbine*, *To Kill a Mockingbird*, *Good Will Hunting*, *Saving Private Ryan*, *Citizen Kane* and *Schindler's List*.

Many other stories will become available to swell these lists. The wise selection of reading material and films can go a long way to stimulating discussion on morality.

Morality in sports

Many boys love to play sports. Within sports, there are opportunities to explore ethical and moral issues. Athletics teach a boy to play within prescribed rules—at least it should. Unfortunately, cheating and bad sportsmanship have taken on such a plurality that sports don't always provide an arena for the exercise of noble deeds.

Therefore, a son will benefit from understanding something about the three R's of sports: rules, respect, restraint.

Rules

Sport is a test that examines whether a person, or a group of people, can achieve certain goals while keeping to specified rules. However, it is a test of something far greater than this. It is a test of character. A boy who finds it difficult to play within the rules can become the man who finds it difficult to work within the rules.

Respect

With the stakes in sports being so high in terms of monetary reward and recognition, there is a temptation to see any who stand in the way of such riches as hated beings. It is not good enough to beat the opposition; you must crawl down their throats and rip their hearts out.

While vigorous competition is acceptable, failing to respect the opposition is not. A son will not learn to respect the opposition if he hears his parent vilify them. A boy must be able to shake hands with his opponents—whatever the result.

Restraint

Winning is not good for a boy unless he is able to win with grace. Neither is losing. Likewise, learning to exercise restraint when an umpire's call goes against him is important. A son needs to learn that character is not revealed when things go well; it is revealed when things go badly.

AN IDEA

Share case studies of sportsmen behaving well

Lutz Long was the champion German long-jumper who participated in Hitler's Olympic Games of 1936. His main opposition was Jesse Owens, an African American. Hitler wanted the Games to prove that the Germans were the Master Race, particularly those who were blue-eyed and blond-haired. Long was blond. Owens was black—and considered by Hitler to be racially inferior. When Owens double faulted in the qualifying round of the long-jump, Long advised him to move the start of his run-up farther back. Owens followed the advice and went on to qualify and win the Olympic gold medal. The first to congratulate him was Long, who picked up the silver medal. Owens acknowledged that it would have taken a lot of courage for Long to have befriended him in front of Hitler.

John Landy was the second man to break the "four-minute mile." He did this a short time after Roger Bannister achieved this milestone in 1954. While racing in the mile at the 1956 Australian National Championships, Landy was running against the 19-year-old Ron Clarke, who tripped in front of him. Landy jumped over Clarke but clipped him with his running spikes. Landy stopped and helped Clarke get to his feet before racing off to recapture the lead and win the event in four minutes and four seconds.

More recently, in the 2012 Olympics in London, Andy Turner of Great Britain and Jackson Quinonez of Spain were running in the 100-meter hurdles. Also running in their heat was the former gold medalist Liu Xiang of China. Unfortunately, Liu Xiang hit the first hurdle and tore his tendon. Determined to finish the race, he began to hop to the finish line. Unaware of Liu Xiang's disaster, both Turner and Quinonez completed the race, but, on seeing their adversary hopping to the finish line, they immediately went back and put their arms around Liu Xiang in order to help him finish. This moment was one of the highlights of the London Olympics.

In a world of conflicting moral codes and confusing ethics, boys need firm reference points in relation to proper behavior. Many of their role models say one thing but demonstrate another. This suggests an important truth. A son will fail morally. So will his parents. The important thing is to acknowledge these failures, learn from them, and get on with the business of trying to live happily with others.

SUMMARY

The most important things to keep in mind during this conversation are:

- The consequences of moral failure can be significant.
- The concept of values is probably more attractive to discuss with a son than morality. Morality is how we ought to live; values are the chosen code we live by.
- When conversing with a son on this topic, it is as well to remember that no one is perfect. We must look for opportunities to praise as well as to punish our sons.
- The two major sources of direction for moral living are to be found in divine directives and in directives decided by man. Both have merit in some areas.
- There is value in sharing examples of different kinds of moral codes with a son, and in deciding on a moral code to live by as a household.
- There are a variety of philosophies that can back up a parent's advice to their son about what he should value.
- Share stories with a son about the morals shown and values chosen by his heroes and heroines, and study the morality to be found in sports.

CONVERSATION FOUR

Leadership

Having touched on what a boy's moral code should be, we need to look at the issue of responsibility. Why? Because knowing what should be done is one thing, but doing it is an entirely different matter. A son must translate theory into practice. In short, he has responsibilities. However, talking about responsibility is likely to be as attractive as root-canal work. The term reeks of repressive obligation and tiresome duty.

Another way to tackle the topic is to focus on the rather more alluring idea of leadership. Leadership is sexy.

Leadership is not only expressed in the management of others; it involves the management of self. If a son is able to take control of his life, he is showing leadership.

The assumption that our sons are currently taking responsibility for their own lives needs to be tested. The food is enjoyed by them, the shirt is ironed for them, the lift is given to them, the school is built for them, the lessons given to them, the work done for them, the money spent on them, the chores done for them, the treats given to them—a lot is typically done for our sons.

Quite properly, sons need to be given things, particularly love, nurture and nourishment. Children, by virtue of their tender years, are dependent on others to provide for them. However, there seems to have developed a sense of entitlement in some of our young that results in them not appreciating their bounty. The holiday is not enough; there must be ice-creams on the hour and chocolate on the half-hour. The clothes are not enough; they must have designer labels. The cell phone is not enough; they must have the latest bit of electronic hardware.

The product of this indulgence is not always attractive. Having learned the art of consumerism in their early years, some sons grow into adults with the same habit. Material expectations are huge but willingness to work for them can be limited. For this reason, many young adults continue to be a drain on their parents.

Our sons need to explore the delights of giving instead of getting. Making beds, cleaning rooms, setting tables, washing up, helping in the garden should not be rewarded as extraordinary behavior but should be seen as the normal contribution a son should make to his home.

Similar expectations should be evident at school. A boy must learn to complete assignments without minute-by-minute support. He needs to be able to learn independently and contribute positively to the learning climate of the classroom. There are some children who are far too dependent on teachers, who are incapable of adding value to their education, who prefer to be entertained rather than informed.

Whether it be at home or at school, our sons need to be introduced to the concept of responsibility. They need to hear conversations that encourage them to add value to society rather than just take from it. They need to learn that a boy takes but a man gives. They need to grow up.

Encourage a son to lead

It's difficult to know how to advise a son who is suspicious of leadership except to reassure him that he is not alone. There are many who don't want to engage in an activity that might be demanding, but our sons need to be encouraged to accept the challenges of leadership and not live a cushioned existence in which they limit themselves to voyeurism.

A boy needn't worry if he is neither a superhero nor a varsity athlete. Not all leadership is about heroics. Leadership can be quiet and unassuming. It can be found in a gentle word of encouragement, helping another, steering a conversation, offering a suggestion or some small service. These are tasks that all can fulfill, and, thus, everyone should give consideration to leadership in some form.

To an ongoing protest of "You must be joking. Just look at the idiot in charge of my school," a boy can be reminded that, although endangered, leadership is not yet extinct. Effective leadership can still be found in society. It's just that those who are leading are not necessarily in leadership positions, and those in leadership positions are not necessarily leading.

A leader is not always someone with an impressive badge, significant responsibilities and an invitation to dine with the gods. A leader need not even be someone with rank, power or position. If our words direct and our actions inspire, we are leading. If we cause another to follow our example, we are leading.

Having encouraged a son that he can be a leader, care must be taken not to inflate his ego to an inappropriate degree. Little is served refining the arrogance of those hell-bent on securing a life of privilege and power. "Followership" is also an important skill. It is a concept sometimes described as "teamwork."

Teach them when they're young

Some may suggest that instruction in leadership is best left until a boy is in his late teens. This view needs to be challenged. It has been said, "Give me the child until he is seven, and I'll show you the man." The perfect time to teach the skills associated with leadership is when our sons are young. It is in these early years that they may be most influenced for good or for bad. These years should not be wasted, but, tragically, they often are. Leadership skills can remain underdeveloped if they are not allowed to be exercised in the formative years. By the time a boy reaches adulthood, most of his capacity to learn profound, character-building attributes has been lost.

Most worthy ideas can be taught at almost any age in some way. The challenge is to find the appropriate way.

Can any conversation really encourage leadership skills? There are no miracle words. Any initiative that claims to give the magical incantation necessary to turn every son into a gifted leader needs to be treated with some suspicion. However, a son can be encouraged to: take responsibility for the pet, mentor a younger sibling, learn to set the dinner table, organize themselves for school . . . and that sort of thing.

Individual power

We need to remember that, even without training, each and every son has an awesome amount of power. This power should not be underestimated. Even if a boy thinks himself a bottom-feeder in the sea of life, he needs to understand he still has power, and this power must be used wisely. He has the power to grant life. He has the power to let things live or die. On seeing an insect, he has the power to squash it or allow it to live. He can also plant seeds, tend gardens and feed the cat. These activities may seem silly and inconsequential, but not to the cat.

A son also has the power to control other people. By simply sticking up a finger, he can give someone a bad day. By offering someone the larger slice of cake and taking the smaller piece, he can control that person's attitude about him and get them to think he is nice (or on a diet). By emailing a thank-you to parents who have hosted a party, he will get a lot of them wanting him to marry their daughter.

Our sons need to be encouraged not to waste their power or do what normal people do . . . which is to take the larger slice of cake and to forget to say thank you. These small, trivial initiatives can determine character and forge reputation.

Bullies have long learned they have great power. With a few hurtful words, they can cause a dramatic reaction in others, including tears, sleepless nights and depression. This is real power, which is why some get high on this sort of behavior. For this reason, one of the best ways to deal with bullies is to ignore them. If a son is going to give power to anyone, he must give it to those he loves and admires.

The question for sons is not whether they have power; the question is how they decide to use their power. Will they use it for good or for evil? Will they use it for themselves or for others?

AN IDEA

Embark on a program to transform someone

A worthwhile project can be to get your son to consider the unpopular person who is on the fringe of their social group, the person who does not have the social skills to fit in well. The power a boy has to transform the well-being of that person is enormous. A warm word of greeting, a kind comment, an effort to include them can literally change a life. Let no one say a boy has no power when there are those about him whose lives can be changed by just a few words of encouragement. Everyone can be an agent of healing.

A fellow headmaster, who once taught at my school, told me that he kept hearing about a particular Old Boy who had an amazing reputation as a school prefect. He longed to meet this man and discover his leadership secrets. One day, he did meet him, and was disappointed. The man had no charisma. When he asked others why it was they thought this man remarkable, he was told, "As a prefect, he was kind." It was this kindness that had caused him to be remembered so fondly as a leader. We can all be kind.

Can leadership be taught?

There are many who describe themselves as leaders but may not be. At best, they might be managers, but they are certainly not leaders. A leader has followers. This rules out half the people who have a reserved parking space, a secretary and a six-figure salary. Being a leader is about initiating change. The very idea of change can frighten the living death out of some who wear suits—or anyone else for that matter.

Some suggest that leadership cannot be learned. *Either you've got it or you haven't. You can't put in what God left out.* There is truth in this comment and there is error. Yes, there is a need to acknowledge the powerful influence of nature, but it is also important to acknowledge the powerful influence of nurture in the formation of leadership skills.

There is no question that genetics (nature) plays a great role in determining leadership skills. Enough powerful dynasties exist to bear testimony to some families having rich leadership blood flowing through their veins. Think of the Kennedy clan, the Mountbattens and the Churchills. Yet, failure to recognize the capacity to learn leadership skills, and failure to acknowledge the influence of nurture is to risk lapsing into fatalism. Some leadership skills can be taught, can be acquired and can be realized in every son. It is particularly important to recognize the influence of nurture because it reminds us that we can be masters of our own destiny and that all can be leaders in some way.

Leadership is not necessarily waving a sword, charging the enemy and hoping the cavalry will follow. It can mean a quiet conversation with a friend and encouraging them in their search for an answer to a problem. It can mean showing some initiative in a situation, be it dealing with a bike accident or calming an angry friend. The truth is that most of our sons, at some time, will be invited to lead in some way. Whether they accept this invitation is another question entirely.

Leadership is a science for all, not just for a chosen few. Not all will be privileged to lead in grand ways, but all will have opportunities to lead in small ways. These small expressions of leadership should never be underestimated. Collectively, they determine the character of a boy and of a nation.

The hard bit of leadership

It is worth reminding a son who has leadership aspirations that, although this is admirable, leadership is not always easy:

- The easy bit of leadership is to use your gifts to help yourself.
  The hard bit of leadership is to use your gifts to help others.
- The easy bit of leadership is to be popular.
  The hard bit of leadership is to be unpopular.
- The easy bit of leadership is to wear the badge.
  The hard bit of leadership is to deserve the badge.
- The easy bit of leadership is to do what is popular.
  The hard bit of leadership is to do what is right.
- The easy bit of leadership is to deal with policy.
  The hard bit of leadership is to deal with people.
- The easy bit of leadership is to enjoy its success.
  The hard bit of leadership is to endure its failure.
- The easy bit of leadership is to follow consensus.
  The hard bit of leadership is to follow conviction.
- The easy bit of leadership is administration.
  The hard bit of leadership is inspiration.
- The easy bit of leadership is to cope with friendliness.
  The hard bit of leadership is to cope with loneliness.
- The easy bit of leadership is to judge others.
  The hard bit of leadership is to judge yourself.

The changing concept of leadership

Leadership as a concept has changed a lot. In the early days, a leader was a heroic sort of person who would visit merry hell on others if they did not do what the leader wanted them to. They were strong, even ruthless people who were followed as much because of fear as out of respect. However, things have changed and this style of leadership has now been superseded by a very different approach.

The old style of leadership

- The accent is on individualism, which empowers the leader.
- The leader is on top of the organizational pyramid.
- The leader is a dictator and insists on conformity.
- The leader creates a sense of dependency in followers.
- The end matters more than the means by which it is achieved.

The new style of leadership

- The accent is on empowering a team rather than an individual.
- The leader is collaborative and is in the center of the organization.
- The leader is a facilitator and values diversity.
- The leader creates a sense of empowerment in followers.
- The means by which objectives are met are important.

The new style of leadership is different. It is also difficult. It can require our sons to do unnatural things such as pick up rubbish rather than drop it, wait until last to get their meal in the cafeteria or spend some time talking to the unpopular boy with the body odor problem and interpersonal skills of a brick. Our sons need to be shown appropriate definitions of leadership and leadership behaviors.

AN IDEA

Share stories about leadership that made a difference

A chat with your son about leadership can often be enriched by a story. There are many stories that can be told to inspire a boy and cause him to emulate his heroes. One example is the story of Major-General Sir Peter Cosgrove, AC, MC.

When the Australian Government was looking for a leader for its peacekeeping forces in East Timor, they agreed on Major-General Peter Cosgrove. In the 1990s, East Timor was in a mess. Attempts to achieve independence from Indonesia were being frustrated by armed pro-Indonesian militias. Killings and terrorism were rife. A number of influential people in Indonesia were also unhappy with the loss of a country that had long been under their control.

Therefore, it was a tense moment when Cosgrove flew into the troubled capital of Dili. Waiting for him was a well-armed Indonesian army under the command of Major-General Kiki Syahnakri. Cosgrove decided not to match the display of lethal force and stepped off the plane without his side-arm or his SAS bodyguards. So began a successful posting that saw Cosgrove, in his trademark slouch hat, assume the role of soldier and diplomat.

This mix of strength and subtlety is often found in great leaders. Under Cosgrove's amiable demeanor was a determined commander who oversaw the rapid deployment of more than a thousand troops in Dili. Thirty Hercules aircraft arrived in the first 24 hours, something that the Indonesian traffic controllers refused to accept was possible. Cosgrove was able to bring his aircraft in by getting his pilots to use night goggles. He wanted to create an immediate impression that there was a powerful force in place that could enforce the United Nations resolution that East Timor should operate as an independent nation.

The purpose of INTERFET (International Forces for East Timor) was to oversee the birth of a new nation. This was no small task. Fortunately, Cosgrove was not your average bloke. He had already distinguished himself as a soldier in Vietnam. In 1971, while serving in the 9th Battalion, Royal Australian Army, he won a Military Cross. The citation read:

Lieutenant Peter Cosgrove was commissioned on December 11th, 1968 and was allotted to the Royal Australian Infantry. He arrived in Vietnam on August 3rd, 1969 and was posted to 9th Battalion, The Royal Australian Regiment on August 20th, 1969.

On October 10th, 1969, Lieutenant Cosgrove was commanding 5 Platoon, B Company. The platoon located an occupied bunker system in an area where, because of the proximity of allied troops, indirect fire support was difficult to obtain. In spite of this, he led his platoon in an assault on the bunkers without indirect fire support, capturing the system and killing and wounding at least four enemy without sustaining any casualties.

On October 16th, 1969, 5 Platoon located another bunker system occupied by about a platoon of enemy. Lieutenant Cosgrove silently deployed his own platoon for an attack. His assault completely surprised the enemy causing them to flee, abandoning large quantities of food, stores and documents.

The following day in the same bunker system a party of enemy approached his right forward section and was engaged by the sentry. Knowing that the remainder of the section was elsewhere on other tasks, Lieutenant Cosgrove ran to the contact area and personally conducted the fight against the enemy. As a result of his actions, two enemy were killed and three weapons and four packs containing rice were captured.

On every occasion, Lieutenant Cosgrove has shown determination, aggressiveness and outstanding courage. His actions have been an inspiration to his platoon and company, and accord with the highest traditions of the Australian Army.

After serving in East Timor, Cosgrove was promoted to Chief of the Australian Army and then Chief of the Defense Force. He was awarded Australian of the Year in 2001. In 2006, Australia turned to Cosgrove once again to lead the taskforce to clear up after the devastation left by Cyclone Larry in Queensland.

Peter Cosgrove was a man who made a difference.[1]

*

Lest it be thought that leadership is the sole preserve of adults, sharing the Judeo-Christian story of David, as told in the Old Testament, is a great way to illustrate that the young can also lead.

David had a fair bit in common with many boys today. He was the product of a second marriage and he was the youngest in a big family, a family in which he had to fight in order to survive.

David was also an underachiever and was often overlooked. Despite being intelligent and a natural musician, he was often sent from the home to mind sheep in the hills.

David's leadership qualities were to emerge when he was sent to the battlefront to bring food to his older brothers and their commanding officer. On arrival, he found his brothers, and the rest of King Saul's army, drawn against a hostile Philistine army. The two forces stared at each other from either side of the Elah Valley. Neither seemed anxious to launch an all-out attack, but on most days the Philistines sent their champion soldier down to taunt Saul's army.

This champion soldier was huge. His name was Goliath and he came from an area called Gath where genetic abnormality combined with some in-breeding to produce a small community of giants. The behemoth of a man would swagger down with his shield-bearer and shout, "Come and fight me. If I win, you must serve us. If you win, we will serve you."

There were no takers to Goliath's challenge. This was hardly surprising, for he had a spear whose point alone weighed 15 pounds. He also wore a coat of armor made of bronze that weighed 125 pounds. The Israelites shrank from Goliath. This spurred Goliath on to shout more taunts. The Israelites had to bear the insults, for they were far too afraid of Goliath to take up his challenge.

When action ceases, talk begins, and Saul's soldiers talked of the glory that would come to the man who killed Goliath. There would be riches, tax concessions and even the hand of King Saul's daughter in marriage. Despite these rewards, no one would take on Goliath.

Into their conversations wandered David, who, with all the impetuosity of youth, blurted out the opinion that Goliath was a bag full of wind and should not be feared. This view earned David a stern rebuke from his elder brother Eliab, who told David to clear off back to his sheep and stop shooting his mouth off about something he was too young to understand. Eliab thought David was both proud and insolent, and suggested that he had only come to visit his brothers in the hope of catching sight of a fight.

Eliab was not the first boy to try to put a heavily opinionated younger brother back in his place, and David was not the first younger brother to refuse to back down. Word of David's defiance spread, and he was summoned to appear before King Saul. In the presence of the King, David's defiance was not checked. Indeed, it grew, and he said, "Let no one be afraid of Goliath. I will fight him."

Saul's response was predictable. "You are not able to go against this Philistine, because you are a youth and he is a man of war."

There is within many of our sons a passion for justice and a preference for action. Sometimes, these qualities have to be curbed because youthfulness and lack of experience can get a boy into trouble. At other times, these qualities can be an asset.

Adults can sometimes underestimate the young. In this case, they forgot that, even in the menial task of looking after sheep, skills can be formed and strength acquired. In the course of his shepherding, David had fought off lions and bears that came to eat his charges. David was used to fighting dangerous beasts, so he was not being arrogant in wanting to take on Goliath. He was well aware of his ability, even if his elders were not.

David explained his experience to the King, who was impressed and clothed David in his own armor. It was state-of-the-art military hardware but totally unsuitable for David; the boy could hardly walk in the heavy brass helmet, coat of bronze and sword. David removed King Saul's armor, went to the stream and chose five stones for his sling, took his shepherd's bag and staff, and strode forward to fight the taunting giant.

Our sons, in taking on responsibilities, might do things differently. They might challenge conventional wisdom. This is not necessarily them being irresponsible. It's them wanting to do things their way.

It was now Goliath's turn to be insulted. Here was a mere lad defying him—and with nothing more than a shepherd's staff and sling. Goliath roared, "Am I a dog that you come against me with sticks? Come to me and I will give your flesh to the birds of the air and the beasts of the field."

David, however, fought with a weapon of which he was a master. He did not mess around. After running toward Goliath, he took out a stone from his pouch, put it in his sling and whirled it around his head. The stone thudded into the forehead of Goliath, who fell to the earth. David then took Goliath's sword and cut off the giant's head.

This was the lead the Israelite army needed. This was the break in the stalemate and the end to the war of words. The Israelites charged at the Philistines, who panicked and fled.

So began the public life of a boy who would ultimately become King of Israel.

*

We need not turn to the pages of history to find examples of a boy exercising leadership. Rather, more contemporary stories can be shared. For example, the story of Akram Azimi.

Akram did not have an easy start in life. He was born in war-torn Afghanistan, but, in 1999, he had to flee when the Taliban assumed control of his homeland. As a refugee child in Australia, life was not easy. Racism was part of his early experience. However, Akram did not respond with bitterness or self-pity. He resolved to overcome his rejection by working hard and being helpful to others.

With the emergence of his leadership skills, Akram became the top-performing student in his class and was elected Head Boy of his school. This led to a triple major in law, science and arts at the University of

Western Australia. While a university student, Akram used his leadership skills to help teach young people in rural communities, particularly in the remote Indigenous areas of Western Australia. He acted as fundraiser, mentor and teacher in the Kimberley region and elsewhere.

In 2013, Akram Azimi was elected Young Australian of the Year.

Teach responsibility through the giving of tasks

Not every boy is going to have opportunities to serve in the remote areas of Western Australia. However, they can still undertake tasks that are helpful. Although not quite as romantic as the sun-blasted region of the Kimberley, the bedroom presents several opportunities. They can clean it!

It can be useful for parents to detail in writing the responsibilities they expect their son to take on. The idea of chores seems to have gone the way of hula hoops and pogo sticks, but as a concept it still has much to commend it.

Parents who—out of misguided affection—become slaves to their son are at risk of breeding a selfish monster whose sense of entitlement may make him a liability for the rest of his life. When parents list the tasks expected of their son, they show him that he is part of a family team whose well-being is predicated on every member doing their bit to help.

The sorts of responsibilities that can be listed for a teenage son include: making his bed daily, changing the sheets weekly and sorting his laundry into dark and light items. To these specific tasks can be added behavioral expectations such as being thoughtful, kind, honest, trustworthy, pleasant, sociable, tolerant, positive and reliable.

A son can participate in a family conversation about this process and help create the list of responsibilities.

*

A friend of mine had an urban-reared nephew who expressed a desire to learn how to erect a barbed-wire fence. This exercise took the boy into the country and into a world of stays, battens and braces. It also introduced him to an incomprehensible bit of gear called a wire strainer. With its levers, hooks and chains, this hand-held device tensions the barbed wire to the extent that an amorous bull can be kept away from the cows.

"How does it work?" asked the boy as he held the wire strainer in bewilderment.

"You'll figure it out," said the farmer airily. Then he hopped into his ute and drove off. Predictably, the city-softened boy panicked, experimented, despaired, experimented again, worked a bit of it out, experimented further, then got it right. He will now regale any within hearing distance that he is a "gun" fencer and can fence a paddock quicker than a cyclist on steroids.

AN IDEA

Develop a life-skills curriculum

Much of leadership is about accepting responsibility, and accepting responsibility is about living positively and productively within a community. It is about acting in a manner that enriches.

Chatting to your son about responsibility is important because he needs to understand that taking responsibility is the prerequisite to you giving responsibility. And give it you must, lest your son fail to develop those skills considered essential to independent living.

The sorts of skills an 18-year-old son should include being able to do the following:

- Cook at least three nutritious dinners.
- Clean a bathroom properly.
- Sew on a button and iron a shirt.
- Tend a garden.
- Paint a room.
- Budget.

- Manage debt, credit cards, phone plans and loan schedules.
- Change a tire and give a car a basic service.
- Use modern technologies and social-networking sites in a competent and responsible fashion.
- Cope with the etiquette related to fine dining, dating and the writing of letters.
- Dress well, do up a tie and clean shoes properly.
- Converse well and exercise good social behavior.
- Manage personal hygiene and health matters.

To go on adding to this list runs the risk of causing alarm. However, even drawing up a list of this length suggests there should be no problem designing a life-skills curriculum and evaluating your son's progress against that curriculum.

Consequences

I'm not sure that contemporary society likes taking responsibility for its actions. The word "consequences" appears to have morphed into two and become "con sequences."

It often seems that our children no longer have to bear the punishment due to their manifold sins and wickedness; they can now retreat to a sequence of cons, a line in deception that prevents them having to suffer punishment.

It is the lot of a headmaster to deal with instances of unacceptable behavior in students. Sometimes, parents are supportive in these matters; sometimes they are not. I never like it, but at times I have to punish a boy. This is because I happen to believe in consequences, I happen to believe in justice, and I happen to believe that one of the things that a school must do is to stand for something. It must be prepared to defend its standards.

So must families.

Excuses, excuses

A son learning to accept responsibility will not find it an easy task if his parents make a habit of rushing in to defend his behavior when any dare criticize it. When confronted with irrefutable evidence that their son's behavior is not perfect, some parents' forensic search for reasons fails to extend to looking at their own son. "My son is never like this at home." "This is the first time we have had this problem. I blame poor supervision at school." "My son has obviously mixed with some bad company."

The father of Richard Reid, the man who attempted to blow up a plane with explosives hidden in his shoes, said of his son, "He's not a bad lad." The parent of American John Lindh, caught fighting against his own country for the Taliban, said, "I don't think John was doing anything wrong . . . We want to give him a big hug and then a little kick in the butt for not telling us what he was up to."

The contemporary age often has difficulty accepting the concept of accountability. Our "It wasn't my fault . . . I was dropped on my head as a baby" society revels in being able to choose personal standards, but bitterly resents not being able to choose the consequences of those standards. When asked to excuse the behavior of someone because "they were tired," we may need to say, "No, I will not *excuse* the behavior, but I now *understand* the behavior." A brittle response, perhaps, but a necessary one lest our sons believe that bad behavior is permitted when tired. It is not.

IT'S NOT MY FAULT

It's not my fault I got drunk, you see.
So you can't put the finger on me.
Get those who went and gave me the beer.
Let the lawyers earn their fee.

It's not my fault I'm a gambler, you see.
So you can't put the finger on me.
Get the guys who went and placed my bets.
Let the lawyers earn their fee.

It's not my fault I can't get to college, you see.
So you can't put the finger on me.
Get the teachers who failed to teach me well.
Let the lawyers earn their fee.

It's not my fault I'm delinquent, you see.
So you can't put the finger on me.
Get the ones who urged me to break the law.
Let the lawyers earn their fee.

It's not my fault I do drugs, you see.
So you can't put the finger on me.
Get the blokes who went and sold me the stuff.
Let the lawyers earn their fee.

(T. F. Hawkes)

Freedom and responsibility

The greater the age and maturation of a boy, the greater the responsibility he can be given. Just how much responsibility a boy can handle is a matter of some debate—even among educators. For example, should a boy be given the responsibility of deciding his subjects and even his teachers at school?

The Sudbury schools allow their students to choose their courses of study and to select their teachers. A democratic model pervades these schools, with students permitted to choose how they spend their time, and with whom. There is no teacher tenure. Staff nominate for teaching roles, and staff and students vote as to whether a teacher should be employed. Tenure for teachers lasts only a year, after which the positions are declared vacant and another voting procedure then takes place.

I have to admit to not yet having the courage to institute the level of student responsibility seen in the Sudbury school system. The Sudbury Valley School was the first such school. It was founded in 1968 in Framingham, Massachusetts. There are now more than 30 Sudbury schools scattered around the world.

The delicious freedoms of the Sudbury schools include freedom of choice and freedom of action. However, the alacrity with which sons thrust Sudbury enrollment forms at their parents might be tempered by the third freedom: the freedom to bear the results of action. Ouch!

Herein lies a timeless truth. Freedom is linked to the chain of responsibility, which in turn is welded to the stanchion of accountability. It is vital that sons learn that the delights associated with increased responsibility come at a cost. Freedom must be paid for by the acceptance of accountability. Unless a son is prepared to pay that price, he surrenders the right to be granted the keys to the car, the use of the credit card and the trust of his parents.

AN IDEA

Prove you are ready

It is a useful idea to ask your son to demonstrate he has the skills to enjoy a privilege. For example, if he wishes to own a car, he needs to have demonstrated that he has the skill to drive a car safely and maintain a car well. The burden of proof must rest with him.

As a boy grows older, a presumption of entitlement can creep in. This will require a conversation that reminds him that the steady ticking of a clock does not impart entitlement. Age does not always make a person responsible. It only makes them older. When asking for more responsibility, a son needs to provide evidence to support his case.

"REFER" them

Conversations with a son that center on him wanting dispensation might be enriched if the discourse aims to REFER him: **R**equest **E**vidence **F**used **E**vidence against **R**eply.

Request

What is the request? It must be specific and its limits clearly understood. For example, a freedom given once will often be interpreted by a boy as a permanent entitlement.

Evidence

What evidence can a son provide that the request is fair and appropriate? Reasons need to be given. Recourse to petulant accusations that a parent is the "only one who says no" does not constitute evidence.

Fused

Evidence *for* granting the request needs to be fused with evidence *against* granting the request.

Evidence against

The evidence against granting the request needs to be considered. All too often, teasing out the reasons for not granting a request is the sole preserve of the parent. This is a mistake. It promotes an adversarial approach. Both parent and son need to evaluate the evidence *for* granting the request and then both need to evaluate the evidence *against* granting the request. This approach can increase an understanding by both parties of the variables that must be considered before arriving at a proper decision.

Reply

A request requires a resolution. A son may not get the response he wants, but his ire might be assuaged if the reply is thoughtful and open to review at an agreed point in the future. A parent should explain the reasons for a decision, but only to a certain extent. Sons often say, "I don't understand . . ." when they really mean, "I don't agree . . ."

The advantage of the REFER approach is that it invites both parties to acknowledge different points of view. It can also unite parents and son in the task of finding a solution to a problem. As parents, we mustn't deprive our sons of the obligation to think. When a son presents a problem, he gifts his parents with the obligation to fix it. His job is done, he has told Mom and Dad. If we wish to promote leadership in our sons, we need to invite them to be partners in finding solutions to their problems.

Let him be a boy

I have described the virtues of a boy exercising leadership and taking responsibility, but we also need to acknowledge that there are times when exercising leadership and taking responsibility is neither wise nor appropriate.

A boy is a boy is a boy. He cannot be expected to have accumulated the same amount of wisdom and experience as his parents to make the right call on many of life's questions.

Yes—we need to encourage responsibility in a son, but we must not rob him of his childhood or expect him to be an adult too soon. He will spend enough time as an adult without having to rush him into this state prematurely. Let a son play, particularly a young son. Let him enjoy a few delicious years without care. Let him be a boy.

SUMMARY

The most important things to keep in mind during this conversation are:

- A son must learn that he has responsibilities—these can be taught using the more attractive topic of leadership. Failure to teach responsibility can result in our sons becoming a liability in society.
- Leadership is not just about the management of others; it is about the management of oneself.
- Leadership is not just for those who are heroes. Leadership skills *can* be taught, and all our sons can be encouraged to exercise them.
- Sons need to recognize that they have a great deal of power. This power needs to be used wisely.
- The concept of leadership has changed from being hierarchical to being more collegial, and there is a difference between nominal leadership and authentic leadership.
- Leadership can be encouraged in a son by giving heroic examples of great leadership.
- Allotting tasks to a son can help teach the acceptance of responsibility.
- Sons can be given certain freedoms, but, if they are, they must also bear the consequences of their actions. If a son wishes to enjoy a certain privilege, he has the obligation to demonstrate that he is ready for that privilege.

CONVERSATION FIVE

Living together

A PARTICULAR AREA of responsibility that a son needs to accept is the fact that whatever he does or doesn't do will have an impact on others.

There is a natural egocentricity in a boy, particularly a young boy, that needs to be tempered with conversations that remind him he is a social being. Living with others and benefiting from their respect is great, but here's the rub: others need to receive that same respect. Communities offer much. However, they also require much.

Communities offer: membership, belonging, identity, connectivity, support, protection, security, goods and services, relationships, friendships and love. Communities require the same things.

What is being described is a symbiosis, a mutual enrichment, which sees a boy supported by the communities of which he is a member. It also reminds us that membership brings obligations. There is a reciprocity expected that requires a boy to give as well as receive. Alas, there exist a number of boys who could be described as being at the selfish end of the give–take continuum. If a boy wishes to enjoy the benefits of community membership, he must be a benefit to that community and not anger its residents.

Empathy

Much of living in a community involves the giving and receiving of kindnesses that, together, bind that community in reciprocity and love. For this to work, there needs to be empathy.

Empathy is related to many virtues, including kindness and mercy. These are good qualities to encourage in a son. Shakespeare knew this. In *The Merchant of Venice*, we read:

> *The quality of mercy is not strained*
> *It droppeth as the gentle rain from heaven*
> *Upon the place beneath: it is twice blest;*
> *It blesseth him that gives and him that takes*

And it does. Living well in a community blesses everyone.

Empathy is the ability to identify with, to have compassion for and to know the unspoken feelings of others. Those who don't have empathy are sociopaths who can cause pain without guilt, psychopaths who are unable to feel another's hurt. These sorts of people are dangerous because they can remain unmoved by the hurt they cause in others. Put in scientific terms, the neural pathways between the verbal cortex and limbic brain are damaged, making them immune to parasympathetic arousal. In less scientific terms, they are selfish beings who blunder through life causing harm to themselves and to others.

It's not just the people whom a son loves who should feel the benefit of his empathy and kindness. It should characterize a boy's relationship with everyone.

Most people say they are kind and empathetic because they help their family and friends. This is no great achievement. So do dogs. The true test of character lies in whether a person is prepared to help those who are not family or friends.

Some are quick to say they are kind, compassionate and empathetic, when they are merely average in their mindfulness of others. If there were a "compassion scale," they would give themselves a high score. They need to be reminded that there might be more accurate evaluations as to how compassionate they are, such as the following.

A seven-point compassion scale

1. Totally without compassion.
2. Generally insensitive and without much compassion.
3. Minimal compassion and none toward those they do not like.
4. Generally only compassionate toward friends and family.
5. Reasonably compassionate toward others but it tends not to translate into giving any practical help.
6. Compassion shown by some acts of service to others.
7. Very compassionate as shown by many acts of service to friends and strangers alike.

*

When one of my past students was seriously injured in a terrorist attack, I got upset. Headmasters, when they get upset, tend to write things. And I did.

OUR WORLD

I want to stroll up to the hate-filled and hurt, and say that I am sorry the world has brought them to this state. I want to soothe the indignant zealot and allow the heated barrels of war to cool by taking them all on a journey.

First we would travel to the kitchens of our enemies, and there amid the intimacy of a home we would dine on a different story and play with different children. Then we would journey to the great libraries of the world and be reminded that there is very little that is new under the sun. Thereafter we would talk to the women who have lost their children to a man's cause.

Our pilgrimage would then take us to those with a foot on either side of the grave to find out what is important in the life of those

*facing death. Then we would travel to space to play with the planets.
There, we would learn that of the billions of trillions of yellow stars,
only one has been identified with the blue bloom of life.*

*We would then journey back and ask any who wish to change the
world to check first that they know what they are doing. Our planet
is a miracle, our life on it limited, and our capacity to ruin it great.*

*We have borrowed the future from our children. How shall we
return it? Will we wrap it in toxic clouds and hand it back fractured
by war? Will the planet reflect the dull indifference of neglect so that
it no longer shines with the polish of loving attention? Will the
accompanying card be anything other than an angry scrawl of self-
justification?*

*If earth's history were encompassed by our outstretched arms, a
snip with the nail clippers would remove the period of human existence. Let us make the most of our 650,000 hours and ensure that,
like 99.9 percent of world species that no longer exist, we do not
become the fossil of an animal whose ferocity is to be wondered at, and
whose demise was inevitable.*

Living in a community

Throughout his childhood, a boy undergoes socialization. This is a
process that introduces him to community norms. But whose norms
are they? Are they the norms of the family, or are they norms modeled by the media? Are they the norms of the cyber world, or are
they the norms of peers?

It can be helpful for parents to map the community influences on
their son. An audit might determine whether these influences reinforce or erode the values of the home. If a son is adopting peer norms
that are not family norms, it might mean a quiet conversation is required.

There are skills associated with living in a community, and these
skills need to be taught lest our sons blunder through life with an ex-

alted sense of entitlement and a diminished sense of obligation. Mind you, it's a lesson we all need to be reminded of, even in the adult world.

*

I had a sensational mom. She was intelligent, caring and hugely creative. My birthday cakes were three-dimensional extravagances of sponge, cream and lollies artfully sculptured into boats, trains and planes. She also made several of my presents. Offerings were typically alarming, such as fake-leopard-skin waistcoats and similar accoutrements. My mother was an actress before she met my dad, which meant that she smoked like a chimney.

"It's my life and my choice," she would say loftily, when lectured on the subject of smoking. I struggled to counter this logic—until she developed lung cancer and died. My mom was taken away on a gurney that smelled of antiseptic. She was one of three bodies in the undertaker's van. I remember wondering if the other two had been smokers.

It may have been her choice, but it wasn't her life. It was *our* life. Her smoking took her away from meal tables for "a little smoke-aroo." Her smoking took her away from her husband. Dad died of renal cancer—probably brought on by passive smoking.

What we do affects others.

Individual rights

Our sons live in an age that glories in individual rights. "It's my right" is a common refrain, and one frequently used by sons bartering for privileges. Rather less frequent is an appreciation of duty. Less common is the realization that what we do impacts others. For this reason, others have the right to expect certain behaviors of us. Giving bed baths, administering enemas and wiping up coughed blood isn't much fun when protecting the rights of those who want to live "their life" their way. And I miss her.

A son needs to be reminded that he is designed to live with others. Despite the "My room, My mess, My problem" sign on the bedroom door, a son is part of a family. Despite the wire fence being replaced by a six-foot-high wall, a family still has neighbors. Despite living much of his time in the virtual world, a boy will gain his true identity from the real world.

There is a great deal of truth in the African saying "A person is a person because of other persons."

In an age of rampant individualism, it is good to be reminded that we all have obligations to the group. The poet John Donne knew this:

> No man is an Island,
> Entire of it self;
> Every man is a piece of the Continent,
> A part of the main;
> If a clod be washed away by the sea,
> Europe is the less,
> As well as if a promontory were,
> As well as if a manor of thy friends
> Or of thine own were;
> Any man's death diminishes me,
> Because I am involved in Mankind;
> And therefore never send to know
> For whom the bell tolls;
> It tolls for thee.

"No Man Is an Island" by John Donne

Being a gift to others

The word "community" comes from the Latin *communitas*, which is an amalgam of two words meaning "together" and "gift." This is a rather charming sentiment that suggests we could do worse than think of ourselves as needing to be a gift to others. Given that a gift can reasonably be expected to bring pleasure, we can ask the question of ourselves, "Are we bringing pleasure to other people?"

Much of the secret to being able to live well in a community re-
lates to the capacity to see things through the eyes of another and to
adjust behavior so that others are enriched rather than hurt by it.
Living within a community requires mindfulness. Living in a community requires one to get along with others. Living in a community requires one to consider the needs of others. Parents can teach
this by modeling this sensitivity themselves.

*

Ernest Gordon was an officer in the Argyll and Sutherland High-
landers during the Second World War. He had participated in the
disastrous Malayan Campaign and witnessed the fall of Singapore. In
seeking to escape, he put to sea in a native boat, but was captured by
the Japanese and sent to work on the infamous "Death Railway" in
Burma. Disease and wounds put him in "Death Ward," where the
Japanese put the prisoners not expected to survive. There, he was
treated by "Dusty" Miller, a soldier who had been a gardener in a
previous life. The other person to care for him was "Dinty" Moore.
They never gave up on Gordon and nursed him back to health. Gordon survived the war. Those who had nursed him did not. Dusty
was crucified by his captors and Dinty was drowned.

Gordon's chronicles of what happened on Death Railway are a
lesson in cruelty and kindness. For many prisoners, the only reason
they survived was because others never gave up on them. Even when
a prisoner was in solitary confinement and was not allowed to speak,
fellow prisoners would devise a way to be in adjoining toilets when
the prisoner was given a toilet break. Silently, they would extend
their arms into the prisoner's cubicle and grip his shoulders.

He was still a part of them.[1]

This is why

Some time ago, I was driving behind a car in the school grounds. It
was a Saturday and we were playing several sports games against

another school. The window of the car in front was lowered and rubbish was thrown out.

Headmasters are neurotic at the best of times, but when someone chucks rubbish in their school, it is taken personally. How dare they! I overtook the car, swerved in front, stopped, got out and walked to the offending car. I was appalled to see that it was not a car full of air-headed students. It contained a father and son from the visiting school.

I told them haughtily not to throw litter in the school grounds. I then shared further sentiments before allowing the boy and father to drive away. As my anger subsided, I wished I had responded rather better to the boy's statement, "It was only some paper. It wasn't a bomb!" All I had managed to say was a rather stuffy, "We don't do that sort of thing around here." (Although I fully recognized that we sometimes did.) This is what I wish I'd said.

We don't throw litter out of a car because we are all members of society, and society can reasonably expect our contribution to the rest of society to be positive for as long as we wish to enjoy the benefits of belonging to that society. If you want to drop litter, fine, but make sure no one else sees it, or is upset by it. This will probably mean you have to live in a community that numbers only one.

If you become a litter-bug, you may get into trouble from someone. The litter could fester and breed germs and people could get sick. You might slip on the rubbish and it might ruin the look of your garden (or school). You might even get stopped by someone for dropping it and he might want to write an essay on the paint of your car with some blunt keys. In short, there are usually good reasons for rules being in place. Ignore them at your peril.

Dropping litter makes a statement that you are seriously bad news. It tells people you don't care about the world in which you live. It tells me that you are uncaring, spoiled rotten or both. Either way, you expect others to clean up after you. This sort of attitude suggests you must be an unpleasant person. It wasn't just a piece of paper you threw out. It was an exam paper. And you failed!

An educational whine

While on this topic, indulge me with an educational whine.

I sometimes feel alarmed at the contemporary design of many boarding schools. As an educator who has spent much of his working life in boarding schools, I've seen a drift from dormitory accommodation to individual bed-studies. The use of single bed-sits for senior students can be justified, but only after serving an apprenticeship of living in shared accommodation with others.

Part of the magic of a boarding experience is learning to live in community. Nauseating habits and antisocial tendencies can be quickly pulled into line by the main body of boarders. To provide a boarding environment that prevents this socialization is a tragedy. Although the offering of individual rooms can look wonderful in an enrollment brochure, it can be a wasted educational opportunity in teaching how to live in community.

End of whine.

Joining the herd

Of course, most boys will not be offered a boarding experience at school. This does not mean that opportunities cannot be found that require a boy to learn the skills of living in a community. Scout camps, church camps and even family camps offer experiences that can knock a few antisocial habits out of a boy. Traveling with a tour group and staying in youth hostels can have the same effect.

One of the great joys I have had as a headmaster was to admit into my school a number of boys who were in the care of the government owing to their disastrous family circumstances. I remember one such lad—I will call him Jim—whom I enrolled because it was cheaper for the government to send him to my boarding school than to place him in foster care.

It was a risk. Jim's specialty was stealing cars, which he would sell to get money for drugs. He had stolen more than 14 cars and was barely 15.

Things did not start well. Jim broke into a classroom and stole a computer. Other infractions occurred that suggested Jim's stay with us would not be long. Then we had our "Head of the River" rowing regatta. Jim painted himself in the sky-blue-and-white colors of the school and joined with hundreds of others to cheer our crews home over the 2,000-meter course. It was maritime warfare. It was tribal. It was glorious.

Other schools were there. Their defiant flags, drums, bagpipes and different colored war paint challenged our contingent, who responded with chants, trumpet blasts and war cries. Jim had never seen anything like it—and he loved it and wanted to be a part of it. Over time, he became a fearless ambassador of the school. He grew to love the place and its customs and traditions. He never stole again. He wanted to belong. When Jim finally left the school on completion of Year 12, I shook his hand with watered eyes and gave him a reference. He was off to join the police force.

AN IDEA

Consider the implication of the horse whisperer's success

To illustrate that we are all herd animals, a parent could share with their son the work of a horse whisperer. Just what a horse whisperer does and how they operate varies somewhat, but, essentially, they are skilled horse-trainers who develop a close relationship with a horse based on respect and understanding. They can break in a horse in a matter of minutes. More impressive is the fact that it is done without brutality. The technique used to bring a horse under control is to appeal to its desire to belong, rather than its desire to avoid the whip.

I once witnessed a horse whisperer in action. A wild horse was let into the enclosure and immediately galloped around the perimeter, completely ignored by the trainer. After a while, the horse calmed down and became curious about the man in the middle. But the trainer remained uninterested and even flicked his reins toward the horse to shoo him away. This led to the horse feeling rejected. It would approach the man and try to connect by putting his nuzzle on the trainer's shoulder, but the trainer did not cooperate. Eventually, the trainer acknowledged the presence of the horse and stroked its head. He then saddled the horse and rode it away, to the applause of the astonished crowd.

Our sons may be wild but they still want to belong.

Friends

You can't choose your family, but thank goodness you can choose your friends.

If this saying is true, then why is it that I know too many boys who come from good families but have had their lives ruined by bad friends? Of course, it is next to impossible to tell a son, particularly a teenage son, that he has made an unfortunate choice of friends. If a parent were to be indiscreet in this regard, a son may well receive this judgment as particularly good news.

If the topic of friendships has not yet been raised with a son, it probably means that the parent has yet to stumble on what their son's friends are saying on Facebook. It also means a parent has been well protected from news of what happened at the weekend party. I had a friend in Melbourne whose son borrowed his parents' holiday house for a drunken revel that lasted several days. The kids needed to get in professional cleaners when they finally left the house and took three carloads of bottles to the dump. "I'm so proud of them," cooed the boy's mother. "I only found one champagne bottle in the garbage!" Clever.

Friends are vital for a boy. They represent his world, his choice, his arena. Although choosing a friend is the absolute right of any individual, it is of such importance that parents must take an interest in the sort of people who are becoming friends with their son. This interest is likely to be tolerated by a son if the happy situation exists that sees parents approving the friendship. Where things can go pear-shaped is when parents do not approve of a friendship.

If a parent suspects the formation of a troublesome friendship, certain strategies may have to be entertained, such as reviewing the choice of playgroup, kindergarten and school. They can also encourage the growth of alternative friendships by saying, "Why don't you invite young Ben to join us when we go fishing tomorrow?"

If, despite parents' best efforts, destructive friendships are formed by their son, other tactics may become necessary. "You will not invite that boy into my house" is the resort of the desperate. It seldom works, for it merely invites social mischief to occur in a place over which the parental shadow does not fall.

If the timing and occasion are right, honestly sharing fears about a son's friendships can work. A useful approach can be to start the conversation with "Which of your friends do you think you'll keep for life?" or "Which of your friends do you really respect?"

If it is not stretching things too much, it might also be possible to ask a son what he feels the characteristics of a true friend are, and then ask who, of his friends, have these characteristics.

Who's packing his parachute?

Charles Plumb was a US Navy jet pilot during the Vietnam War. While on his 75th combat mission, Plumb's F4 Phantom was shot down. He parachuted out of the fireball that had been his aircraft only to be captured and imprisoned for six years by the communist Vietnamese.

After the war, he was dining in a restaurant back in America when a man recognized him and came over to introduce himself. By way of greeting, the man explained that he had been the person who had packed Plumb's parachute.

Reflecting on this remarkable meeting, Plumb now publicly

shares his conviction that we must never take for granted those who help us. Every one of us needs to support each other.[2]

AN IDEA

Who is packing the parachute?

It can be useful to ask yourself, "Who is it that is packing my son's parachute? Who is it that is giving my son the means to survive in this world?"

Parents will usually play the key role. But, there should also be others to give intellectual and mental support, social and emotional support, physical support and spiritual support.

Sometimes, a mentor can fulfill more than one of these tasks, but it is wise to ensure that there are several who are "packing the parachutes" of a boy. It can also be helpful to have different types of people mentoring your son, such as friends who are a similar age, adult friends and grand-adult friends, mentors of either sex, and specialist advisors as well as generalists. Aunts, uncles, grandparents, godparents, neighbors, ministers . . . they can all be used to help pack your son's parachute.

AN IDEA

Encourage your son to watch the news and read all about it

Not many teenage boys read newspapers, either in print form or electronically. Some catch a few of the headlines on the television news, but, in general, too many have too little understanding of national and international affairs. Parents who watch the evening news with their son, who talk about the events making the news, are doing much more than forging a sense of belonging in the home.

They are forging a sense of belonging in the world. As an added bonus, a veritable gift is offered by the media's coverage of the news for parents who struggle for things to talk to their son about. Engagement with the news also offers other benefits—not least, a better appreciation of the events that are shaping the community our sons will inherit.

*

A son is part of a concentric ring of communities. It starts with a single person. These individuals are usually set within a family, which, in turn, is set within a local community. Then, encircling them are national and international communities.

Just when we have the sociometrics nicely arranged in a pattern, along comes something that messes it all up. The cyber community. Some things cut across all boundaries.

The cyber community

Of the six billion people on this planet, 4.8 billion have a mobile phone, which is more than own a toothbrush.[3]

When talking about living in a community with a son, no conversation would be complete without reference to the cyber community. The use of electronic social networking is endemic in the lives of our sons, yet parental knowledge of how sons are engaging with this world can be dangerously close to zero.

*

The parents were outraged when I showed them the message on the phone. The message was not pretty.

yor fuked
"why"
yor a shitbrain
"?"

goin to smash yor face in an screw yor sista

There was more, but you can get the sense of it.

"This is vile," said the father with forced calm. "The reference to my daughter is particularly disgusting. She is only 14."

"Who sent this?" demanded the mother. "Who do you think sent this to you, darling?"

The boy was about to respond but was prevented from doing so by a question to me from the father.

"Do many other boys get targeted like this?"

"No—I don't think so."

"Who sent it, son?" the father asked.

The boy looked despairingly at me. I gave him a slight nod.

"I did," he said.

*

Many parents have no idea of the persona their son adopts in the social-networking world. They have no idea of the language used, the morals espoused or the attitudes shown by their son. Neither do many have any idea what their son watches online or which websites he visits. The best brought up of sons can have a cyber identity that is alarming. Just as significantly, they can be interacting with others who may be even worse. Online harassment and unwanted sexual solicitation is rife in the lives of our children.[4]

As far back as 2008, a third of 10- to 15-year-olds were reporting online harassment. This figure is increasing.

Quite apart from the morals issue, the time issue is also significant. The cell phone can become a time thief, robbing our sons of a proper engagement with learning and with living. Research shows that 23 percent of social networkers check Facebook five times a day or more. With many of our sons, it is much more frequently, and small wonder when the top five hash tags used in social-media searches in 2013 included #love, #me and #cute.[5]

And Facebook is just one of many distractions to be found online.

Cyber bullying

Some of our sons have been victims of cyber bullying. Estimates vary, but figures of 33–43 percent are commonly reported on cyber-bullying surveys.[6] The rate of cyber bullying tends to increase through the school years. The reason bullying takes place varies, but the top reported explanations are: for fun, to show off, to be mean, to embarrass, because "they deserved it," and to get back at some-one.[7]

The last point is significant. Those who are victims of cyber bully-ing are often likely to become a cyber bully. The desire for revenge can be powerful.

The expression of cyber bullying can vary, but it includes cyber stalking, reputational damage, impersonation, exclusion, threats, den-igration and the disclosure of personal information or embarrassing pictures.

The most common means of cyber bullying is via instant messag-ing. Other means include emails, chat rooms and text messages.[8]

What can parents do?

Parents need to have ongoing conversations with their son about us-ing social-networking sites and about the standards and protocols that should be adopted online. However, parents need to recognize that, for every conversation they have with their son on this topic, he is likely to hear and see many more examples of different standards. That is why constant reinforcement is necessary.

Some parents have tried to stay engaged with what their son is doing in the cyber world by linking into the same network of con-tacts. Examples include having their son as a Facebook friend or sharing Pinterest material with them. This is admirable, but it is no guarantee. A son can set up more than one account and can easily "unfriend" their parents.

Getting a son to do all his computer work in a public area of the house is also admirable but is probably not going to achieve much given the prevalence of mobile communication devices. It is unrealistic to require a son to activate his phone only when a parent is present.

In the end, a parent cannot rely on external controls. They have to build the internal control capacity within their son.

The sort of advice parents can give their son in this area includes the following:

- Never say anything in the cyber world that you would not say in the real world.
- Anything said or posted in the cyber world can stay there forever and come back to haunt you in years to come.
- There is no such thing as cyber anonymity.
- Be nice.

If a son is suffering cyber bullying, then he should be advised to:

- Tell someone immediately.
- Not retaliate.
- Seek counseling.
- Try to preserve the evidence, and give it to the police.

If a son is being a bully, then he must be instructed to:

- Stop it.
- Take measures to ensure he does not do it again.
- Recognize that there are consequences. Losing his ISP or IM account could be the least of his problems. He could go to jail.

Acquire other contemporary means of help, such as the BOB (Back Off Bully) phone app.[9]

Further advice on the matter of bullying is given in Conversation Ten, which deals with the issue of resilience.

Reciprocity

Whether operating in the cyber world or the real world, it is as well for a son to be reminded that there are consequences to actions. It is suggested that the flutter of a butterfly wing in one part of the world can cause typhoons in another part of the world. It is also suggested that if we wipe out a forest we may have wiped out a cure for cancer. We need to be careful.

Sometimes, boys find it difficult to understand ripple effects and consequences. It is not always easy for a parent to provide an antidote to this, particularly in younger children, who are naturally egocentric. However, help may be at hand by the simple expedient of appealing to a son's self-interest.

Communities are built around the concept of reciprocity. *I will give you this if you give me that. I will behave this way if you behave that way.* For this reason, a conversation with a son that reminds him of what he is receiving can be useful. Even more useful is to ask him what he is giving in return. The simple inquiry "Dad's doing this, Mom's doing that, big sister is doing the other . . . what are YOU doing?" can be quite an eye-opener.

When a community deserves support

To be fair to sons, encouraging them to adopt behaviors that enable them to be accepted by their community is not reasonable if that community is dysfunctional. It is asking a lot of a boy to save a family blighted by parental feuding, afflicted by illness or complicated by a parent who is required to leave the home for extended periods of time. Of course, the obligation to behave in a responsible manner is not removed by such circumstances, but it can be unrealistic to expect a son to be unaffected by such problems.

Therefore, when we expect a son to support a community, we need to add a few caveats. The "community" can only expect a boy's support if it is worthy of it—it is not fair to expect him to adopt behaviors wanted by his community if that community has done little to deserve it.

SUMMARY

The most important things to keep in mind during this conversation are:

- The natural egocentricity in a boy needs to be moderated by him being reminded that he lives in a community.
- A boy's community can offer him much, but he has an obligation to give to that community. That said, there is an obligation on the community to deserve that support.
- Parents must monitor the community influences on their son.
- Friends are an important part of a son's community. Choosing the right friends is vital.
- A son needs a range of diverse people in his life to mentor him: intellectually and mentally, socially and emotionally, physically and spiritually.
- A son needs to know how to navigate the cyber world safely. In particular, cyber bullying is a growing problem. Therefore, parental engagement with how their son is operating within the cyber community is important.

Achievement

MOST BOYS WANT TO ACHIEVE and be successful. Poor things. They often don't realize that success can be a bugger. Not long ago, my school had one of those stellar sets of Year 12 exam results that caused me to consider hanging up my mortar board and gown and start zigzagging golf balls down a fairway. Impetus for retirement was added when a fellow headmaster mournfully said, "You're stuffed now, Hawkes. The governors will want those results every year." As I said, success can be problematic, and our sons might need to be reminded of this in their quest for fame and fortune.

To be considered successful

It has been suggested that to be successful as a teacher you need to be able to drink three cups of coffee before 8 a.m. and keep it in your system until after 5 p.m. To be successful as a teenage boy is rather more demanding. It requires the following:

- The body of a Greek god (usually male).
- The sporting ability of an Olympian (preferably without steroids).

- The mind of Einstein (but without the hair).
- The sex appeal of Leonardo DiCaprio.
- The social charm of Casanova.
- The wealth of the average banker before the Global Financial Crisis.

All this can be a touch daunting for the average boy struggling with C grades, uncoordinated limbs, a mumbled conversation limited to football and a propensity to blush in the company of a girl. He might also be struggling with acne and a Facebook page devoid of any female friend who could be remotely considered genuine.

Heaping coals on the head of the average youth is the implicit expectation that they should do at least as well as their parents, and probably better. I distinctly remember as a teen being in awe of the fact that my parents had learned to drive a car, got reasonable jobs and saved enough moolah to secure a modest home. Furthermore, their dinner conversation was made up of the relaxed banter of those who had read well, traveled a bit and knew a thing or two about contemporary literature. How had they done it? I was flat out learning the road rules for my learner's permit, holding down a part-time gardening job and buying myself the latest Hendrix offering. And I knew sweet nothing about *foie gras*. Evidently, it's not a form of artificial grass.

A boy can be overwhelmed by the task of growing up. Comfort is not provided by schools that hold "The Future is Unlimited" sorts of mottos (usually in Latin). Neither do schools help when they wheel in a steady procession of inspirational speakers who have all sorted themselves out and become famous. As a boy in 4B (the bottom grade), I found it all rather depressing. School prizes won in my early teens were limited to a dictionary given at Speech Night. I think it was for effort.

Some parents offer little comfort to their son. Several have quite unrealistic expectations, and this problem can be made worse by a parent who is professionally successful. Being expected to climb the same pinnacle of success can be particularly frightening for a son, and even more so if he suffers vertigo. Some boys do not cope well with living on the top of a mountain. It can get cold and windy up there.

Parents must be careful not to visit upon their son their own neuroses. More than one father has tried to assuage his failure on the football field by screaming advice at his son from the sidelines. More than one mother has tried to deal with the demons of career disappointment by hounding a son to improve his school grades.

Sons can be quite different from their parents. They must be allowed to be different and to find success in their own way. While on this topic, it is worth noting that a son can be quite different from another son—and, even more significantly, from a daughter. Mars is not Venus.

*

I've only ever done it once. It was while I was teaching at a boarding school.

Like many farmers, these parents were generous of heart. They had popped in to the housemaster's flat with some pickled this and preserved that. It was a heartfelt gift, given that their son was a difficult child. As the conversation moved from the weather (could do with a few points of rain) to their son (could do with a few better grades), I sought to reassure them.

"Look, he may not be strong academically, but he is quite good at . . ."

I could not think of a single thing the boy was good at, and stood there umm-ing and ah-ing when, to my infinite relief, both parents laughed. As I said, he was a difficult child.

In nearly 40 years of teaching, this has happened only once. Normally, I am able to find some virtue in a boy. Even in the most challenging of students, there is usually some redeeming quality.

Back in 1983, the educationalist Howard Gardner wrote a book titled *Frames of Mind*. It is a book that has had a huge impact on schools. It now deserves to have a huge impact on homes. Gardner argues that we are too consumed with IQ (general intelligence). We see a low IQ reading as indicating low all-round ability. Gardner suggests that this is not true, because there are many ways a person can be intelligent. A son's intelligence can focus on the following areas:

- Math, reasoning and logic.
- Spatial tasks such as map reading and visualization.
- Language, in both spoken and written form.
- Sport, dance and coordination.
- Music.
- Interpersonal skills, such as being able to relate well to others.
- Interpersonal skills, such as having a good understanding of oneself.
- The natural world, in being able to understand plants, animals and the physical geography of a place.
- Spiritual and religious matters.

Okay—a son may not be topping his class in English, but he may be outstanding in sports and in looking after animals, even the cat.

Success can come in many forms.

Defining success

There are some well-known anecdotes, reflections and pithy sayings that can be shared with a son struggling with the "Will I ever make it?" question. Chief of these is the poem "Success," which has been attributed (wrongly) to Ralph Waldo Emerson. Here, in a slightly adapted format, is one of the best definitions of success.

SUCCESS IS

To laugh often and much;
To win the respect of intelligent people
and the affection of children;
To earn the appreciation of honest critics
and endure the betrayal of false friends;

To appreciate beauty, to find the best in others;
To leave the world a bit better, whether by a healthy child,
a garden patch or a redeemed social condition;
To know even one life has breathed easier because you have lived.
This is success.

Although lovely in sentiment and redolent in truth, this poem might need to be customized and contemporized if connection is wanted with a teenage son. Try something like:

hi son
try 2 leave people u meet ! by a kindness 2day
when i do—i find u end the day more ☺
hv a gr8 day
dad

Yes—it doesn't have quite the same literary punch, but there you go. A parent can't quite be expected to match it with something attributed to RWE himself.

Other literary gems exist, such as Rudyard Kipling's "If."

IF

If you can keep your head when all about you
Are losing theirs and blaming it on you;
If you can trust yourself when all men doubt you,
But make allowance for their doubting too;
If you can wait and not be tired by waiting,
Or being lied about, don't deal in lies,
Or being hated, don't give way to hating,
And yet don't look too good, nor talk too wise:
If you can dream—and not make dreams your master;
If you can think—and not make thoughts your aim;
If you can meet with triumph and disaster
And treat those two impostors just the same;

If you can bear to hear the truth you've spoken
Twisted by knaves to make a trap for fools,
Or watch the things you gave your life to, broken,
And stoop and build 'em up with worn-out tools:
If you can make one heap of all your winnings
And risk it on one turn of pitch-and-toss,
And lose, and start again at your beginnings
And never breathe a word about your loss;
If you can force your heart and nerve and sinew
To serve your turn long after they are gone,
And so hold on when there is nothing in you
Except the Will which says to them: "Hold on!"
If you can talk with crowds and keep your virtue,
Or walk with Kings—nor lose the common touch,
if neither foes nor loving friends can hurt you,
If all men count with you, but none too much;
If you can fill the unforgiving minute
With sixty seconds' worth of distance run,
Yours is the Earth and everything that's in it,
And—which is more—you'll be a Man, my son!

But, there's the problem . . . "If." It implies a condition, a prerequisite, an obligation to do something if the prize is to be bestowed. This can be an uncomfortable truth for our sons. Attainment is elusive—except, perhaps, in the home, where superlatives from well-trained parents can be heard, even for performance that is quite modest.

Unfortunately, outside of the home, the judges are harder, and their grades are less generous—unless undisputed genius is displayed. For this reason, a son needs to be encouraged in the home but not to the extent that mediocrity is adulated. The world can ill afford to have its ranks swelled by little princes who think that everyone beyond the front door adores them. Therefore, a parent must tread that difficult path between encouragement and exhortation, between "Well done" and "I think you can do better."

Depression

Rather too many of our sons face a barrage of negativity and put-downs, particularly at school and on social-media sites.

> *You brain-dead moron. You have absolutely nothing to offer except an apology. You would be out of depth in a moderate-sized puddle.*

Or more realistically:

> *u r a shit*

There will be very few sons who have avoided putdowns. They are heard with such a frightening degree of frequency that their brain can become saturated by negative thoughts. Parents might think of them as being part of the normal rough and tumble of life and something that should not be taken too seriously. Yet, deep down, and possibly even unknown to our sons, the putdowns can erode confidence and begin to infest minds with doubts and negative thoughts.

> *"You dork."*
> *"Hey, airhead."*
> *"Out of my way, pizza-face."*
> *"We have a bunch of wogs and rice-eaters here."*
> *"What mark did you get, you remedial?"*
> *"You're a waste of space, four-eyes."*

When comments such as these are repeated often enough and said with enough constancy and venom, a son can begin to believe it all. He may even become depressed and start to hate himself as well as his tormentors.

Although the subject of resilience is tackled in Conversation Ten, it is worth reinforcing here that any sign of low mood, long-term depressive behavior, act of self-harm or talk of suicide must be taken very seriously by a parent; expert medical attention should be sought over any concerns about a son's sense of well-being. Above all, a son needs empathy and compassion. He also needs expert guidance and counseling, and this will need to happen as quickly as possible.

If a son thinks he is an underachiever to the extent he is giving up and becoming apathetic, a very important conversation is necessary. Clear warning signs that a son is at risk include giving away his prized possessions, engaging in deliberate acts of self-harm or participating in high-risk behaviors such as substance abuse; at this point, intercession is even more urgent. In either case, professional medical help should be sought.[1]

In the United States, teen suicide is the third leading cause of death. In Australia, suicide by those aged 15 to 24 trebled between 1960 and 1990, and remains the second most common cause of death in this age group today. In the rural sector of Australia, the problem is even worse, with teen suicide rates being twice as high as in the city. A similar tale can be told in India. A third of India's suicides occur in the 15 to 29 year age range. These stats are not pretty.[2]

If the warning signs described above are not present in a son and all his parents have to deal with is an episodic whine, professional help is generally not necessary. Parents are usually quite capable of sharing with their son the knowledge that everyone is a loser and everyone is a winner at some time in their life. Losing now does not disqualify from winning later. Okay—not everyone will be able to motivate a crowd before breakfast, storm enemy strongholds before lunch and establish a moderately sized empire before dinner. Deal with it.

*

A few years ago, I was on the receiving end of a mega gripe from one of my senior soccer players. He was complaining that far too many of the accolades in sports were being given to the rugby players and not nearly enough to the soccer players.

"It's just not fair," he said. "We should have the soccer players up on the stage at assembly just as much as the rugby players." I digested the accusation carefully and then I invited the boy to join me on a stroll to "The Place of Pain," otherwise known as the weights room in our school gym. It is an extensive facility with all manner of machines designed to cause you to puff a lot. It was full of rugby players. On the wall were aerobic and nonaerobic exercise regimes for each of those in the rugby team. "Where are the soccer players?" I asked.

Happily, I can now report that my soccer players are puffing a lot in the gym. They are also on stage a lot.

Famous failures

It is slightly worrying that we sometimes take comfort from the failure of others. But we do. Reminding our son of the lackluster history of some of the more famous icons might be just the thing to cheer him up:

- Socrates was condemned as an "immoral corrupter of youth."
- Isaac Newton performed poorly at school.
- Albert Einstein did not speak until he was four years old and did not read until he was seven. He was described by his teacher as being mentally slow and forever in a dream world.
- Beethoven was described by his teacher as being hopeless as a composer.
- Charles Darwin was dismissed by his father as liking little else than shooting, being with his dogs and catching rats.
- Louis Pasteur was ranked only 15th out of 22 in his undergraduate chemistry class.
- The opera singer Enrico Caruso was told by his teacher that he could not sing.
- Rodin's father described his son as an idiot, and Rodin tried (but failed) to get into the School of Art three times before becoming a world-famous sculptor.

- Henry Ford was bankrupted several times before going on to develop the Ford Motor Company.
- In fourth grade, a teacher called Mrs. Phillips constantly said to a boy that he was no good and would not amount to anything. The boy remained illiterate until he was 26. Then Peter J. Daniel learned to read, made a fortune and wrote a book entitled *Mrs. Phillips, You Were Wrong.*

Recently, my school was visited by Cadel Evans, winner of the 2011 Tour de France. He has become a good friend of the school and has helped design our mountain-bike track, spoken at a few of our "manhood" workshops and handed out the odd prize on Speech Night.

Cadel's life has not been without setback. Although he was the world champion mountain biker in 1998 and 1999, his switch to road racing in 2001 saw him fail in his initial attempts to win the Tour de France.

There is one thing worse than not winning, and that is *just* not winning, and Cadel was to experience this several times. He came second to the Spaniards Alberto Contador and Carlos Sastre, respectively, in the Tours de France of 2007 and 2008.

That would have hurt, as would subsequent failures in the Tour de France brought about by poor form, poor team support and injury. Then, in 2011, at the age of 34, Cadel Evans became the first Australian to win the Tour. It was a win celebrated for many reasons, but not least because Cadel achieved it without performance-enhancing drugs and with the courage to ride again after previous failures.

Goal setting

It is said, "We don't plan to fail; we just fail to plan."

Many do not plan and prefer to drift along in life's currents and be washed up on whatever shores the gods choose. Too many of our off-spring trust in fate, luck and star signs rather than their own initiative and ability. They believe their future is somehow pre-determined and that it is pointless to try to change things. Others are just lazy and never get around to working out their goals. They get so distracted with the present, they never allow themselves to consider the future.

A son needn't worry if his chosen goals are ambitious. They often are in the teen years. Big goals are simply a large number of small goals. The journey of a thousand miles begins with a single step. The writing of a book begins with a single word, and the ability to run like the wind begins with the first training session. One of the most effective ways of coping with an ambitious goal is to divide it into a series of achievable steps. As a wise person once said, "The way to eat an elephant is one mouthful at a time." Concentrating on the next step, visualizing it and remaining positive are three important elements in the quest to reach a large goal. The important thing for a son is to set goals to help him achieve his dreams.

AN IDEA

Get your son to consider his future career

You can choreograph a conversation about goals by chatting to your son about what job he would like when he leaves school. The terrifying relevance of this topic for older sons may mean that they will be particularly prepared to talk about it.

Shown here are a few questions that can be helpful in guiding your son through a career-planning exercise:

What subjects did you do well in at school and what sorts of careers relate to these subjects?

_____

_____

What subjects did you not do well in at school and what sorts of careers would this possibly disqualify you from pursuing?

_____

_____

Do you prefer working in a team or on your own? What sorts of careers relate to your answer?

_____

_____

Were you stronger in the sciences or the humanities? What sorts of careers make use of these strengths?

_____

_____

Do you classify yourself more as an introvert (prefer your own company) or an extrovert (like the company of others)? What sorts of careers relate well to your answer?

_____

_____

Do you enjoy performing in front of others—for example, giving speeches or getting involved with drama or debating? To what extent do your preferred career options rely on these sorts of skills?

_____

_____

Do you have any physical limitations, such as bad eyesight, that might disqualify you from some jobs? What careers might not be available because of these limitations?

_____

_____

_____

How strong are your academic results? Some jobs require university training as well as good school grades. Is it realistic that you can get the necessary grades to be allowed to train for your preferred career?

_____

_____

_____

What employment have you already been engaged in? Does this suggest a possible career option?

_____

_____

_____

Do you enjoy administrative tasks, organizing things and helping others to sort things out? What sorts of careers match your answer?

_____

_____

_____

Would you classify yourself as being able to cope well with working in an office, or do you prefer to work outside? What careers does your answer suggest?

_____

_____

_____

Are you prepared to travel? What sorts of careers relate well to your answer?

_____

_____

_____

Which of these describe you?

- ❏ Copes well with stress
- ❏ Doesn't cope well with stress
- ❏ Likes looking after others
- ❏ Prefers to look after oneself
- ❏ Social
- ❏ Private

- ❏ Likes manual tasks
- ❏ Dislikes manual tasks
- ❏ Prefers poorly paid but enjoyable work
- ❏ Prefers well paid but less enjoyable work

Rate yourself on a scale of 1 to 10 (10 being excellent) on:

Oral communication

Art

Mathematics

Written communication

What career options are suggested by your answers?

What are your interests and hobbies? Do any suggest a possible career?

What careers would you definitely not undertake?

What types of careers interest you?

Are you prepared to complete a university degree, apprenticeship or any other type of tertiary training?

Having reviewed your answers, write your ideal job description.

What jobs come closest to meeting your ideal job description?

_____

Remember that it is quite okay for a boy not to be sure of a career when in his teen years. It is also worth remembering that he will probably change his mind several times before choosing a career. Even after choosing a career, it is likely he will have many changes throughout his life. The important thing is for him to keep his options open.

However, it might also be worth warning a son that some careers are quite hard to get into. There is strong competition for certain jobs. Therefore, any initiative a boy takes now to advance his future career, such as doing work experience in that area or getting the necessary school grades, will help. On the other hand, every time he decides not to put in the effort to secure a good career, that sound he can hear in the background is of closing doors.

The ABCD of goal setting

When parents engage in a goal-setting exercise with their son, it can be useful to ensure they have gone through the ABCD of goal setting. In other words, a son may benefit from being asked the following questions:

A   Is your goal *achievable*? Is it realistic?

B   Do you *believe* you can do it? How certain are you that you can really achieve this goal?

C   Do you *comprehend* the goal? Do you understand what needs to be done to achieve it?

D   Is the goal something you really *desire*? Are you hungry for it?

When going through the ABCD of goal setting, it is important that the goals discussed are the son's and not the parents'. This may not be easy if a son is considering a career as a curbstone on the motor-way of life. Likewise, it can be hard to suggest that a son may need a reserve career if his first choice is to pop down the nearest black hole to discover the origin of time.

After the goals have been set

Going through the process of setting goals is hardly a new idea, but sons must do more than decide on a goal—they must take steps to achieve it. This can be encouraged by: thinking through ways the goal might be achieved, timetabling activities that will help meet the goal, and monitoring progress in reaching the goal.

In other words, encourage a son to build a "GATE."

G   Set a realistic GOAL.
A   Think of ACTIVITIES that will help meet the goal.
T   TIMETABLE those activities.
E   At an agreed time, EVALUATE progress in meeting the goal.

Goals may be set:

- Each day
- Each week
- Each term
- Each year
- For a lifetime

In other words, setting goals requires a son to think through the following questions:

- Where am I now?
- Where do I want to get to?
- How am I going to get there?

These exercises are useful in giving direction to a son who might otherwise become something of a drifter. Success cannot be guaranteed but it can be encouraged by focusing on those things that a son uses to define success. That said, it is worth remembering that a boy will change his mind many times about what he wants to achieve in life. That's okay. What is not okay is to be blighted by regret in later life because options were not kept open in early life.

Use your brain

A frequent topic of conversation between parents and sons is that of academic achievement—or the lack of it.

Being a teacher, I am heartened by this, but I believe that these conversations might be made a little more effective if parents knew more about what it takes to optimize academic performance. Among other things, this will involve an appreciation of the importance of looking after the brain.

Success in life requires many things, not least the ability to think. The capacity to plan, evaluate, create and learn is a common prerequisite for achievement. The locus of these skills is the brain, so the brain is something our sons need to look after. Tragically, some boys do the very opposite and adopt a lifestyle that is damaging their brain and reducing the efficiency of its operation.

It is entirely possible for a boy to undermine any chances of success in life by getting involved with activities that damage his brain. Not for nothing is the brain wrapped in a thick protective shell. We call it a skull. Blows to the head and concussion in football games can reduce the capacity of a boy to learn. We often treat concussion rather too casually in contemporary society. It can kill. More than once, I've stood at the bed of a boy who has had a large section of his skull removed to reduce the pressure caused by swelling. Sometimes, this has saved his life. Sometimes, it has not. At other times, it is somewhere in between.

Any head injury needs to be treated seriously.

It doesn't always take a blow to the head to damage a brain—a toxic lifestyle can have a similar impact. Some activities poison the brain, and others can cause "die-back" in a brain and reduce its capacity to function. A poorly functioning brain is not going to serve a boy well in his quest for fame and fortune.

If a boy is addicted to adrenalin rushes, if he eats rubbish food, if he starves his brain of sleep, if he fails to stimulate his brain with thoughtful challenges, if he poisons his brain with recreational drugs, then his brain will reward him by not functioning at its optimal level. Its neural pathways will be reduced and its function limited. This is not good news for a boy who wants to conquer the world.

An inefficient brain is one that wants to be fed experiences and is preoccupied by seeking out activities that are pleasurable. It is a brain that doesn't like to be exercised much by reading or by academic challenge. It is a brain that wants thrills. It is a brain that is frequently awash with alcohol or fed toxic drugs. It is a brain whose neural pathways are made less efficient by a hamburger-and-chips lifestyle.[3]

By contrast, an efficient brain is one that seeks meaning. It bathes itself in experiences that help it grow and become more efficient. It is a brain that is well used, that is employed in thought, that is made efficient by constant use in new and enthralling ways. It is a brain that is hungry for meaning, that is inquisitive, that likes to find out things and understand the world. It is a brain that is nourished by a good diet, by brain food such as fruit, nuts, vegetables and fish.

The cry that comes from exasperated parents of wanting a boy to "grow up" may be a diagnosis of a brain malfunction caused by a poor lifestyle. A poor lifestyle can render a son's brain just as inoperable as that of a patient with a recognized mental disorder. In both cases, the symptoms can include childlike behaviors and a boy not being able to adapt well to new situations. In these cases, parents may need to seek professional medical help for their son. However, they can also do a great deal to help by encouraging their son to look after his brain properly.

The capacity for a boy to grow his brain, as well as shrink it, should not be underestimated. "Plasticity"—a word that comes from the Greek meaning "molded"—suggests that a person has the ability to enrich or damage their brain. If a boy wishes to engage in experiences that "blow his mind," he will succeed in more ways than one. High-risk behaviors, thrill seeking, binge drinking, drug taking and overeating will all damage the brain and render it less effective in being able to guide its owner toward mature behavior. The result can be a permanent childish state that can trap a man as a boy.

The number of brain connections grows dramatically until a child is aged about six. Thereafter, a pruning occurs, with unused neural pathways dying off and well-used pathways developing further. In other words, a use-it-or-lose-it principle is at work. This explains why it is easier for a young child to learn a foreign language than it is for an adult.

For a brain to be healthy and functionally efficient, it needs to be exercised and kept free of bumps, drugs and too many baths of dopamine. Dopamine is an addictive chemical, much like cocaine, which is released in the brain when the body engages in thrill-seeking "fight or flight" behaviors. So, getting high on adventure is a literal truth in the lives of some boys. The high can also come from drugs, drink, sex, food and dangerous activities, all of which can become addictive. The price paid for these highs, however, can be poor cranial performance.

Of particular significance to the contemporary boy is evidence that an excess of electronic social networking, computer gaming and TV watching can also promote an infantile brain.

Typically, the world of a video-gamer is filled with violence without empathy and behaviors without consequences. The danger is that these qualities become learned and transferred to the real world. The video-gamer is constantly bombarded with pictures, sound bytes, changing images and compelling action. How can the teacher or parent compete? Armed only with a whiteboard marker, the teacher is no match for the visual delights of the computer screen.

Small wonder that the number of boys being treated for attention deficit disorder is growing dramatically.

Social networking, video gaming and TV watching typically occupy a boy's life more than the classroom does. The battle of the real world against the virtual world is being lost. The result may be a generation of boys who show the symptoms of electronically induced autism.

It is easy to sensationalize this thesis, just as it is easy to dismiss it. The truth lies somewhere in between and requires a boy to counteract those activities that have little meaning in his life with activities that have great meaning. This is not going to happen if a son is an under-exercised, jelly-bellied video-gamer with an affection for junk food and late nights.

When it is recognized that a boy now engages in between four and five hours of TV watching, computer gaming and electronic social networking each day, parents have every right to be concerned about the possibility of a brain-damaged son.[4]

To this must be added the desensitization to violence (by the age of 18, a boy will have watched about 20,000 murders), a premature sexualization (12- to 22-year-old males are the biggest users of sex-chat lines in many countries) and exhaustion due to constant social networking (the peak use of teenage networking in some countries is just after midnight)—and the disaster is complete.[5]

There must be a renewed urgency to ensure that our sons are not adopting lifestyles that promote brain-deadening experiences. They must be readers of books as well as watchers of screens. To fail in this challenge is to risk our sons remaining in a state of perpetual boyhood.

Our sons need to learn that they must take care of their brains so that their brains can take care of them. Keeping the brain healthy involves many things, including the following:

- Avoid bumping the head, and rest properly if it does get bumped. If a parent is worried about their son receiving a blow to the head, they should seek immediate medical advice.

- Ensure a brain is stimulated not so much by the thrill of cranking up a car to 100 miles an hour, but by cranking up the brain to engage in problem-solving exercises that are new and interesting.
- Exercise a brain in different ways. A brain likes variety. A boy must read books as well as watch screens. A boy must talk as well as listen.
- Adopt a healthy diet. *You are what you eat.* If a boy eats junk food, then he is in danger of having a junk mind. What is eaten impacts mental efficiency.
- Ensure the brain is well oxygenated. This can be assisted by regular exercise.
- Rest the brain and make sure it is not exhausted by inadequate sleep.
- Keep the brain free of toxins found in recreational drugs, including alcohol.
- Employ the brain on tasks that edify and enrich rather than sully and despoil.

If any parent needs further advice on this matter, they should see their doctor.

Academic achievement

Parents can often be in awe of schools and feel that they must necessarily leave all things educational to the trained teacher. A touch of awe is no bad thing, but parents must recognize that they must not disqualify themselves from giving good academic advice to their son. These conversations can be rendered even more useful if they are guided by the following principles.

Facilitate rather than tell

There can be a temptation to simply provide a son with the correct answer. Sometimes, this is unhelpful. Learning can be better enhanced by helping a son arrive at the answer himself. Use questions to prompt and show a son the steps that can be taken to get to an answer, rather than telling him the answer.

Stimulate interest

The parent who can awaken the intelligence of their son, who can stimulate wonder and interest, is someone in the wrong place. They should be teaching in my school! Good use of questions, painting mental pictures, using all the senses, engaging with a son's emotions: these are all tricks to stimulate academic engagement in a son.

Encourage creativity and problem solving

Being able to present an issue as an intriguing question that needs to be answered is a real gift. *Why is it so? Can this be done another way?* These are the sorts of questions that can encourage creativity and problem-solving skills.

Teach thinking skills

Sometimes, boys are content to limit themselves to shallow thinking. Parents can help prevent this by challenging their son to exercise deeper thinking skills, as shown in the following diagram.

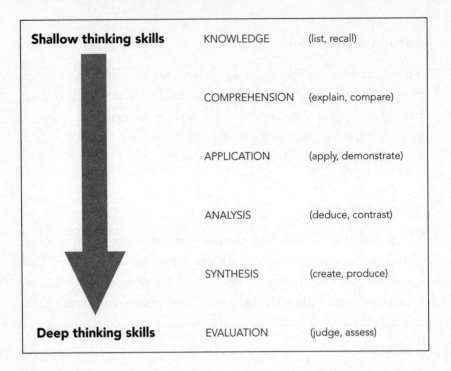

Shallow thinking skills	KNOWLEDGE	(list, recall)
	COMPREHENSION	(explain, compare)
	APPLICATION	(apply, demonstrate)
	ANALYSIS	(deduce, contrast)
	SYNTHESIS	(create, produce)
Deep thinking skills	EVALUATION	(judge, assess)

Stimulating deeper thinking skills can be done with the use of questions such as:

- What would you have done?
- Can we trust the source of this material?
- What do you think caused this?
- What other ways can this be done?

The sorts of thinking skills a parent can encourage in their son include the ability to solve problems, make decisions, see relationships, be creative, reason and judge wisely.

Do not encourage mediocrity

Sometimes a son can develop the habit of doing just enough school work to stay out of trouble, rather than extend himself. The discipline needed to work to an optimum level goes AWOL in some boys, with the result that they need external pressure to get them to produce work that reflects their best ability. Given that this is not always a pleasant experience, some will hide their ability and convince their parents they are dull. A parent can then become lulled into thinking that mediocre is the norm for their boy. Parents must be awake to this ruse and be prepared with sufficient incentives to encourage their son to produce work that reflects his best.

At other times, the reverse is true. A son believes his rather pedestrian effort is a stellar performance worthy of commendation and an increase in his allowance. Some boys have an entirely unrealistic understanding of the quality of the work they hand in. Even though sourcing examples of better quality work can be discouraging for a son, and even more so if that source should be his big sister, such initiatives should not be ruled out. It can appeal to the competitive streak in a boy.

Be flexible in expectations

Boys differ in personality and in preferred learning styles. Some like to work individually, others in groups. Some prefer a literacy-based approach to learning, others an activity-based approach. Some like to use multimedia approaches when presenting their work; others do not. Some like quiet; others like noise when they are working. Parents need to recognize the preferred learning styles of their sons.

Set goals

Academic goals should be set by our sons. This exercise should also detail how the goals are to be met. A useful approach is to get them to agree on a contract, which could use the GATE approach described earlier (see page 169).

G	=	Goals:	What are the academic goals this term/semester/year?
A	=	Activities:	What activities will be undertaken to reach these goals?
T	=	Timetable:	Exactly when will these activities be done?
E	=	Evaluation:	How will I know I am on track?

Teach time management

Some sons can have difficulty in managing their time and need to be taught how to use it effectively. Planning each day is important. A good way to do this is to devise a weekly timetable that covers not just the school hours but all the waking hours. It can be useful to get a son to record how he typically spends each 30-minute period of time throughout the week. Then he needs to think through whether he likes what he sees. After completing this task, he can write out a new timetable that will better enable him to reach his goals. Having the revised timetable pinned up in a prominent place or put as a screen saver on his computer can be a useful reminder to use his time more efficiently.

Look for learning windows

It is not often that one finds in constructive alignment a son, a momentary sense of interest, and someone willing to develop that interest—but it does happen. Props can be used to create a learning window such as a holiday trip to the zoo, diagnosing a gooey thing on the lawn and inviting a son's opinion on why the fish has died.

Make use of modern technologies

Computers and electronic learning devices are now a feature in most homes. What these bits of technological wizardry mean is that the home can now be a school. Instead of parents seeing formal education as something that happens to their son *outside* the home, parents can now partner with their son in educational tasks *inside* the home.

Educational institutions around the world are waking up to the "flip" method of learning. Flip learning means that things traditionally taught at school are flipped to the home, and the academic work traditionally done at home is flipped to the school. In other words, normal learning is flipped on its head. With this development comes many more opportunities for parents to enter into conversations with their sons on educational matters.

Eric Mazur, a Harvard professor of physics, started delivering his lectures using the flip method, and his academic results skyrocketed. When a state school in the low socio-economic area of Newark, New Jersey, introduced the flip method of teaching, their Advanced Placement scores in physics leaped to 50 percent. This wasn't bad considering the national average was 1.5 percent.[6]

Much of the pioneering work in flip learning was done by Jonathan Bergmann and Aaron Sams. They developed online lessons that their students could access and work on from home. Students could then network online with their classmates and make use of online learning resources such as "Wolfram Alpha," which is a knowledge engine that gives instruction on a huge range of topics. Other sites exist such as L4M and those designed by the Khan Academy.[7]

These online resources create opportunities for parents to enter into academic discussions with their son. Before any parent disqualifies themselves from this task because they feel unable to teach quantum physics, calculus or the digestive features of a cow, the good news is that they are not required to be the repository of all knowledge. However, they may be required to help their son to find that knowledge. For example, a problem in mathematics might be solved by visiting the Mathtrain website: www.mathtrain.com.

Probably the most exciting thing that modern technology does is create a culture whereby learning can be a lifelong adventure that can happen at time-of-need and place-of-need. A son who sees his parents excited at discovering new things is a son who is likely to engage in similar quests.

Finally, it is also worth remembering that, sometimes, all that is needed for effective teaching in the home is some healthy curiosity in a son and the back of a grocery receipt on which a parent can scribble an answer to a question.

AN IDEA

Teach your son how to remember

Getting your son to learn stuff is hard enough, but getting him to remember stuff can be even more difficult.

A huge amount of a boy's success at school depends on his ability to remember things. There are things you can talk to your son about in order to improve his memory.

Techniques for improving memory are linked to the three areas the brain uses to store information:

1. THE SENSORY MEMORY	Receives information from the five senses: sight, sound, smell, touch and taste.
2. THE WORKING MEMORY	Tries to integrate the information from the sensory memory with stored knowledge in the long-term memory. Information will only be stored in the working memory for approximately 18 seconds unless it is recognized as useful, or unless it is reinforced in some way.
3. THE LONG-TERM MEMORY	Made up of: Procedural memory, such as remembering how to ride a bike. Declarative memory, such as remembering French vocabulary. Long-term memory is heavily influenced by the frequency with which the material is used.[8]

Developing a good memory requires stopping the memory "leaks" from each of these areas.[9]

STOPPING THE LEAKS IN THE SENSORY MEMORY

You can help your son by encouraging him to use as many of his senses as he can when digesting information. For example:

- If it had a taste, what would it taste like?
- If it had a smell, what would it smell like?
- If it made a noise, what would it sound like?
- If it had a shape, what would it look like?
- If it were an object, what would it feel like?

Encourage your son to record the information in an interesting way, and in several different ways. The brain pays attention to information that is interesting. For example, he could record the information in written form and then record it in a diagrammatic form.

STOPPING THE LEAKS IN THE WORKING MEMORY

Remind your son about the relevance of the information being processed. Link what you want him to remember with something he already knows. For example, "The arm is a lever," "The heart is like a pump." You could also use poetry, rap, chants, music and rhymes. For example, "Thirty days has September, April, June, and November. All the rest have thirty-one . . ."

- Use word puzzles, acronyms and acrostics as memory aids. For example, to learn the planets of the solar system, use the mnemonic:

MY	VERY	EASY	METHOD	JUST	SPEEDS	UP	NAMING	PLANETS
Mercury	Venus	Earth	Mars	Jupiter	Saturn	Uranus	Neptune	Pluto

- Reorganize information so it makes more sense. List the items alphabetically, or by age, size or importance. For example, 43235463 can be remembered as spelling HEADLINE on a phone.

- Remember things in as many ways as possible. For example, when introduced to Mr. Peabody, remember: the sound of the name, the spelling of the name, the picture of the name, i.e., a pea with a body.

STOPPING THE LEAKS IN THE LONG-TERM MEMORY

There is no easy way for a boy to stop the leaks in his long-term memory. It requires the grind of repetition and review:

- Encourage him to write out revision cards. He will need to look at them regularly if they are to work.
- Flash cards, posters and notes can also help if they are stuck on a noticeboard, back of the cupboard door or appear as a screen saver on the laptop.
- Discuss the topic regularly. Reinforcement is good. Nagging is not.
- Try to get your son to use the new information as quickly and as often as possible. Get him to teach it to Dad, to little sister and to the cat.

*

It has been known for the occasional boy to want achievement without action, excellence without exertion and progress without pain. Parents might need to remind their son that things of great worth are seldom achieved without the down payment of a lot of diligent work. In other words, "No pain, no gain!"

Thoroughly finishing something will not be possible unless it is thoroughly started. A son must know what he wants to achieve. He needs a dream to work on.

SUMMARY

The most important things to keep in mind during this conversation are:

- Most boys want to be successful.
- The expectations that parents put on a son to succeed can be daunting and the expectations a boy can put on himself can be even more frightening.
- Depression and suicide can be the tragic result of boys who fail to meet these expectations.
- Failure is normal. How we respond to failure is what defines us.
- There are many ways a son can be intelligent, and there are many ways a son can succeed. Achievement is not always measured in fame and fortune. It can be measured in leaving the world a better place and in the development of good character.
- Boys need to be affirmed in their strengths and in what they have to offer.
- Success can be made more probable by setting clear goals.
- For many boys, success is measured in how well they perform at school.
- Academic success can be assisted by parental involvement in a son's learning.
- A key instrument in determining success is the brain, so it must be properly looked after.
- Success can be influenced by the capacity to remember things. Memory skills can be improved in the sensory memory, working memory and long-term memory.
- Dreams *can* be turned into reality.

CONVERSATION SEVEN

Sex

Oʜ ᴅᴇᴀʀ. But, you knew this chapter had to be written.

The birds-and-bees chat is a must between parent and son. If a parent is not going to speak openly with their son about sex, a son will cobble together his own understanding from sources that may not be appropriate.

In chatting to a son about sex, conversation needs to be extended beyond the biology of it all to other sciences including sociology, psychology and a lot of other "ologies" as well.

First, there are a few basic truths to put on the table when talking to a son about sex. These include sex being: pleasurable, normal, biologically important and instinctive.

Having got that out of the way, it's time to consider the sorts of things a parent (both parents, preferably) can chat about with their son on the topic of sex.

It has been suggested that boys are driven more by lust than by love and are more interested in conquest than commitment. This may not be entirely fair. What many boys are looking for is not just sexual satisfaction but a degree of intimacy that parents—even the most loving and devoted of parents—cannot give them. A boy needs to love and be loved, not just within the home, where affection is unconditional, but outside the home, in the beguiling world where acceptance is conditional—on looks, character, values and a host of other factors that lead us to make judgments about one another. In short, a boy needs to know he can find love outside the home as well as in the home.

Sons are often not just hunting for sex; they are looking for identity. They are on a voyage of discovery. They are seeking affirmation that they have the means to attract a mate. They are searching for evidence that they are a man.

What exactly is sex?

Former US President Clinton was more than a little vague about the definition of sex, so parents can be forgiven for being somewhat uncertain about what is defined as "sex" these days.

A penis being inserted into a vagina has been the bog-standard definition of heterosexual intercourse for some time. (Note—for sexual intercourse to have happened, it does not require ejaculation. Therefore, withdrawal from a vagina before ejaculation is still sexual intercourse. So, bedroom lawyers beware.)

Oral sex is growing in popularity among some groups of young people. Indeed, there is a suggestion that it is now so commonplace that some teens do not even consider it as sex. "Rainbow" parties, where a boy tries to collect as many different colored lipsticks on his penis as he can, are not unknown and neither are teenage girls practicing oral sex on soft-drink bottles. Boys need to know that oral sex is still sex and that it carries with it many risks as well as pleasures. Although pregnancy can be crossed off the list, sexually transmitted diseases (STDs) cannot.

Partners masturbating each other using fingers, hands or any other means, including sex toys, are also engaging in sexual acts. More than one boy has been charged with rape and/or sexual assault believing he was not actually engaged in a sexual act. Wrong. Very wrong.

Going significantly up the Richter scale of sexual exploits are other behaviors such as anal sex. This is still sex. Whenever sex is engaged in outside of the conventional biological norm of putting a penis in a vagina, particular care is needed.

Sexual assault

It is a sobering necessity that our sons need to know what constitutes sexual assault. Legal definitions vary around the world, but most countries define sexual assault as engaging in a sexual act without consent that leaves a person feeling frightened or uncomfortable. If a sex act is engaged in with someone who is incapable of giving proper consent, such as being too young or too drunk, then this may also be interpreted as sexual assault and possibly even rape.

It should be remembered that a number of boys will become victims of sexual assault and a number will perpetrate sexual assault. Our sons must be certain that, when they engage in any sex act with a partner, it is transparently consensual.

Speaking of legal matters, a boy also needs to understand the frightening ramifications of entering into sexual behaviors associated with the cyber world, such as "sexting." For those a touch vague on what sexting is, it is the distribution of pictures of a sexual nature using electronic means. A son sending a friend a picture of his girlfriend's breasts would constitute "sexting," as would swapping nude photos with the girlfriend using a cell phone. The legal fallout from such behavior does not exclude prison.

Other things to chat about

Perhaps one of the greatest dangers for boys in their initial sexual relationships is that they move toward a physical intimacy unmatched by a psychological intimacy. The problem can be increased by a desire by boys to keep up with their friends and the "leader of the sack," who may be setting the pace in terms of sex. Even if many of the claims about sexual conquest are hot air and bravado, the effect on boys can be much the same: a propulsion into physical intimacy for which some may not be equipped. Our sons need to be encouraged to be their "own man" and not just follow the behavior of others.

Sexual energy

Although not entirely accurate, there is probably some truth in the saying that men give love to get sex and women give sex to get love. The expectations in relation to sex can differ between men and women. It is not always true that men want sex whereas women want relationships, but there is some evidence to suggest that the need to release sexual energy may be stronger in males, with males registering higher irritability when going without sex. This may explain accusations that boys are born more promiscuous than girls.[1] There are very real sexual tensions in our sons' lives, and boys can often be aroused more quickly than girls. The fairer sex knows that it is her looks that turn a boy on. The pornography industry bears testimony to the strength of the visual thing with guys.

It might come as a surprise to many that the average teenager may not be quite as promiscuous as some would have us believe. About half those finishing their school days are virgins.[2] This news is important lest some of our sons feel that unless they are bonking energetically on most nights and on a significant number of days they are not really a man.

The value of sex is all too often measured by what is gained rather than by what is given, and by short-term pleasure rather than by long-term joy. Yes, there is very real pleasure to be gained from sex. Yes, it's good for a young man to know he can "do it." Yes, there's satisfaction in having the skill to excite another person sexually. No, not everyone is "doing it."

Also complicating things is the fact that boys are trapped between religious codes and secular codes; between boy codes and man codes; between heterosexual codes and homosexual codes; between lust codes and love codes. Therefore, our sons need to be encouraged to make wise choices in relation to sex.

The right time to "go all the way" and become sexually active is a boy's own choice, and his choice alone. However, it must also be the informed choice of his partner. A girl losing her virginity is not just a mental or emotional issue. There is usually a physical change, with the rupture of her hymen. This change cannot be reversed, even if the girl should wish it. The physical change can remain a permanent reminder of the first instance of sexual intercourse. Therefore, a boy must understand if a girl wants the memories of her first time to be particularly pleasant.

Guys also need to consider the unfairness of the contemporary judgment that labels a promiscuous boy a "stud" and a promiscuous girl a "slut." A girl can make herself vulnerable to social criticism if she agrees to sex, particularly the sort of casual sex that sees the boy doing nothing in the afterglow except shouting confirmation to his friends that he has "scored."

It is worth noting that, for some boys, losing their virginity is not always a triumphant "rite of passage." It can be an awkward, unsatisfying act that can leave them scared and guilty. So, a boy needs to be careful what influence they have on their friends—some might not be quite ready to go where he has gone.

AN IDEA

Tackle the sex conversation carefully

Charging in and asking a boy if he is having sex is unlikely to be received well. Remaining mute and allowing him to make his own choices in this area is also not helpful. Somewhere in between is the right level of involvement by a parent.

A good way to tackle conversations about sex is to start off by asking questions of a nonpersonal nature. These questions relate to other people's sex lives, rather than his own. Following are some examples:

- What did you think about the love shown between the leading couple in the movie?
- It says here that teen pregnancy is becoming a bigger problem. What do you think, son?

When the time is right, the use of semi-personal questions can become appropriate. These are questions that do not directly relate to your son's sex life, but rather relate to his opinion about sex. Following are some examples:

- When do you think it is right for a person to start having sex?
- Do you think some people regret their first sexual experience?
- Why do you think some people feel guilty about sex?
- Do you think it's true that girls give sex to get love, whereas boys give love to get sex?

Even these sorts of questions can be a touch confronting unless introduced naturally. A conversation that has been exploring the topic of who is going to feed the cat is probably not going to provide a good introduction to the topic of sex (unless the cat has just been de-sexed). On the other hand, if your son confesses that one of his pals has got his girlfriend pregnant, it might be a good time to talk about such matters.

Is your son ready for sex?

When I was at school, a friend of mine received an interesting gift from his father on his 16th birthday: a packet of condoms and the instruction to "Be careful." We all thought it deliciously daring. "Go and bonk," the father appeared to be saying. Needless to say, the son obliged. Unfortunately, he failed to heed all instructions, resulting in getting his girlfriend pregnant.

Parents need to give more effective advice to their sons about sex. This advice should, quite properly, be colored by many things, including cultural and faith issues, family values and so on.

Is a boy ready for sex if he has been given a packet of condoms by his father? Possibly, but only if a number of other things have been discussed in relation to when it might be right to become sexually active.

When discussing whether a son is ready to become sexually active, parents could focus on the following questions.[3]

1. Do you BOTH want sex?

If there is any disagreement about it being the right time for sex, then having sex is a serious no-no. Coercion is not wooing. Coercion is coercion and may be illegal if it can be interpreted as putting inappropriate pressure on a partner.

Those who want sex have often learned the rhetoric to get it. However, a boy needs to be strongly counseled not to use any of the following sorts of lines:

- "You would if you loved me."
- "It's only natural."
- "Everyone else is doing it."
- "Don't you want to make our relationship stronger?"
- "You'll have to do it sometime—why not now, with me?"
- "It'll be really great, I promise!"

Boys who want sex must not put psychological pressure on a partner to engage in it before the partner is happy to do so.

Nor should a boy have sex just because their friends are saying things such as the following:

- "You mean, you've never done it?"
- "I lost it when I was 14 . . ."
- "I've had sex loads of times . . ."
- "You're still a virgin!"
- "No one'll be interested if you're frigid."
- "You don't know what you're missing!"

If there is any hint of pressure, any suggestion that any party is not certain it is right, then it is not right . . . irrespective of what the hormones are saying.

2. Is this the right person?

If a boy does not know his partner well, then it may be unwise to engage in sex with them. Even if both are keen and agree that sex will meet their mutual needs, if a boy is not sure he can trust his partner, then it may not be wise. First-time sex can be a vulnerable experience, so it is better for a boy to enjoy it with someone in whom he has confidence.

3. Are you breaking the law?

The age of consent for sex differs between countries. In much of the western world, it is 16 years. In some Muslim countries, sex is illegal unless the parties are married to each other. Therefore, intercultural liaisons can be problematic when traveling overseas, so great care is needed. It is also worth remembering that you don't have to go overseas to encounter different cultural perspectives on premarital sex. Care and sensitivity are needed.

It is also worth noting that anyone who takes sexual advantage of another when their partner's judgment is impaired through disability, alcohol or drugs can find themselves in prison. Don't go there.

Sex obtained by blackmail, threats or harassment is also illegal and is morally abhorrent. Parents must be sure to share these obvious facts with their son, because some boys still don't get it.

Another point worth reinforcing is: no means no!

4. Do you want to give pleasure as well as receive it?

There are some predatory people who seek sex for their own satisfaction rather than to provide mutual enjoyment. This can be a particular problem with boys who watch a lot of porn. Becoming sexually active should not be entertained unless there is a preparedness to give pleasure as well as receive it.

For this reason, males need to be taught not to go straight to the erogenous zones. Sex is too special to rush. It's better for them to take things slowly and to give their partner many reassurances of affection before consummating the experience.

It is also as well for a boy to be reminded that a well-executed kiss can be infinitely more arousing for a girl than a grope. Great sex is not always about gymnastics. It is often about tenderness. Yes— there can be animal passion, but never at the expense of respect.

What happens after sex is also important. In the post-coital afterglow, there has to be a wind-down. A boy needs to learn how to take a partner to the "mountain top," and they need to learn to take a partner down from the mountain top in a manner that leaves the partner with an abiding memory of a great journey. This often requires some minutes of cooing and cooling afterward, together with expressions of tender appreciation.

5. Do you know enough?

A boy needs to know something about the biology of it all before he is ready for the physical exam. He needs to know what goes into what and what can happen if it does. There are lots of mistruths out there, such as not being able to contract an STD via oral sex and not being able to get a girl pregnant if you have sex standing up. Both partners must know what constitutes "safe sex" and know how to practice it. Boys need to be able to pass the theory before taking the practical.

6. Could you have regrets?

A boy needs to ask himself, and his partner needs to ask themself, whether they will be able to bask in the glow of pleasant memories after having sex, or whether they might be haunted by regrets. This is particularly important in relation to losing one's virginity. Understandably, this is an experience that most want to remember with some fondness. A condom may protect from pregnancy, but it can't protect from regret. So . . . our sons need to be careful about rushing in and losing their virginity, and they need to be careful about taking another person's virginity.

7. Does sex fit in with your personal beliefs?

It may be that a boy, or his partner, has religious beliefs that shape attitudes about premarital sex. These beliefs need to be respected. However, the decision to have sex should be that of the son and his partner. While other people may influence their decision, they shouldn't make it for them.

*

Not everyone will agree with all of the advice above. Good. Parents should compile their own compendium of wisdom on the topic. If these words have encouraged a parent to undertake such a task, then they will have served their purpose.

Like, lust and love

One of the more interesting homework talks I have given my students in the past is to have them discuss with their parents, or carers, what the difference is between like, lust and love. Just when is it that a person can know for sure they are in love?

Okay—it's not an easy question to answer, so it's only fair I have a shot at it. If my son had asked me when I thought I was in love, I think I would have said something like this:

I knew I loved your mother when:

■ She totally dominated my thinking. Everything I did was referenced against what I thought she would think, what she would do and what she would like.

- I thought she was "hot." There was no denying it, there was a chemistry, a mutual attraction between us.
- I realized that, if she left me, I would be shattered, particularly if she left me for another guy. I felt that I was made complete by her. When she wasn't with me, I felt that something important was missing.
- I was proud of her. A casual relationship need only be proud of the partner's body. A good relationship must also be proud of the partner's mind. A great relationship must also be proud of the partner's soul. I was proud of your mom physically, emotionally, socially, intellectually and spiritually.
- I recognized that I wanted her to be the mother of my children. There were some girls I may have been attracted to because they looked promising in terms of sex, but in your mother I saw someone who looked promising not just in terms of sex but also in terms of what happens after sex.
- I knew she liked me. Vanity is seductive.
- I smiled more when she was with me and I enjoyed her conversation.
- I had found someone from whom I did not want to have any secrets.

Puppy love

When chatting to a son about love, it is important for a parent not to dismiss their son's profession of love for someone as anything other than the real deal. To dismiss it as "puppy love," and something that they will soon get over, is unfair. Teenage love can be just as intense as adult love and needs to be treated with respect.

Loving more than once

A boy falling in love for the first time can be a bittersweet experience. His mind can become totally consumed by passion and he can be besotted to the extent he can think of no other future than to be in the everlasting arms of his beloved. *This is the real thing, Dad, we want to live together.*

Somewhat gently, a parent might need to remind their son that being in love does not necessarily mean he has found his life partner. There is a very real chance that he will fall in love more than once.

The seasons of love

The passion, intensity and expression of love can change over time. It doesn't necessarily get better or worse—it just changes. This is particularly true of long-term relationships. In short, there are seasons of love. A boy who fails to recognize this—who expects that love will always be in spring—puts at risk his long-term relationships. Part of the magic of a relationship is that it has different seasons, all of which can be enjoyed in different ways for different reasons.

When one first commits to a partnership, it is spring. There is vigor and growth. Everything is new, green and full of promise. Then summer comes, which sees a ripening of the relationship. The season may end with the harvest of children. The following season is autumn. The stubble is plowed into the ground to return wisdom and nourishment to a new generation. Then there is winter and the huddling together for warmth and protection. There is limited activity and, eventually, death.

Parents must teach their son that the successful relationships are those that are able to adjust to all four seasons.

What attracts a lifetime mate?

Most boys want to know if they have what it takes to attract a mate. When parents chat to their son about this matter, it can be useful to get him to reflect not just on whether he needs to put peroxide tips in his hair, but whether he needs to put goodness into his character.

He will, of course, say something like, "?," to which you might respond that peroxide tips may get him a girlfriend, but character will get him a partner.

AN IDEA

Use a character test to help your son understand what qualities he might need to attract a life partner

It is not possible to predict with any accuracy if a boy has what it takes to secure a life partner, but the clues rest more in character than appearance. If he should need further illustration, try him out with the following questionnaire—or something like it.

Are you the sort of guy who:

1. Pours himself the largest drink?
2. Sulks when he doesn't get his own way?
3. Has difficulty controlling his impulses?
4. Takes out the garbage without being asked?
5. Fantasizes about his friends' girlfriends?
6. Gives the minimum when there is a collection for a charity?
7. Asks people how they are instead of talking about himself?
8. Trashes other people if they trash him?
9. Tries to get out of the washing up?
10. Teases girls?
11. Becomes aggressive when angry?
12. Has an addiction?

13. Engages in random acts of generosity?
14. Gets on well with children?
15. Cares well for his pets, including the cat?
16. Gives blood?
17. Disciplines himself to eat a reasonable diet?
18. Has difficulty liking people of other races?
19. Leaves the toilet seat up?
20. Judges quickly and forgives slowly?

Most will not agree with the appropriateness of all these questions and they shouldn't. However, they serve to make the point that it is the combination of little things, the seemingly trivial things, that make a life partnership work. This is because "trivial things" betray the biggest thing of all—the heart of a person.

For a life partnership to succeed, it needs work. When the lust wears off, the love must go on. A marriage is kept alive by small acts of thoughtfulness, by personal sacrifices gladly made to honor and support a mate. A strong marriage is found in the inability to maintain a hurt or a grudge for very long. It is in being faithful. It is in the two becoming one. It is in the unity found in diversity. It is in the continual demonstration of kindness, the maintenance of a sense of fun and the ongoing sense of completeness when in the company of the other.

The prefrontal cortex

A girl looking for a boy to love is not always turned on by a bulging bicep or a washboard stomach. She is more likely to be attracted by a gooey mass of crinkled jelly at the front of a boy's brain called the prefrontal cortex (PFC). This may come as a disappointment to some of our sons, particularly those relying on their time spent in the gym.

It might also be a disappointment to be told that the PFC tends to develop more slowly in boys than in girls and may not fully mature until a boy is at least 20. No amount of how-can-they-resist-me gel in the hair or compelling man-fragrance on the chin can make up for an underdeveloped PFC. This is because the PFC is the seat of many of the qualities that turn a stupid boy into a good boy.

The sort of thing that wrecks marriages and destroys romances is, as often as not, selfishness, poor self-control and thoughtlessness. The part of the brain that contributes most significantly to the presence or absence of these qualities is the PFC.

For some boys, the PFC is a "Pretty Fantastic Center" of the brain that contributes to their reputation for good judgment and being fine company. In other boys, the PFC is a "Positively Foul Center" that contributes to their reputation for high-risk behaviors, poor social skills and bad impulse control.

The son who is gay

Parents of a gay son may find it particularly challenging to talk to him about sex.

Anger, denial and sorrow are among some of the feelings that a parent can experience when they learn that their son is homosexual. In some cases, the news comes as no surprise. Their son may have displayed signs of sexual ambiguity for some years and, thus, the "coming out" merely confirms a long-held suspicion.

It can be difficult for the heterosexual parent to accept that the fruit of their loins and the product of their parenting has resulted in a homosexual son. This is entirely understandable and highlights a very important fact. No one can predict with any degree of certainty that they will have a son who is "straight." Being gay is not the preserve of any group of people.

Typically, when a son announces that he is gay, he is making himself enormously vulnerable. He is putting at risk relationships that are precious to him. It threatens the closeness he has had with his parents, with the reference points and refuge places he has enjoyed throughout his life. Parents need to recognize this before they say anything by way of a reaction.

That said, parents have a right to their own feelings on the issue. They have a right to express themselves honestly as well. So—what to do?

Hug, thank and go.

An immediate reassurance of love and affection is needed (hug), and an acknowledgment of the courage and honesty shown (thank). Then, lest anything be said that might be regretted later, it might be good for parents to have some time by themselves (go). Say that you will chat further on this matter once you have digested the news. Then it is time for the parents (preferably together) to go on a long walk with the dog, or to retire to the living room with no-one other than the cat to witness them pour a very large whiskey.

Sometime later—and it should not be much later because it would be cruel to a fretting son—the conversation must recommence. It should be opened by more assurances of love before a parent shares their feelings on the matter. Structure can be helpful at times of high emotion, so in thinking what to say, parents might like to divide their conversation into three parts: the past, the present and the future.

Some questions about the *past* will be helpful. "For how long have you known you are gay?" Some questions about the *present* will also be useful. "How are you feeling?" Other comments will deal with the *future*. "How do you want to handle telling your sister?"

Questions about the past often relate to the *facts*. How long? How do you know? And so on. This last question is important because it is not unknown for teens to go through short times of experimentation with homosexuality. It is also worth recognizing that the degree of homosexual orientation can vary a great deal. Some people are bisexual.

Questions about the present are useful because they give an opportunity to share *feelings*. How are you feeling? This is how I'm feeling. In doing this, a parent should remember that a son is not able to choose his personal orientation. So—any expression of anger, judgment or disgust would be entirely inappropriate.

Issues about the future must also be discussed. Parents need to ensure the ongoing *well-being* of their son in these circumstances. Decisions will need to be made on how to manage the "coming out." At some stage later, there will also need to be clarification about the codes of behavior expected in the house in relation to boy-friends and so on.

The past-present-future approach to conversations can be useful in these sorts of circumstances, but not so much as a big hug.

The difficult topics about sex and relationships

Talking about sex is hard enough, but there are some associated top-ics that are particularly difficult to broach. Sometimes, that difficulty is a result of social sensitivity, such as divorce. At other times, the difficulty rests in the extremely personal nature of the topic, such as masturbation and pornography. But, regardless of how uncomfort-able parents may feel, they must let their son know he can chat to them about these topics.

The following thoughts are shared on divorce, masturbation and pornography in the hope that they might offer parents some guide-lines for what they can share with their son.

Divorce

Although not directly related to the topic of sex, divorce is a topic of conversation a parent must have with a son when the boy is of an appropriate age. When this conversation should happen will also be influenced by circumstances, such as whether the parents are actually going through a divorce.

The link between sex and divorce is not always strong, but the quest for sex and a better quality of intimacy has wrecked more than one marriage, hence the placement of divorce in this chapter.

Divorce can be intensely painful, and therefore great sensitivity is needed by a parent when sharing with their son on this topic.

A reticence by a parent to talk about divorce is entirely under-standable, as is a hesitance by a son to want to hear anything about it. Some boys are already very aware of the impact divorce can have, but others don't know a great deal about it, and this can be problem-atic when they have a 30–40 percent chance of being divorced or separated from a life partner themselves. However sensitive a boy may be, he needs to know something about divorce, and it is prefer-able that he learns about it from his parents.

For the purposes of this conversation, "divorce" will relate to the break-up of de-facto relationships as well as marriages. In many countries, the law makes very little distinction between the two.

*

Divorce is not much fun. Those divorcing will probably have to deal with multiple miseries. First, they may have to deal with the misery of declining warmth in a relationship. Then, they may have to deal with arguments and fights. They may experience betrayal. Thereaf-ter, there are lawyers' bills, court proceedings and the painful busi-ness of dividing assets and finalizing custody arrangements. There may also be a heavy financial burden due to court costs, mainte-nance payments and the loss to the household of a breadwinner.

The post-divorce period can be challenging too. There may be loneliness. A parent may only be allowed to see their children on given days. There can be emotional complications. The children may become angry and suffer a variety of conditions, including sep-aration anxiety.

A divorced parent might then be tempted to overindulge their children to show that they still love them—and love them more than the ex does. The result can be catastrophic in terms of children learning the art of parental manipulation. The progeny of a failed relationship can also experience poor school grades and develop be-havioral problems.

New relationships are a possibility, but they can bring their own problems. Blending families can bring complications, with each partner trying to be accepted by the other's family, and parents having to cope with different parenting standards. No two families have the same standards in parenting.

Other complications can occur, such as having to work out ways to protect the inheritances of each child. In short, just because divorce is common, it does not make it pretty, and it is best avoided if at all possible.

Having noted the above, some families sail through divorce with the minimum of harm and with the minimum of fuss. It also needs to be acknowledged that a family that has suffered divorce may well be in a far better place than they were when the relationship was intact.

Although the stigma of divorce is declining, there can sometimes be a residual element in society that do not accept divorced people with ease. This is regrettable, particularly because some divorcees are total innocents in a failed marriage. Contrary to popular opinion, it does not always take two for a relationship to fail.

While divorce can sometimes be a blessed relief, the lead-up to and process of a divorce are seldom happy experiences. For this reason, talking about divorce with a young son is generally not a good idea unless the matter comes up naturally. A premature discussion about divorce can cause anxiety in those who do not have the maturity to talk about the topic.

That said, a son needs to learn that breaking up with a life partner can have all sorts of consequences. Given that not many of these consequences are pleasant, the experience is best avoided. Although there are no guarantees, choosing the right life partner and cherishing them on a daily basis is to be recommended as a means of reducing the chances of divorce.

For the son whose parents are divorcing, or have divorced, there are a number of things that should be discussed. These include the following:

1. Reassurance that, although his parents may have stopped loving each other and/or can no longer live together, this does not mean that his parents have stopped loving him.

2. Reassurance that anger and grief are entirely normal under such circumstances. (Be prepared to seek expert help in dealing with this.)
3. Reassurance that the divorce was not caused by the son. A divorce is an issue between two adults, and they should do everything they can to avoid their children feeling any guilt.
4. Reassurance that, if another partner appears on the scene, they will never replace a loved parent. Nonetheless, it is worth expressing the hope that the son will get to know and like the new partner in time.
5. Realistic explanation that divorce means some things change. This cannot be avoided. It is understandable not to like these changes, but there is still a need to cope with them. There may be changes in such areas as parental access and custody, financial and living (including schooling) arrangements along with general family make-up—a blending of families may be necessary.

Divorce is traumatic enough for a son without it being made more so by his parents fighting in front of him. There must be an agreement not to fight or trash each other in front of any children. However tempting, it is important for a parent not to enter into a conversation with a son that is designed to get him to take sides in a parental dispute. Neither is it right to overindulge a son and try to win favored-parent status.

Clear behavioral rules must be set by *both* divorced parents, and these rules need to be observed consistently. This applies to such things as homework, bedtime, diet, and so on.

Divorce is usually upsetting. Tears and depression are not unknown. Open displays of grief by a parent can be unsettling for their son, so these should be avoided if possible. Let the grieving be done privately. That said, a son should be aware that his parent has feelings and is not immune from the same sadness he might be feeling.

In the fullness of time, and when a son is in his late teens or early adulthood, it might be appropriate to talk with him about those things that make a marriage work and those things that can cause it to fail. There is little more powerful than personal testimony—and if something good can be salvaged from something bad, then great.

Masturbation

Although not the easiest topic to chat about, parents must have a conversation with their son about "wet dreams" and why they occur. A son needs to know that masturbation is perfectly normal in a teenage boy. Figures vary on this question, but anonymous self-reporting by teenage boys suggests that masturbating about four times a week is normal in the late teens. However, sexual appetite varies a great deal, so care should be taken not to put too much weight on these sorts of figures. It is enough to know that masturbation is normal. As it has been said: masturbation is engaged in by about 90 percent of men, and the other 10 percent are lying.

The male of the human species is designed to mate with the female in order for her to bear children. To assist with this task, both have sexual organs. The male has a penis that swells when sexually aroused in order to facilitate the more effective impregnation of the female. When sufficiently stimulated, the penis will ejaculate semen. In order to ensure the species reproduces regularly, the experience of ejaculation has been made pleasurable, and this pleasure is, quite understandably, sought after, even if there is no female available or willing to be impregnated.

In other words, a son must understand that the desire to jerk off is perfectly normal.

However, like many activities, it is one that is best done in moderation. A boy must not become a slave to sexual fantasy to the extent that it interferes with his normal day-to-day function. He must learn to steer a responsible course between being crippled with guilt at the presence of "impure thoughts" and jerking off every hour.

Not ejaculating can cause irritation in a sexually mature male. Masturbation can therefore bring relief. Where it can all become a bit naughty, in the eyes of some, is when sexual fantasy accompanies masturbation. However, without a partner to make love to, it is difficult for a boy to avoid fantasy in bringing themselves to a point of ejaculation. So, parents need to be understanding.

Some advice about ways to deal with the hygiene of it all is wise. A box of tissues is better than a bed sheet. Enough said.

Pornography

Another topic difficult to talk about is pornography. However, the prevalence of pornography in the lives of our sons makes it imperative to discuss.

The premature sexualization of the young has never been more rampant. The raunch culture is affecting even "tweenagers"—those in their preteen years. To this can be added the normalization of sex in the media and the easy access to porn on the net. For these reasons, parents must talk about pornography with their sons.

Understanding the attractiveness of porn

Not many red-blooded males are indifferent to pornography. Our sons should be great admirers of God's creation, particularly when it is displayed attractively in human form. To appreciate human beauty is one of the great privileges of life.

The capacity to appreciate this beauty is happening earlier than in previous generations. Most boys develop the ability to father children in their early teens or even their preteen years, yet the average age of marriage in western cultures is about 30. The period in between represents the need for a lot of cold showers.

Our sons also have to wrestle with easy access to porn in a manner no other generation has had to. To this state of affairs can be added evidence that males may have a stronger tendency than females toward sexual promiscuity and a greater capacity to be sexually excited by alluring images. A society that wears clothes to seduce, uses sex to sell and preaches a "just do it" mentality has created the conditions to foster a great deal of sexual tension in boys.

The problem with porn

To understand a fascination with pornography is one thing; to approve of pornography is another. This is because:

- Some pornography exploits women and reduces them to sex toys sold for profit.
- Pornography can encourage unhealthy fantasies associated with power, violence and rape scenarios. This thinking can be carried over into normal sexual relationships and can harm them.
- Our sons suffer enough sexual tension without adding to it in an irresponsible manner.
- An unhealthy preoccupation with lust may hinder a healthy appreciation of love.
- Pornography can encourage promiscuity in some, which results in a growth in physical intimacy not matched by a growth in social maturity.
- Unrealistic expectations may develop about lovemaking, which may leave our sons and their partners feeling frightened and inadequate.

*

A few years ago, I raised a few eyebrows when I wrote about porn in one of my fortnightly missives to the school community:

> Society has lost its battle against pornography and with it the mystery of women.
>
> I am a great fan of the female form. I love the complexity and character of women as well as their beauty. I think this is why I find pornography so disappointing . . . the complexity and character of a woman goes missing in favor of the carnal and compliant.

Call me old-fashioned, but something deep within me is inspired by the attitude to women found in great stories such as Alfred Lord Tennyson's *Idylls of the King*. Let me quote some of it. It's about the Knights of the Round Table . . . Sir Lancelot, King Arthur, swords and all that sort of thing. Their aim was:

> *To ride abroad redressing human wrongs,*
> *To speak no slander, no, nor listen to it,*
> *To honor his own word as if his God's,*
> *To lead sweet lives in purest chastity,*
> *To love one maiden only; cleave to her,*
> *And worship her by years of noble deeds,*
> *Until they won her . . .*

"Won her," not bought her for $8 at the adult video store. Winning someone implies a struggle. It requires grit. There is the need to present oneself as worthy.

I know, I know . . . I'm going a bit far here, but let's settle for developing a level of respect and even reverence for women.

Steve Biddulph writes:

> *Sexuality, when fully allowed to unfold, has many aspects. It merges the sacred, the intimate, the sensual, the emotional, the creative, the funny, the tender and the intense.*[4]

Biddulph goes on to write:

> *There is little poetry left in the culture thrown at young people. For boys, conditioned by online porn and compliant but disengaged girls, sex may come to have no more meaning than an ice-cream or pizza.*[5]

Biddulph is not alone in his concerns. Writing in *The Guardian* newspaper, Sandrine Levêque, an advocacy officer at Object, a human rights group that challenges the sexual objectification of women, also warns:

Pornified culture sends out a disturbing message that women are
always available. It dehumanizes women into a sum of body parts,
reinforces valuing women for their "sex appeal" and undermines
healthy sexual relationships . . .[6]

Thirty-five percent of Internet downloads are for pornography.[7] This is not an attractive revelation about the human condition. If we are defined by what we do in private, then rather too many of us are sordid individuals grunting at sad fiction.

When the door is closed, the computer on and the porn at hand, a question is asked: "What are you really like?" Too often, the answer is: a sleazeball, someone with a porn addiction, someone who has sacrificed a manly nobility for a squalid and voyeuristic world.

Pornography comes from the Greek words *porno* and *graphia*. And it is everywhere. It is on TV and in magazines. It is sent over phones. It is collected under beds. No matter what net filters are put in place, pornography cannot be kept out. Unfiltered cell phones, bypassed filters using alternative proxy servers, shared porn brought in on DVDs and thumb drives all contribute to porn seeping into the lives of our sons like a beguiling miasma. And no wonder. The sex drive should never be underestimated in the life of a teenage boy.

The only thing that will keep porn out of the life of a boy is a decision by that boy not to revel in the world of voyeurism but to seek the integrity of the real world even though it may hurt. The faux world of porn is for those who can't cope with reality.

Doyle and Doyle of Choicez Media remind us that Hollywood releases 400 films a year. The porn industry releases 700 "films" a month. They go on to suggest that:

Many people feel ill-equipped to deal with the issue of pornography.
The complacency surrounding this issue means an entire generation of
young men are being reared in a pornographic culture with no moral
boundaries.[8]

Doyle and Doyle warn of the uncontrollable craving that porn can arouse in a boy, to the extent that it can interfere with his normal life. It is suggested that sexual arousal followed by sexual relief can be addictive and that the neuro-chemistry involved is not dissimilar to drug dependency. The brain is affected by porn. New neural pathways are formed and pornographic images can be imprinted that can last for a lifetime. Detoxing from porn can be problematic. The "high" given by porn needs to be satiated, and this will only happen if the porn becomes more and more "hard core."

The challenge for parents, suggest Doyle and Doyle, is to help their son decide whether he wants to become a porn man or a real man.

PORN MAN	REAL MAN[9]
Self-gratification	Self-denial
Self-indulgence	Self-control
Lives a fantasy	Lives a reality
Into domination	Into protection
No commitment	Committed
Secretive	Open

Most parents do not want sons who are sad, whose only conquests are in the mind, who are sold sex when they want love, who are encouraged to take rather than give.

Not many parents like to think their son is into porn, but many are—in a big way, robbing them of self-control, self-esteem and a decent night's sleep. We must talk to our sons about porn.

Suggested sex-related topics to be discussed with a son

For those parents who want to know the sorts of sex-related topics to talk about with their son, the following are included as a suggestion. The list is by no means exhaustive and the suggested timing of these conversations is not written in the law of the Medes and Persians. In the end, parents are the ones to decide which sex-related topics they will talk about and when.

1. Early- and mid-primary-school years

- The parts of the body and their function.
- Physical differences between males and females.
- Respect and care of one's body and other people's bodies.
- Circumcision.
- Stranger danger.
- Good and bad touching, kissing, hugging.
- What to do if approached or spoken to in a way that makes a child feel uncomfortable.
- Basic theory of reproduction by animals, plants and humans.
- Elementary discussion on relationships between people and how they vary.

2. Late-primary-school and early-secondary-school years

- As above but in greater detail.
- Good friendships, bad friendships.
- Menstruation, fertility, pregnancy.
- The function of intercourse.
- The biology of reproduction by humans.
- Basic differences between like, lust and love.
- Masturbation, its normality and associated hygiene hints.
- Introduction to the concept of contraception.
- Introduction to the topics of STDs and AIDS.
- Respect for the other sex and appreciation of individual differences in size, shape and maturation.
- Virginity—what it means physically, emotionally, spiritually, socially.
- The proper use of social media, the net, cell phones/cameras.

3. Early- to mid-secondary-school years

- As above but in greater detail.
- Care of the body, particularly the skin.
- Safe sex.
- The influence of drugs on sex, promiscuity, fertility and health.
- The emotional and social differences between boys and girls, and how they might vary on a "monthly" cycle.
- Identification of STDs and AIDS, and treatment for such conditions.
- How to cope with lust as well as love.
- What girls find attractive and unattractive.
- Testosterone and how to cope with it.
- Attitudes toward people with a different sexual orientation.
- Celibacy.
- Responsible dating.
- Looking after a relationship while maintaining platonic friendships.
- Agencies specializing in helping teenagers.
- Guidelines and rules associated with pornography, cyber-sex, virtual sex, sexting, et cetera.

4. Mid- to late-secondary-school years

- As above but in greater detail.
- Hints on how to "pleasure" a partner.
- How to cope with love as well as lust.
- How to cope with thwarted love and being in love.
- The desirable qualities of a life partner.
- Legal responsibilities and rights associated with relationships, including de-facto relationships.
- Looking after a sexual relationship while maintaining platonic friendships.
- Home rules such as where the girlfriend/boyfriend sleeps.
- Online dating.

SUMMARY

The most important things to keep in mind during this conversation are:

- If at all possible, when talking to a son about sex, *both* parents should be involved. It can be useful to broach the topic using questions of a nonpersonal nature.
- Teenage boys should understand that sex is pleasurable, normal, biologically important and instinctive, and that their interest in and an appetite for sex is normal.
- Boys are often not just looking for sex; they are looking for identity and an affirmation that they have what it takes to be a man.
- Boys must understand what sex is from a legal perspective and must ensure that they keep to the law when engaging in sexual acts. Additionally, the cyber world presents a legal minefield for boys in relation to sex.
- A son should be reminded that, generally, physical intimacy should be matched by a psychological intimacy.
- Boys also need to be reminded that the loss of virginity is not always a triumphant rite of passage; it can leave both girls and boys feeling scared and guilty.
- When a boy is ready to become sexually active will depend on many things.
- It can be helpful for a son to know the difference between like, lust and love.
- A son needs to understand that he will probably fall in love more than once, and parents need to understand that "puppy love" can be just as real as adult love.
- A boy must understand that there are "seasons" of love: spring (vigor and growth), summer (maturity and fruitfulness), autumn (preparing for a new generation) and winter (hibernation).

- Parents can help their son understand what it takes to attract a lifelong mate—and it is more than a washboard stomach.
- There are a range of difficult topics related to sex that parents should talk about openly with their son, including homosexuality, divorce, masturbation and pornography.
- A good way to deal with a conversation that has a high degree of emotion associated with it is to adopt the "hug, thank and go" approach. Giving structure to an emotionally charged conversation can also help.
- Conversations about sex should be done in an age-appropriate fashion.

CONVERSATION EIGHT

Money

Let's assume you have a 16-year-old son. Would he be able to comment intelligently on the following?

1. Agreed value
2. Third-party insurance
3. Excess
4. Premium
5. Executor
6. Power of attorney
7. Portfolio
8. Salary sacrificing
9. Fixed interest
10. Credit rating
11. E-commerce
12. Profit-and-loss sheet
13. Compound interest
14. Critical literacy
15. Tax return
16. Diversification
17. Mortgage

18. Bankruptcy
19. Financial asset

If the score on this challenge is likely to be in the southern region of possibilities, there is a risk that the degree of financial literacy in your son may not be quite as it should be.

Yes—we can blame the schools. The fact that schools release children into the world knowing important things about metaphysical poets but sweet nothing about money is close to irresponsible. If money is meant to make the world go round, then not many of our sons are going to circumnavigate the fiscal landscape with much confidence . . . and schools must accept part of the blame.

Having scolded schools on this matter, we can't abrogate our responsibility as parents in preparing our sons to operate responsibly in the financial world. Many parents seem to think financial matters are a bit like sex. *It's private, excitingly grubby and you'll figure it out when you grow up.*

When my father died, I was in the unenviable position of being his executor. Not only did I have no idea of what an executor did, I had no real idea of my father's financial affairs. As I waded into the task, I was surprised to find he had small bits of money stashed away in a variety of not-so-hollow logs. He had all manner of insurances and annuities and little pots of cash here and there.

My father had never discussed these matters with me in any great detail. In fact, we never really discussed anything about money. He once became cross with me when I took out a mortgage on a house— being a child of the recession, he didn't believe in borrowing.

Having noted the above, let me say that it is entirely appropriate for some confidentiality to be maintained by parents about their finances. A young son trumpeting his father's tax-file number at school and the amount in the family bank account is not likely to enrich his parental relationships.

However, it is appropriate for parents to reveal the mysteries of the financial world in general terms. Why not let your son see the tax-return form before you fill it in? Why not let him listen to discussions about the affordability of the next family holiday? Why not explain why buying the bigger pot of marmalade for $3.50 instead of the smaller one for $2 could be a good deal?

Talk to your son about financial literacy from a young age

Any discussion about money needs to be age-appropriate. This does not require parents to wait until their son is in his late teens and wanting to buy a car before introducing him to the harsh realities of a limited income stream. A boy needs to know why $275 in the bank and a lawn-cutting business that nets $20 a month is unlikely to acquire a Ferrari 599 GTB Fiorano. Even a boy well under the driving age can be taught elements of financial literacy.

The preteen son

A preteen son has many opportunities—including the examples below—to learn about financial matters:

- The principle of money, i.e., that it can be used in exchange for the sticky bun sold in the school's cafeteria.
- The importance of wealth security, i.e., there is little that can be done to secure that sticky bun if the 50 cents is lost on the way to school.
- The realization that selling ten marbles for 50 cents could secure the sticky bun.
- The appreciation that the power of money is limited and that, despite a cute and winning smile, 50 cents will only get you *one* sticky bun.
- A painful understanding that there is a difference between need and greed when Mom does not allow you to buy a sticky bun every day.

In no particular order, here is a smorgasbord of topics that parents might chat about with their son in order to enhance his financial literacy, even though he may not yet be in long pants:

- Money comes in different amounts. A certain numbered bill will buy five sticky buns. A different numbered bill can buy 15 sticky buns.
- The power to buy things is not limited to different numbered bills, but also extends to coins and to credit cards.
- You have to be careful using a credit card because, if people knew that Mom's PIN was 1839, she could be in trouble. Some things must not be shared with anyone else.
- Having money is a good thing, but, like many good things, it is not always easy to get. Pocket money is conditional on: a tidy room, feeding the cat and stacking the dishwasher twice each week.
- Extra money can be accumulated by watering Mr. Jones's garden when he is on vacation and sucking up to Aunt Matilda in the months leading up to Christmas.
- There is both pain and pleasure in giving some of your money away to a good cause.
- Advertising makes you want to buy stuff.
- Saving up and not spending can be great—particularly if Dad matches what you save dollar for dollar.
- Shoplifting and stealing is wrong—very wrong.
- Read the small print. Some things do not come with batteries.
- When batteries are promised and they are not included, you have the right to complain and get the batteries.
- Stuff bought over the Internet can be seriously dodgy, so you have to be careful.
- Use-by dates are worth looking at.
- Often, you have to buy tons of cat food if you want to buy it cheaply.
- Borrowing money is great at first, but paying it back can be a drag, particularly if it involves cleaning out the cat litter every week for three months.

Yes—it can be quicker for a parent to find the right amount of money from their wallet rather than allow their son to complete the transaction at sloth-like speed. Yes—it can be easier to give into a son's request to buy something rather than explain that not all impulses should be accommodated. Yes—it can be faster to choose a packet of toilet rolls if you work out the best deal rather than allow a barely numerate son to do the calculation. However, inviting a son, even a young son, to discuss money and its management can sow the seeds of financial literacy in later life.

The teenage son

When a boy is a little older, the possibilities for meaningful discourse about financial matters increase significantly.

It is worth reminding ourselves about some of the features of the contemporary teen.

The contemporary teen is:

- *Reasonably sophisticated.* The days of them being palmed off with imitation and generic brands are over in many households.
- *An avid consumer.* Pester power, product awareness and peer influence combine to make teens a real purchasing force.
- *Sometimes spoiled.* Perhaps an unfair comment, but with more double-income parents, parents who are older and well established in their careers, and with smaller family sizes, some teens are well provided for in the western world. Teenagers can be plied with all manner of goods and services, to the extent that some see them as a birthright.
- *Unfazed by authority.* The post-modern world, with its accent on individual rights, has combined with youthful precociousness to produce many teens quite comfortable in matching it with authority figures.
- *Morally ambivalent.* A decline in religious faith and a growth in ethical ambivalence have contributed to many teens being less certain about what is right and wrong.

- *Assertive*. Probably no need to say much more about this!
- *Connected*. Social media and friendship groups mean the contemporary teen engages in a great deal of "social swarming," both virtually and in reality. This results in a significant influence by peers on what the contemporary teenager wants.
- *Celebrity focused*. Football heroes, singers, actors, wrestlers, cage fighters—they can all influence the way a teenage boy wants to spend his money.
- *Tech savvy*. The "app" generation knows where to find anything they want on the net. They also know how to purchase and sell online.

The list could go on, but this is enough to remind parents that a teenage son has many influences on his financial predilections.

AN IDEA

Use pocket money to teach financial lessons

There are no hard and fast rules about pocket money. Some parents give no pocket money but will be more generous with periodical handouts. Others give buckets of pocket money but require their son to buy his own clothes and put a proportion away as part of a saving regime. Other parents increase pocket money by a dollar a year, i.e., $6 a week when six years old and $12 a week when 12 years old.

Pocket money can be a useful means to teach a boy a few of the home truths associated with finances, including the following:

- *Reciprocity*. Pocket money will only be paid if certain chores are completed.
- *Saving*. The amount saved will be matched dollar for dollar.
- *Giving*. A weekly contribution will be required to finance the education of a sponsored child overseas.

- *Investment.* A few lucky sons may find themselves able to earmark some funds to start a share portfolio.
- *Interest.* A certain amount will be placed in a fixed-interest term deposit.

The list could go on, but the point is that pocket money can be a useful means to teach a son a thing or two about finances.

The working son

It is important for a young man who has left school and has a job to learn to manage what money he has very carefully. Money management is also important for the boy who is still at school but has a summer or part-time job in out-of-school hours. At this stage of life, neither is likely to be making much money, so they have to learn to make the little money they have go a long way.

This is not always easy, because Friday and Saturday nights can be amnesia nights. They are the nights when many young men set out to forget the pain of the rest of the week . . . and they succeed. They forget how much effort it took to make the dollars they hand over to entertain themselves on the weekend. They fork out their weekday cash to buy their weekend escape.

Before parents tut and mutter too much, it is important to understand the desire to reward oneself at the weekend, because the working week for a working teen can be rather ordinary. Therefore, the desire to escape and have fun can be particularly strong. Jobs for the average teen can be tedious. Interesting jobs often come with seniority, as does the decent-sized paycheck.

Add to this a desire to escape the harsh realities of life, the wish to be with friends, to be without responsibility and to be where the action is, and one can see why the weekend is important enough for many sons to want to spend a lot of money on it. However, they must learn that going broke on the weekend is only all right if Monday morning brings no regrets. Is five hours of fun worth five days of work?

Some advice on money

Some parents may feel a bit inadequate at the thought of sharing anything meaningful with their son on the matter of financial literacy. *Nil desperandum*. The typical parent knows a great deal more about finance than they realize. Here are a few random thoughts on wealth that could, without any real drama, have come from most parents:

- Beware of the "I'll be happy when . . ." syndrome. Surveys have shown that even those who are millionaires feel they need more money. Enjoy the present. Enjoy the journey. Enjoy the weekdays as well as the weekends!
- More is not necessarily better. (Scene One: I once owned an "S" series Jag. It was British racing green and looked fantastic. I could only afford it because I bought it when it was eight years old and had a clapped-out diff. However, I still worried about the car. When I parked it in the city, I was anxious that someone would steal the badge, scratch the paint or dent the bumper. I never had that worry with my second-hand Toyota. Scene Two: I used to see a 30-meter yacht moored in Middle Harbor, Sydney. I would gaze at the boat. I would admire its sleek lines and state-of-the-art fixtures. I wished I owned it. However, I also noted that it very rarely got off its mooring. Sometimes, a few people would have a party on board, but it only left its mooring three times in the whole year. This was probably not surprising given the owner had to assemble a crew of six to sail her. I also saw an elderly couple potter off with their picnic basket on their small boat most weekends. They would return a few hours later with a contentment I never saw on the faces of those coming off the big boat.)
- About 2.5 billion people in the world live on less than two dollars a day, and many of your peers are significantly poorer than you are.

- The guy who dies with the greatest-looking car, even an "S" series Jag, is still dead.
- There are different ways to be wealthy. Maybe you can't be wealthy in terms of money but you can still be rich in kindness, you can be extravagant in warmth, you can be generous in thoughtfulness.
- Riches do not necessarily come when you are older, because increased wealth is often neutralized by more expensive tastes.
- It's a good thing to learn how to save. It's a good thing to learn how to go without in order to obtain something in the future.
- Learn how to give. A giving heart is a good heart.
- How you decide to spend your money defines what sort of a person you are. You betray your values in what you buy.

AN IDEA

Encourage your son to set financial goals

An unknown wit once said, "I used to be aimless and broke but I have turned my life around. I am now broke and aimless."

It can be worth having a conversation with a son in order to find out what his financial goals are. The chances are that he has a sizable wish list, but the act of articulating financial goals invites discussion on how to prioritize those goals and how to reach them.

Note: The chances are also that a son will change his mind several times about his fiscal goals, but this should not disqualify him from starting to think about them.

Rip-offs and scams

This dour topic is tragically relevant. Our sons need to be warned about those who wish to steal their financial assets. Unfortunately, most parents will have enough examples of larceny to share with their son, but, in case they don't, here are just a few:

- Never trust an email that says it is from your bank and requires you to give bank account or card details via email.
- Never give anyone details of passwords, account numbers and so on—not even best friends and girlfriends.
- Never trust automated teller machines (ATMs). They can be rigged to record your details. Use your other hand to hide the keypad as you punch in your PIN, and never use a machine if someone is looking over your shoulder or if the machine looks odd in any way.
- Never trust anyone wanting your account details in order to pay you mega bucks because you have won the opportunity of a lifetime.
- Never trust anything that is too good to be true—because it usually is.

Rules about wealth creation

Most parents can also share a fair bit of common sense about wealth creation, such as the following three rules:

The golden rule

Do not borrow money unless what you are buying is going to increase in value.

This rules out borrowing money for vacation, borrowing money to finance good times and even borrowing money to buy a car (unless the car is needed to earn a living). In ten years' time, these things will not usually have increased in value.

The things that typically increase in value over the long term are shares (equities) and property, although this cannot always be guaranteed. Great care and good professional advice are needed if money is to be borrowed for these purposes.

Property is probably out of the question for most boys, but, for a few fortunate sons, shares may not be, particularly if they are put into a fund that a responsible adult manages. Sons can be encouraged to build up a portfolio of shares, even if it amounts to only a few dollars' worth at first. Owning shares can enable a boy to engage with financial affairs more than they might otherwise.

The silver rule

Do not go into debt for short-term pleasures. Only get into debt for things that will bring long-term rewards.

When driving a car, a good driver anticipates what might be ahead. They are ready for anything that might happen. A bad driver responds only to the immediate and does not anticipate what might occur farther down the road. With finances, it is the same. Our sons need to look a long way ahead, even decades ahead, and not be totally consumed by what is happening in the short term.

The bronze rule

Do not get out of debt in one area of your life by getting into debt in another area of your life.

The high expectations of some boys, not being matched by high income, make them great targets for those given to usury. Bankers and other lenders can foster a "cargo cult" mentality by making credit readily available to young people who wish to finance their immediate wants.

Dazzled with the promise of heaven by the advertising industry and purported financial salvation by the bankers, our sons can rack up huge debts and end up in real financial trouble if they are not careful.

*

The following topics are also not out of the reach of most parents to talk about with their sons in a helpful way.

Taxes

Parents can let their son in on some of the tasks associated with completing a tax return. This need not require a full declaration of what the parent plans to put on their tax form, but it can involve pointing out the details that need to be filled in when completing it. This can also illustrate the importance of record keeping rather than maintaining a jumbled mess in a shoebox. Filling in a tax return can also prompt a useful discussion about ethics.

Mortgages

Perhaps the best advice to give to a parent as to what to say to a son about mortgages is to explain what a mortgage is. Mortgage is a French word with the rather uncomfortable meaning of "death contract." Because most mortals are far too poor to have enough cash to buy things such as a house, they have to borrow money from a bank or some other lender.

The bank's reward is that they can charge interest on the loan. This enables them to get their money back and a tidy extra amount as well. The borrower's reward is that they can own a house and this asset can gain in value over the years.

Of course, the borrower has to repay the loan to the lender. They also have to pay interest (the financial charge to use the borrowed money). It can be many years before a loan on something like a house is paid off.

If the borrower fails to pay the agreed interest to the lender, the lender can take possession of the house and sell it to get their money back. Then the borrower can be in real strife. They may find it difficult to borrow money again because they can become known as a risky repayer of loans.

It is worth remembering that the interest rate can vary or it can be fixed for the period of the loan. These and other concepts related to mortgages can often be illustrated by a parent talking about their own mortgage. Failing this, the Internet provides much good advice on this matter.

After explaining what a mortgage is, if a son is of an age to understand these things, then share a real-world example, perhaps even details about the family's existing mortgage. If this is confidential, it is not beyond the wit of most parents to present details of a hypothetical mortgage.

Wills

A will is a list of instructions on what to do with a person's belongings if they should die.

It has been suggested that "Where there is a will, there is a relation." This is because those closely related to a person who has died often expect some share of the dead person's assets. Sometimes, there can be disappointments, and this can lead to the ugly situation of a will being contested.

Again, the best way for parents to educate their son about wills is to show him one. If he should quiver with too much excitement at the prospect of inheriting a 14-year-old "S" series Jag with a fully repaired diff, they might want to remind him that wills can be changed and the grass needs to be cut. They need not show their son their own will for instructional purposes; there are many examples of wills to be found online.

Perhaps one of the most vital things to get across to a boy is the importance of *him* having a proper will when he is of an appropriate age—i.e., becomes an adult—and that this will needs to be appropriately witnessed and safely stored. He also needs to understand that an executor must be appointed to make sure the directions in his will are carried out.

Budgets

Many of our financial terms have come from the French, and "budget" is no exception. It is the old French word for "purse." Unless our sons learn to budget, their purses can remain somewhat empty.

The complexities of budgeting from a business perspective can be left until the appropriate time, but the idea of setting a personal budget is not beyond the comprehension of most teens. Essentially, it involves listing the various amounts of money that can reasonably be expected to come in over a set period of time and listing the various amounts of money that can reasonably be expected to be spent over that same period of time. Budgets can be set for a day, a week, a month, a year and even beyond.

Bank accounts

Bank accounts vary a lot. Parents can explain to their son why they have chosen the bank accounts they have. Conversation will probably meander along the lines of the following.

- *Money optimization.* Some accounts offer higher interest rates on savings.
- *Money security.* Some accounts encourage saving by reducing access to your money for a set period of time and by rewarding you if you continue to put money into an account.
- *Money convenience.* Some accounts simplify money management. This can happen in a variety of ways, such as allowing bank accounts to be linked to ATMs. Some accounts also allow telephone and Internet banking, automatic bill payment and so on.

Credit cards

A credit card—especially one that describes itself as being "gold" or "platinum"—can be drooled over by the contemporary teenager with as much covetousness as their father showed for a V8 with bucket exhausts and a metallic paint job. Like the V8, a credit card offers all manner of freedom. And, like the V8, it can be very expensive to run.

The age at which a boy can access a credit card varies around the world, as does the age they can get a bank loan. In Australia, the minimum age to obtain a credit card is 18,[1] and to obtain a loan borrowers generally need to be a minimum of 18; some mortgages set the age limit at 21 or 25.[2]

Joy-oh-joy, a credit card allows a boy to borrow money. Slightly less joyous is the requirement to pay off a set amount of the borrowed money at regular intervals. Even less joyous are annual fees and significant interest rates if the cardholder elects to pay off only the minimum required by the lender.

Credit cards work well if they are used within the interest-free period and if the fees charged for the lending service do not trap the cardholder into escalating debt. A boy needs to learn that money is never free, and, unless he has trained his parents to bail him out each time he loses control of his indebtedness, he could earn himself a reputation as a credit risk at a very young age and find it difficult to borrow money when older.

If it can be reasonably expected that a credit-card debt will be entirely paid off each month, then a credit card that offers a certain number of interest-free days is an attractive option. If the card is unlikely to be paid off each month, then the scissors become an attractive option. Failing this, a boy needs to make sure that the fees for late payment do not consign him to working in a bank-owned salt mine for the rest of his life. Boys must remember that cash borrowed from a credit card is usually very expensive cash.

Therefore, a key task for parents is to share with their son the difference between a credit card used badly and a credit card used well. The principal differences are as follows.

Fantastic plastic

- Is a credit card used to manage money rather than to borrow money.
- Is great when it gives the convenience of buying things without having to carry cash.
- Is great when you never pay interest on your credit card. This will only happen if you discipline yourself to pay the whole amount off when you get the bill, rather than just paying the minimum amount required.

Drastic plastic

- Is a credit card used to borrow money.
- Is encouraged by banks. Banks love to lend money on credit cards so they can then charge a whopping amount of interest, sometimes 14–24 percent, if the cardholder pays only the minimum amount on their bill.

*

A son hell-bent on securing a bank loan to finance his holiday in Bali needs to be careful. Financial institutions love lending money to the young and pleasure seeking because they are: relatively ignorant of the pain in repaying big loans; young, with many decades to pay back large sums of money; and supported, with many having parents who will help them pay any defaulted loans.

Shares (Stocks)

Not all families will have experience in dealing with shares. However, a knowledge of shares is important for a son because the day might come that sees him owning shares. Shares can be a great way for an adult son to start to build his wealth. Yes—there might be the odd global economic crisis that will see the value of shares take a dive, but, over the long haul, a well-managed share portfolio can still deliver the dream.

Shares are simply a "slice of the action." If a company wants to raise money, they offer part ownership—i.e., shares in that company—to those prepared to pay. If that company does well, the value of the shares goes up. If the company does not do well, then put back the anticipated retirement date a few years.

The buying and selling of shares can be done using online methods, or it can be done using a stockbroker. A teenage son is probably best advised to allow the buying and selling of shares to be done by a trusted and informed adult.

What shares to buy is, of course, the question. The tip-off from a guy at work needs to be treated with some caution. Far better to take expert advice and spread the risk by buying shares in very different sorts of companies. For example, shares could be bought in a bank, a retail company, a mining company, a technology company and a property company. Some shares can be international, some not. Some shares can be in established companies, others in more speculative, start-up companies.

Some shares are risky and should not be bought if a person cannot afford to lose on the initiative. For example, those just about to retire should probably not put all their money into shares in a rumored oil-field find in outer Kazakhstan. Less-risky share options would be wiser at this stage of life . . . and even in the early days of building up a share portfolio when a boy hasn't really got the financial reserve to take a hit by the oil field yielding nothing but broken dreams.

There are many sources of advice on how to start buying shares. Many can be accessed online. Just use your favorite search engine.

Insurance

Insurance is unlikely to be an electrifying topic for a boy, but the possible theft of his bike could concentrate his mind.

However gray and dismal the topic, a boy needs to learn about insurance. He might need to insure himself against injury or sickness resulting in him not being able to work. He might want to cover himself against "Delhi Belly" on a trip to India or a broken leg on a trip to the snowfields of Italy. He might own a car that must be covered by third-party insurance.

If a boy feels he does not need to know anything about insurance, his parents can refer him to the three possessions he loves most in life and play out the "what if" scenario.

Insurance is about paying money to an insurance firm so it accepts the risk of loss rather than that risk being borne by the insured person. When seeking insurance, a boy must know what exactly is being insured (the big-print stuff) and what exactly is not (the small-print stuff). It is also important to know the cost (usually described as "the premium') and the "excess" (that bit of the cost of replacement that must be borne by the individual).

One of the most natural prompts for parents to chat to their son about insurance is when he hears the strangled cry of anguish from his parents when the premium to be paid on their insurance policy has gone up yet again. This can happen in relation to home insurance, health insurance, travel insurance and insuring a 14-year-old "S" series Jag.

AN IDEA

Get your son to complete an asset register

Getting your son to complete an asset register is a useful exercise. In other words, ask him to list what he owns, and to put a value on each item. Even undertaking it with some subjectivity, a boy can become surprised at the cost of his wardrobe and even more surprised at what he stands to lose if the house burned down. This can lead seamlessly to a useful discussion about insurance and wealth protection.

Superannuation (Retirement)

Many boys have difficulty enough planning for tomorrow let alone planning for retirement. But that day (health and work permitting) will surely come, so some knowledge of superannuation is needed.

Superannuation laws vary from country to country. Some countries will automatically deduct money from wages in order to pay for money given in retirement. Other countries leave it entirely to the individual to pay into some sort of retirement fund. Often, there is a mixture of approaches, whereby a country requires some saving for retirement (paid by the employer or employee) but also encourages extra funds to be stashed away. Sometimes, governments give tax incentives to encourage people to save for retirement—and small wonder, because the government does not want the responsibility of looking after hordes of retirees when they reach the "walker and cane" stage of life.

Parents can teach their son a great deal about superannuation by sharing details about their own retirement plans. There are also some excellent websites that can give information on the subject. Some will allow a boy to calculate how much superannuation they will need in order to enjoy a sufficient income when retired.

AN IDEA

Use car ownership to teach financial literacy

It can be good to link conversations about fiscal things to the natural rhythm of family activities that revolve around financial matters, such as paying the mortgage, insuring home contents or filling out a tax return.

Failing this, most sons enjoy the prospect of owning a car. A great amount of financial learning can be smuggled into a boy if he wants to own a car. Loans, budgets, insurance and much more can suddenly become very absorbing for the hitherto vacant-headed boy.

Saving

Most parents are able to chat with their son about saving. Although the topic is up there with having to eat green veggies, it is a particularly healthy conversation to have.

The topic of saving also offers a number of finger-waving opportunities about lifestyle choices. For example, if a boy decides to smoke a pack of cigarettes a day, by the time he is 60 he will have spent close to a million dollars. That's a lot of car.

If each day he buys a coffee on his way to work and a $10 lunch, then the car fund is likely to be eroded by close to $4,000 a year.

There is a lot of truth to the adage that, if you look after the cents, the dollars will look after themselves.

SUMMARY

The most important things to keep in mind during this conversation are:

- The degree of financial literacy in our sons can be frighteningly low, so parents must help their son learn from a young age.
- Boys are unlikely to earn much money in their younger years; therefore, they need to manage what little they earn very well.
- Boys can be encouraged to set financial goals.
- As soon as a boy is managing his money, he needs to be taught about rip-offs and scams.
- Sons need to be taught not to: borrow money to purchase depreciating assets, go into debt for short-term pleasure or solve debt in one area by getting into debt in another area.
- Parents are in a good position to teach their sons about everyday financial issues, including taxes, mortgages, wills, budgets, bank accounts, credit cards, stocks, insurance and superannuation.

CONVERSATION NINE

Health

"Son, I think I know how you are going to die."

Now, *there's* a line that is likely to capture a boy's attention.

Guessing how a boy is going to die is more than a touch morbid, but talking about death may be the instrument needed to get him to stay alive.

Too many of our sons think they will live forever, that they are immune from the accidents and diseases that curtail life. They haven't been to enough funerals; if they have, they haven't been to enough funerals for young people.

I have had to attend several funerals of my students. They are unhappy affairs. Watching sobbing lines of young people shuffle forward to write shaking messages of loss and love on the lid of a coffin is a distressing experience. The bewilderment of those laying flowers at a railway crossing where a boy lost his race with a coal train is beyond healing. Seeing a boy buried prematurely because he has been eaten away by cancer is also hugely distressing.

One of the reasons a funeral is a shock for the young is because not many students are used to them. In their screen games, if anyone is killed, the "reset" button will allow them to play again. Then, without warning, someone changes the rules. They are not allowed to play again. Ever.

A body is made up of a lot of soft tissue that will leak life-giving fluid if punctured. This tissue is fastened to a skeletal frame that can break. For this reason, it needs to be looked after, and all the more so given that the body is prone to diseases and various forms of ailment. Therefore, we need to take care of our bodies. *Use no hooks. Fragile. This way up.* To these handling instructions we need to add a number of other imperatives. *Feed regularly. Water. Keep clean. Exercise. Cuddle.*

Our sons need to learn about the uncertainty of life and to treasure each minute as a gift. A number of years are allocated to a man. About 80. However, the presumption that a boy will live this long needs to be challenged, and all the more so if he engages in life-threatening behaviors.

It can be useful for a boy to think in terms of "Years of Potential Life Lost" (YPLL). Let them start with 80 years. Then, knock off ten years if they decide to smoke. Take away more years if they have unprotected sex. Prune further if they are given to binge drinking. Reduce yet further if veggies only make an occasional appearance on the plate. A further subtraction of years is needed if their lifestyle is given to any other high-risk behaviors.

Too many boys try to cheat death. But not all will escape. However, a personal appointment with the grim reaper can sometimes be delayed if we talk to our sons about common health threats and specific health threats.

General health threats

Statistically, cardiovascular disease (blocked arteries and so on) and coronary heart disease (often leading to a heart attack) are the most likely things to kill our sons. If they avoid these, then throat cancer, lung cancer or stroke will, on the balance of probabilities, claim their lives.

Ailments such as heart disease, stroke, cancer and diabetes are more likely to trouble our sons when they are older. But, before the young breathe a sigh of relief, they need to bear in mind that their lifestyle now can determine their health later.

In many developed nations, the leading causes of death among older teenagers are accidents and suicide. In Australia, suicide rates in males aged 15 to 24 trebled between 1960 and 1990. Today, about 20 percent of male deaths in the late teens are due to suicide.[1] This last bit of information should *not* be shared with a son. It is for parents alone—to keep them mindful of the importance of monitoring their son's mood. If there should be any worries in this area, parents must seek expert medical advice.

Many cancers and heart problems can be avoided by good diet and exercise, and through regular medical check-ups. Guys need to understand this because research indicates that many males only see a doctor when it is too late. Our sons must be taught to see a doctor immediately if they are the least bit concerned about their health.

About 50 percent of people in western countries are overweight and about 20 percent are obese. In fact, the rate of obesity has doubled in the past 20 years, and this will kill many of us earlier than is necessary.[2] If our sons are overweight, they will be more prone to illness. It can also make them look like a jellied blob and interfere with their hunt for a life partner. All this can combine to make them feel rotten about themselves, and this can open a whole new can of worms, such as depression. So—it's worth not going there.

We must encourage our sons to eat properly, rest appropriately and exercise well.

Food for thought

We are what we eat. If our sons put junk into their body, they can only expect junk to come out . . . in terms of sloppy thinking, reduced memory, poor concentration and loss of motivation.

A proper diet can have a huge impact on academic performance. If boys want to do well at school, they have to eat well. Here are ten tips parents can share with their son to help him improve his school grades via the lunch box and water fountain.

Note: These guidelines are general and will not necessarily be appropriate for all students, who may have medical or other conditions that must be accommodated in their diet. For example, some students will have a violent allergic reaction to certain foods that can prove fatal if not managed properly. For this reason, parents must seek expert medical advice to ensure that their son's diet is appropriate. What might be the correct diet for one may not necessarily be the correct diet for another.

Ten ways to feed the brain

1. Drink lots of water. About eight glasses a day are required for a brain to function properly. Danger times at school are the end of recess and lunch, when boys have been running around like blurred images. They must drink lots of water to hydrate themselves before going into class. Water gets rid of the toxins in the body and delivers nutrients to the brain. Our sons should also moderate their intake of coffee and sweet, fizzy drinks, and instead choose natural fruit and vegetable juices.

2. Eat breakfast. Brain function can be reduced by up to 30 percent if a child does not have a good breakfast. Quite simply, memory and mental performance will decline if a boy goes to school without "breaking his fast."

3. Eat little and often. A big meal will hijack much of the body's oxygen from being used in the brain and instead send it to the stomach. This is why we can feel sleepy after a big meal. Avoid huge meals at lunchtime, otherwise thinking will be impaired in the afternoon.

4. Eat carbohydrates such as grains, vegetables and fruits. "Carbs" provide energy for the brain in the form of glucose. Without this fuel, the brain will not work properly. Low blood-sugar levels can lead to light-headedness, tiredness and an inability to concentrate.

5. Eat low "glycemic index" (GI) foods. A great advantage of low-GI foods is that they can prevent hunger and loss of concentration. Instead of flooding the body with glucose, as happens when you eat a high-GI meal such as a burger and fries, low-GI foods release their glucose more slowly and for a longer period. Low-GI foods include wholemeal cereals and bread, pasta, corn, sweet potato and several other fruits and vegetables.

6. Eat omega-3 fats. The idea of eating fat is not appealing, but there are good fats and there are bad fats. Avoid the fats in deep-fried foods. These can be delicious and give an immediate "hit" of contentment, but fast foods of this nature can also give the "jitters" in the longer term and can damage health if eaten in excess. Instead, eat the omega-3 fats found in fish such as tuna, salmon and sardines. Omega-3 fats are excellent "brain food." They can help with memory and can improve the immune system.

7. Eat protein found in milk, cheese, fish, nuts and lean meat. Protein not only provides amino acids that influence the efficiency with which the brain functions, it also provides the raw ingredients used to develop many of the organs in the body, including the heart and brain.

8. Eat iron. This does not require a boy to chew on a packet of nails; it requires him to eat lean meat and vegetables such as spinach. (Remember Popeye?) A lack of iron in the diet can lead to tiredness, sluggish thinking and irritability.

9. Eat fruits and vegetables, because they contain, among other things, vitamin C and antioxidants that are essential to neutralizing the "free radicals" in the body. These free radicals are nasty molecules that can damage the brain and many other parts of the body.

10. Don't eat too much or too little. A boy's body mass index (BMI) should be somewhere between about 18.5 and 25. BMI is calculated by weight in kilograms divided by height (in meters) squared. Look up the details on the net. If in doubt, ask your doctor to check your son's BMI.[3] Waist circumference is often a

preferred indicator to BMI. Again, guidelines in relation to appropriate waist measurements can be obtained from your doctor.

AN IDEA

Get your son to test himself about his diet

Invite your son to give himself a score out of 10 against each of the ten tips listed. A score of 10 will indicate that he thinks he eats perfectly in a particular area. A score of 1 will indicate that he feels that he eats poorly in this area. If his total score is near 100, he is doing well and his brain is being well nourished. If the score is lower, he may be stopping his brain from working at its optimum level.

*

Before leaving the topic of food, it is worth noting the value of a boy being taught how to cook. The Y chromosome does not remove the obligation to learn this skill. Parents should teach their son how to cook at least half a dozen nutritious meals. Indeed, he should be encouraged to develop his signature dish, a specialty he can rustle up at a moment's notice and cause those eating to do so with relish.

Note: Being able to turn a few sausages on the grill doesn't count.

Sleep to succeed

Although it is not a popular fact, teenagers need between nine and ten hours' sleep a night—which might seriously compromise some boys' social lives.

For the hours to count as sleep, a son must actually be asleep. Being in the bedroom—even just being in bed—does not count as sleep. This is important to realize given the significant invasion on sleep time that can occur owing to the distraction of 24-hour access to social-networking sites and cell phones.

Anything less than nine to ten hours' sleep a night can lead to fatigue, and fatigue is not good news. It has been identified as contributing to the *Exxon Valdez* oil spill, the *Challenger* space shuttle disaster, the Chernobyl nuclear accident and one in six fatal road accidents in a number of countries.

Just how much sleep is needed by teens and preteens is not always agreed on. Dr. Michael Breus, writing in *SleepNewzzz* in 2012, suggested that research indicates:

- 9–9.5 hours a night for 10-year-olds
- 8–8.5 hours a night for 12-year-olds
- 7 hours a night for 17-year-olds

Other authorities, such as the parenting organization Raising Children, maintain that teenagers need 9.5 hours of sleep a night. Whatever the figure, it is likely to be more than many of our sons achieve.

The trouble is that fatigue and "sleep debt" interfere with the brain's working memory. Judgment can become impaired, a person can become less alert and more accident prone, and irritability and bad-temperedness can occur. There can be a loss in motivation and concentration, and an increase in periods of being "spaced out." Sleep deprivation can also result in micro-sleeps, which are short periods of involuntary sleep lasting a few seconds.

Therefore, studying late into the night to cram for an exam the next day can seriously backfire. Academic performance in an exam will probably decline if a boy does not have his nine hours' sleep the night before.

*

To get to sleep, the body needs to cool off a little and not be full of stimulants, such as sweet, fizzy drinks or caffeine. Likewise, drugs and alcohol can interfere with a deeply restful sleep.

Throughout the night, a person typically goes through sleep cycles that last about 100 minutes. These cycles move from rapid eye movement (REM) sleep to non-REM sleep. Non-REM sleep involves light sleep (drowsiness and sometimes twitches) and deep sleep (the sleep in which bed-wetting, sleep-talking and sleep-walking can occur). REM sleep is important for brain development and non-REM sleep is important for healing.

A person's circadian clock is one of the things that control sleep. It is a type of inner timekeeper. Typically, the circadian clock runs a little later in teenagers than in adults. This means teenagers generally like to go to bed later and sleep in longer. Some schools have recorded improved academic performance when they start their school day a little later.

The military has experimented with giving soldiers glasses that shine white light into their retina. This light is designed to simulate sunrise and can keep a soldier on active duty for up to 36 hours without sleep.

We need to pay conscious attention to the quality and quantity of sleep our sons are getting. Failure to have the right sort of sleep and the right amount of sleep can have an adverse effect on their health and well-being. If you have any worries in this regard, then see your doctor. There are remedies to most sleep problems.

Exercise

Not all boys are greatly attracted to exercise. It can hurt. It is time-consuming. It can be boring and requires one to wash one's hair rather more than usual. However, exercise has the happy knack of keeping us alive, improving academic ability and increasing our general sense of well-being.

In short, we should all engage in some exercise each week. It need not mean running marathons; it can be the discipline of walking to school rather than being driven, walking the dog for half an hour each day or mowing the lawn, especially if it is a big lawn.

Exercise is all the more important in an age that is seeing passive recreation (such as computer games) taking the place of active recreation (such as backyard volleyball). There is a worrying rise in the number of boys whose exercise is limited to pressing the remote control and keyboard.

There are three types of exercise that should be engaged in each week:

1. *Aerobic exercises*. These work on the cardiovascular system. Examples include walking, running, cycling and swimming. This type of exercise enriches the blood with oxygen, with the result that it can improve mental function as well as physical function.
2. *Anaerobic exercises*. These are strength exercises such as lifting, pushing and calisthenics, such as push-ups.
3. *Flexibility exercises*. These are important for balance, posture and movement. This type of exercise is often incorporated in programs such as yoga and Pilates.[4]

*

For specifics on how much exercise and what type of exercise to engage in, seek expert medical advice. However, for most teenagers who do not suffer any complicating medical conditions, light exercise such as walking can be engaged in daily, whereas heavy exercise, such as running and weight training, is better engaged less frequently, to allow the body to recover.

Doctors have recommended getting the heart rate up to 70–80 percent of its maximum for 30 minutes three times a week, but this advice may not be suitable for all people, particularly if they have a medical condition.

After, and even during, exercise, care should be taken to keep the body well hydrated (drink lots of water) and replenished with electrolytes.

It is important that a boy does not charge into a vigorous exercise routine if he is not used to one. He should ease himself in and gradually build up his strength and endurance. Get him to try power walks before going on a run. Get him to do light weights for a short period before tackling heavy weights for long periods.

*

The health benefits of exercise should not be underestimated. Exercise can, quite literally, be a lifesaver. The benefits of exercise have been seen to:

- Improve mental performance, brain function and school grades.
- Help prevent depression (which is one of the fastest-growing illnesses among teens). Exercise releases endorphins, which are rather like opiates, and these can give a "hit" of feeling good.
- Prevent heart disease and Type 2 diabetes, two of the greatest killers in the western world.
- Boost the immune system to make a boy more resistant to illness.
- Reduce the risk of some cancers, such as prostate and colon cancers.
- Reduce obesity.

Faced with this evidence, it really is a no-brainer to encourage regular exercise in our sons. Engaging in exercise with a son can also be very rewarding. Not only are there health benefits, but also opportunities are presented to talk over matters and to stay engaged with each other's lives. A son is more likely to be persuaded of the health benefits of exercise by witnessing it than being lectured about it.

Drugs

A tragic relevance requires the mention of another health-endangering issue: doing drugs.

There are five levels of drug use among boys:

1. No use
2. Experimental use
3. Occasional use
4. Frequent use
5. Dependent use

Of all the drugs our sons might use, by far the most common are alcohol, tobacco and marijuana. This is not to say there are no other forms of drug abuse. It is to say that, to stay within the confines of one book, attention must necessarily be focused on the most common ones.

Alcohol

Some alcohol can be good for you. For example, red wine has antioxidants in it, which, if drunk in moderation by an adult, can be health promoting. However, if a small amount is good for you, a large amount is not necessarily better for you. Getting "rat-faced," "smashed" and "wasted" does not create in a person a feeling of radiant health. To this must be added increasing research that suggests even small quantities of alcohol can impair health—particularly in children.[5]

The body sends efficient hints if it has had too much alcohol. One of them is called a hangover. However, boys need not wait for a hangover to do themselves harm by drinking alcohol. Any amount of alcohol can impair well-being and health, and the capacity for a boy to make sound judgments as to whether it is right to start moderating his drinking can become less clear after each drink.

The focus on getting drunk rather than on having a good time is a growing feature among some groups of teenagers. It seems an occasion is only made special if it cannot be remembered, with the only clues of the evening activities being nausea, a pair of pink panties in the pocket and some vomit on the shirt. It is even sadder that such drinking binges seem to take place on those occasions one rather hopes will be remembered, such as 18th-birthday parties.

The trouble with most teenage sons is that they do not yet have bodies that are able to process alcohol as well as those who are older. This is not a problem that is solved by more practice—it is a problem solved by greater restraint.

The capacity to be able to cope with alcohol varies from person to person and is influenced by a variety of factors, including the amount of water in the body. The generally accepted formula of the body being able to process one alcoholic drink an hour needs to be treated very carefully. Drinks vary in size and a person's capacity to process alcohol also varies a great deal.

Having noted these things, the worry for most parents is not just the direct effect of drinking. It's the indirect effects. Alcohol plus testosterone plus a minor irritation can lead to violence. Alcohol plus fast cars can lead to boys being scraped off a road with a shovel.

By day, all boys are mild-mannered reporters, but on Saturday night they don't so much go into phone booths and emerge as supermen, they get into the beer and become stupid. True, a few will get depressed and moody, but most will be tempted to engage in feats of valor that would not be believed in the sober light of dawn.

*

One of my ex-students, Thomas Kelly, was killed in an unprovoked attack in Kings Cross, Sydney, in 2012. A stranger ran up behind Thomas and hit him. People describe this sort of hit as a "king hit." They shouldn't. They should call it for what it is: a cowardly hit—a hit you land on someone when they are not expecting it.

Thomas was knocked unconscious. His hand slipped out of his girlfriend's and he fell to the ground. Thomas was now brain-dead. Two days later, his parents, Ralph and Kathy Kelly, took the horrendous decision to switch off the life-support system. Thomas died on July 9, 2012. The police were now looking for a murderer.

After graduating in 2011, Thomas had pursued a cadetship in an accounting firm. He also pursued a university degree and a romance. All these dreams were smashed, resulting in a father having to give a eulogy for a son.

What do you say to a school grieving the loss of one of their own? What do you say to the parents of a boy in a coffin?

No words are adequate—but three thoughts came to mind as I informed the school of the tragedy. Sanctity. Fragility. Capacity.

Whenever an individual, organization or nation loses sight of the sanctity of life, the scene is set for atrocity. When people lose sight of the preciousness of the individual, we invite murder.

The imbecilic attack on Thomas was perpetrated by a fool who lost sight of the value of a person. Thomas was not a person, he was a target. When people are seen as targets, we tend to kill them.

We are fragile, and the head is particularly fragile. I remember being at the bedside of one of our past school captains some years ago. He was in an intensive-care unit, his life in the balance after hitting his head on the ground while playing a game of soccer. Fortunately, he survived the accident. However, with Thomas, it was not an accident . . . and he didn't survive.

The trouble with many young men is that they think themselves bulletproof. Our sons need to be persuaded of the virtues of a health-promoting lifestyle and develop an aversion to unnecessary risk. They must also develop a proper understanding of the fragility of the human condition. Otherwise, too many of them will end up in a morgue, or behind bars in a prison.

Some young men need to be taken off our streets and removed from society. They have lost the right to live with us. Some parents need to improve in their duties. They must mentor their sons. They must be role models in anger management, impulse control and in making good choices. Some schools need to do more than grind through mandated curriculums. They need to teach in a values-rich environment. The current moral vacuum in schools is yielding bitter fruit.

The sanctity of the individual, the fragility of the human form and the capacity to learn from tragedy are still an inadequate response to Thomas's death. But, they are good messages to share with a son.

AN IDEA

Advise your son how to drink reasonably

Most of our sons will drink alcohol—many will do so illegally. Whether your son drinks legally or illegally, you can give him advice on how to drink responsibly. However, care is needed to ensure that, in the giving of this advice, a tacit permission is not being given for your son to get into the hooch.

This noted, the sort of advice that you could give to your son about drinking might include the following:

- Always be in control of the alcohol. Do not let the alcohol control you.
- Do not drink and drive. Appoint a designated driver.
- Do not drink anything if you are not sure of its contents.
- Do not mix alcoholic drinks.
- Restrict yourself to only one drink per hour. If you feel any signs of intoxication, move on to soft drinks.
- Match each alcoholic drink with at least one soft drink, or a glass of water.
- Always stay with friends and agree to look after each other when at a party at which alcohol is going to be served.
- If of a legal age to drink, do not be afraid to drink light beer.
- Put in place a plan in case anything goes wrong.
- Be careful with whom you drink.
- Decide the number of maximum alcoholic drinks before going out.
- Be careful of sweet alcoholic drinks. The sweetness can hide the alcohol.
- Drink plenty of water before arriving at a function.
- Drink plenty of water when returning from a function.

*

Before leaving the topic of alcohol, we must acknowledge that there can be enormous social pressure on a boy to drink. A boy who says he doesn't drink alcohol is therefore a courageous person (or the designated driver). Either way, his decision not to drink should be honored and respected. He should not be forced to change his mind and neither should he be asked to explain his abstinence.

Tobacco

Jean Nicot lent his name to the alkaloid found in the leaf of the tobacco plant now known as nicotine. Nicot was an enthusiastic supporter of the plant and ascribed to it many medical and social virtues. One might now forgive Nicot given that Portugal in the 1560s was not alive to the health risks associated with smoking.

But we do know now.

Alarmed by evidence that a number of my students were smoking, I once shared the following garrumph with them and their parents.

SMOKING—A REFLECTION

Why do boys do it? Why do boys smoke when evidence is overwhelming in terms of its harmful effects? It not only yellows fingers and wallpapers lungs with tar, it can bestow upon the smoker ashtray breath, a thin wallet and a shortness of breath. Even more appalling is the preparedness of smokers to allow themselves to be enslaved. While laughing at wowsers [teetotalers] and speaking of freedom, the shackles of addiction snap tight around their lives.

Some boys do it to experiment. This is vaguely defensible, for it has a nice educational ring to it. Unfortunately, some experiments are dangerous, and before the smoke has cleared, another boy has surrendered part control of their lives to a cigarette company.

Others do it to grow up. The socially fragile feel they must win acceptance by sticking white sticks in their mouth. It often takes some years to realize that true maturity is not found in the decision to smoke. Indeed, there is evidence to suggest that the more mature will probably say: "No thanks . . . I don't need it."

Many smoke because of peer pressure. The desire to be accepted by friends is so strong it will dictate what you wear, what you do and even what you breathe.

Some smoke out of rebellion or daring. There is a thrill factor— will I get caught and get punished? Will I get caught and get cancer?

Too many of our young are sending smoke signals asking for help; smoke signals that confess to some personal inadequacy; smoke signals that suggest they don't like society or themselves.

Tragically, smokers are dying out . . . sometimes painfully and slowly. The pathetic, wasted features of those in the cancer wards of hospitals are reminders that the final days of a smoker are not filled with careless abandon, fun and devilment, but rather in wrestling with gurgling tubes, painkillers and bitter regrets.

Often boys find it difficult to believe they are mortal . . . and accordingly take unacceptable risks with their lives. We need to help blow the smoke away and give them a clear indication that smoking is not worthy of them.

Research has found that nicotine is a toxic, addictive stimulant. Cigarette smoke is poisonous, promotes cancer and premature aging of the skin, respiratory problems, heart disease and circulatory problems.[6]

*

It didn't work. Anti-smoking rants rarely do.

The sublime optimism in boys, together with the strong desire to be accepted by the group, will generally mean that anti-smoking lectures are not always effective. Boys already know that smoking is not good for them. But they still smoke.

However, teaching the associated health risks is still important and should not be underestimated in its ability to turn a son away from smoking. That said, logic and knowledge are not terribly effective on a Friday night and in the presence of others who are smoking. Add to this the attraction of the opposite sex (many of whom may be smoking) and the erosion of inhibitions brought on by six bottles of rum and coke, and any "Quit Campaign" rhetoric is lost.

The four approaches I've found to have some impact on stopping boys from smoking are:

1. The deterrent approach
2. The fitness approach
3. The emotional approach
4. The "I don't need it" approach

1. The deterrent approach

Although lacking a certain sophistication, the threat by a parent to limit their son's freedom or expenditure does sometimes work. A few parents have turned the deterrent approach around and offered financial rewards if a son gives clear evidence of not smoking. Care needs to be taken with this approach, for it may do little else than drive the smoking underground. However, it can be argued that underground is better than above ground.

Another potential problem is developing a mindset that sees a boy being rewarded for behavior he should be engaging in anyway. Not smoking is normal and shouldn't necessarily be rewarded, otherwise the dependency may be transferred from nicotine to bribes. Neither is good for a boy.

The deterrent approach can be enriched by regular reminders of the health risks associated with smoking. Lung cancer and respiratory diseases will not only be ten times more likely; there is a long list of other medical problems that can be drawn to a boy's attention, such as heart attacks, blood-circulation disorders, stomach ulcers and the premature aging of the skin. Again, it is as well not to pin too many hopes on the factual approach, for many boys have developed a world-weary immunity to facts, and, even if they believe them, they find a certain thrill in daring the gods to kill them.

2. The fitness approach

Sport is a mainstream religion for many boys. Many want to see themselves as stud-muffins and mega-fit sporting heroes. This is not true of all boys, but it is true of enough to make the fitness approach worth considering. The supportive data is straightforward: to be successful in sports, you need a body that is able to function well, and this will not happen if you smoke.

Smoking reduces the capacity of the blood to carry oxygen and can bring about many other performance-limiting problems, ranging from respiratory problems to gangrene. It is not just sports that might be adversely affected: everyday functions can also be upset. Even the capacity to enjoy good sex. Now, that should scare them!

3. The emotional approach

The testimony of a relative or friend who has been a smoker and who is now having to battle a smoking-related illness can have a strong impact on a boy. It certainly did with me.

4. The "I don't need it" approach

Society has failed to capitalize on the opportunities to discredit smoking as a smelly means for inadequate people to gain social acceptance. This is because not all smokers are inadequate people. However, some of our sons do feel inadequate and believe their social standing to be so fragile they have to burn white sticks in their mouth to gain popularity. Perhaps it is time to say to those offering a cigarette, "No thanks . . . I don't need it."

Such a response implies pity for those who do need a cigarette. Good. There are very few forces more potent than pity in persuading a boy to change his behavior. If the sense can be engendered that the smoker has a problem, then perhaps some ground can be won. *You poor thing, I can see why you smoke* may be the sort of uncharitable thought necessary in the battle against smoking.

*

Parents whose son smokes cigarettes can be forgiven for thinking that drugs other than nicotine might be a feature of their son's life. Surveys have found that half of all tobacco smokers have tried illegal drugs. Among non-smokers, the figure is only a fraction of this amount.[7]

Marijuana

The signs are not good. Cannabis is about as hardy a plant as you can find. It produces a strong fiber that has been used for centuries to make rope, yet if the resin from this plant is injected into its root system, it will die.[8]

That same resin can kill a boy.

The price paid for smoking marijuana can include increased anxiety and paranoia, hallucinations, poor concentration and damaged short-term memory. The longer-term problems make even more depressing reading. They include addiction, respiratory disease, permanent memory damage, schizophrenia, leukemia, weakened immune system, reduced fertility, premature aging and respiratory-tract cancer. Therefore, the only advice that parents can give their son on the matter of marijuana is simple: don't use it. No responsible form of compromise can be considered.

Marijuana comes in many forms—as dried leaves, dried resin and even as oil extract—all from the *cannabis sativa* plant. It is called many names—weed, grass, hash, dope, pot, hemp, to name but a few. The potency of marijuana has increased over the years so that a joint smoked today is likely to be far more dangerous than a joint smoked by a parent 30 years ago.

There will be some who might suggest that marijuana is no more dangerous than alcohol or cigarettes. This may or may not be true, but this should not prevent parents from discouraging their son from using marijuana. There are a number of reasons for this injunction, not least because there is mounting evidence to suggest that marijuana has been linked to schizophrenia and psychosis. It has also been linked to depression, low self-esteem and violence. A further problem with marijuana is that it is generally packaged in an anti-establishment culture and an alternative values system that can damage a boy and society in general.

Unlike alcohol, which is generally removed from the body within 24 hours, cannabis is attracted to the fatty tissues such as the brain and can remain there for up to five years. It is interesting to note that Sweden, which has a strong tradition of liberalism, altered its policy toward marijuana after studies were done using thousands of their military conscripts. The researchers found a strong link between cannabis consumption and schizophrenia, suicide, intravenous drug use and violent crime.

Is my son on drugs?

Parents may be forgiven for suspecting their son is doing drugs if his bedroom wall is plastered with pictures of cannabis plants (with or without Bob Marley), and there are blackened spoons littering the floor together with cigarette papers and strange bottles with funny tubes sticking out of them.

In all likelihood, a son is not going to be quite this careless about betraying his interest in drugs. Not wishing to be disinherited, he will hide his drug use from his parents. So, some sleuthing may be necessary.

Parents have a right to be worried if they see the following signals.

1. Academic

- A decline in academic performance.
- A growing anti-school sentiment.
- Behavioral problems ranging from listlessness, apathy and inattention, to anger and defiance.
- Truancy.
- Increasing vagueness and memory problems.
- Short attention span.

2. Social/emotional

■ Moody, resentful and prone to secretive behaviors.

■ Rapid changes in temperament. Intolerance to criticism, either real or imagined.

■ Growing delinquency.

■ Shortage of money that can lead to involvement in theft.

3. Physical

■ Reduced resistance to colds and flu.

■ Changes in eating habits and weight.

■ Pallid, unhealthy appearance.

■ Sleep problems, both too much and too little.

Care should be taken in putting too much weight on the clues above. They should be recognized for what they are—clues, not proof. Also remember that there are many other conditions that can lead to the symptoms described. In the end, the matter can only be diagnosed properly using expert medical help.

That said, drug-testing kits are now available for private use; they are usually inexpensive and easy to perform. These kits test not only for THC (marijuana) but also for methamphetamines, opiates, amphetamines and benzodiazepines. Testing techniques vary from urine analysis to saliva testing, sweat testing and even hair testing.

There also exist rather more expensive but more accurate measures to test for drug use, such as gas chromatography/mass spectrometry. These can only be administered by specially trained experts. If you need more advice on these measures, you should see your doctor.

Having noted the above, many parents would be appalled at the thought of testing their son for drugs. However, desperate parents who suspect their son has a drug problem might be slightly less appalled.

Some parents who test their son for drugs also make mention of the fact that it empowers their son to say to peers, "No thanks—I'm tested for drugs at home."

Perhaps a responsible compromise on the drug-testing issue is to tell your son that, because you love him, you will fight tooth and nail to stop him ever becoming damaged by drugs. Indeed, you will come down like an avenging angel on anyone who gives your son drugs and will dispense some not inconsiderable judgment toward a son who accepts them.

After explaining why taking drugs is not a good idea, parents might say where they sit in relation to the drug-testing issue. The conversation might go something like this:

Son, it's pretty close to certain you will be offered illegal drugs more than once in your life. I'm going to ask you to say no to these opportunities. I ask this because I love you, and I do not want you to risk becoming addicted to drugs.

If ever you find yourself under pressure to take illegal drugs and feel that saying no is not going to work, then know that I am only a phone call away. I will slay dragons to get you out of a situation involving drugs. Just call.

We operate on a trust system in this house. We have to. Without trust, there is dark suspicion and angst. We don't want that. So, there is no way I will ever test you for drugs. We are going to trust that you make the right call on this issue. Whatever goes on in other homes is their business, but THIS home is a drug-free zone. It is a place that gets its highs from your mom's lasagna, not from bongs.

However, you need to know that, should you ever break this trust, and develop a drug-taking habit, these arrangements will change. I will reserve the right to start testing you for drugs. I will reserve the right to take you to the police. I will even reserve the right to expel you from this house. This is not because I will have ceased loving you; it will be because I will need to love you more—and fight like anything to get my son back to a drug-free state.

Any questions?

High-risk behavior

To the pantheon of general health risks faced by our sons must be added idiocy.

Too many sons are killing themselves because they have been doing "what guys do." The frequency with which males engage in high-risk behaviors does not strengthen their claim to be intelligent. Cranking up a car to explore its maximum speed can be fun. Drinking till you pass out can be fun. Taking a dive from a six-foot jetty into four-foot water can be fun. But, it is not fun going to a best friend's funeral, or to your own, for that matter.

In many countries, the leading cause of male deaths for those aged under 45 is accidents. Many of these accidents are preventable, particularly those that relate to driving. A boy with a driver's license has a license to kill, but, if he exercises that right, he might go to jail for a very long time. It might be worth reminding your son that a lifetime of disability is too big a price to pay for a few seconds of thrill.

Specific health threats

This is the "secret men's business" part of the health conversation.

The health risks specifically faced by males are not trivial, and some of them are not pretty. Although a teenage son needs to know about these health issues, parents need to take care when deciding when and how to talk about these issues. Bringing up this subject prematurely could terrify a young boy. It can even terrify an old man. However, no boy should enter adulthood without knowing something about the following.

Prostate cancer and prostate enlargement

The prostate is a golf-ball-sized gland that acts as a kind of valve for the bladder. It has several functions, including adding important stuff to the sperm. The trouble is that the prostate can get cancerous, and this has the nasty habit of killing off a lot of men.

The prostate can also become enlarged. When guys get to about age 50, the prostate can get bigger to the extent it squeezes the urethra—

the tube that delivers the pee. One of the effects of this is that, when you urinate, only a dribble comes out. This means that the prostate may need to be trimmed, cut or reshaped. If you can write your name in the snow and underline it three times when you pee, you might be okay. If you can only manage your initials and several full stops, you might have an enlarged prostate.

The way doctors diagnose prostate problems will bring tears to the eyes. It can involve, among other things, the doctor sticking a finger up your bum . . . but this is probably better than childbirth, so let's not whinge about it! The important thing to remember is that early detection can avoid early death. So, our sons need to be advised that, when necessary and certainly when they get to 50, they will need to get their prostate checked.

Testicular cancer

This is another thing that can bring tears to a guy's eyes. Cancer is no respecter of private parts, so a boy needs to check his balls from time to time for any unnatural lumps, swelling or pain. If he has any doubts about what he finds, he must see a doctor. Again, time is of the essence.

Erectile dysfunction (not being able to "get it up')

Yes . . . it can happen, even to the most masculine of guys. Although unlikely to kill you, a badly behaving dick is not much fun.

The worry sons have over the size of their penis is generally unfounded. They need to be encouraged that it is not the size that matters . . . it's what they do with it.

A guy needs to have a penis that delivers its sperm in a timely fashion. To "come" early or late when ejaculating can take the pleasure off things somewhat. If this ever becomes a problem for a boy, he needs to see a doctor. There are things that can be done about it.

If a boy passes all the operational issues listed here, he is still not without risk. He might be sterile and not be able to produce children. This can be fine and dandy until, of course, he wants to have children.

About 10 percent of western males have fertility problems. This can be due to a variety of things, such as low sperm count (not enough "tadpoles" in the semen). Again, sometimes there are things that can be done if this becomes a problem.

*

What does all this health advice boil down to? Probably two things. The first is we must encourage our sons not to take their health for granted. The second is we must encourage them to seek immediate medical attention should they have any health issues.

SUMMARY

The most important things to keep in mind during this conversation are:

- Many boys think they are bulletproof and immune from accidents and sickness. They are not. We must encourage our sons to understand that life is a gift that must be treasured.
- The lifestyle chosen now can influence the quality of health tomorrow.
- The most common diseases that kill people in the western world are cardiovascular disease and coronary heart disease. Lung disease and throat cancer are also common.
- In many countries, accidents and suicide are the leading causes of death in older teens.
- A healthy diet can have a huge impact on well-being, as well as promoting better brain function and general health. Our sons need to know what constitutes a good diet.

- The quality and quantity of sleep can greatly influence a boy's health.
- Our sons need to have the right amount of exercise, including aerobic activity, anaerobic activity and exercises that promote flexibility.
- Boys need to know the health risks associated with recreational drugs.
- Alcohol is the drug most commonly abused by children. Boys need to obey the law in this area and, when of an age to drink legally, know how to do so responsibly.
- Tobacco is another popular drug that can reduce the health and well-being of children. Ways to encourage a son not to smoke include the deterrent approach, the fitness approach, the emotional approach and the "I don't need it" approach.
- The health risks associated with smoking marijuana should not be trivialized.
- There are ways to tell if a boy is using illegal drugs.
- A challenge for boys is to curb their natural inclination to engage in high-risk behavior.
- There are certain health issues specific to males that need to be well understood by sons. Examples include prostate cancer and prostate enlargement, testicular cancer and erectile dysfunction.
- Males often only see a doctor when it is too late.

CONVERSATION TEN

Coping

Bᴀᴅ sᴛᴜꜰꜰ ᴏᴄᴄᴜʀs. Unfairness is rife. Disappointment happens. We all know that—but not, it appears, some boys. Several believe themselves entitled to a life of unbridled success, so when they do not get the girl, the place in the team *and* the right grades, they collapse.

Our sons need to learn how to cope with imperfection in themselves and in others. The world requires 50 percent in the bottom half in order to make the top half possible.

Everyone will fail at some stage in their life. Although a boy will be good at some things, the gods rarely bestow all their favors in one place, with the result that he will be bad at other things. A boy must also realize that, although he can control some events in his life, his powers are limited and there will be times he will have to deal with the cat piddling on the carpet.

Just to set the record straight: coping does not necessarily require a boy to like a situation. Coping means putting the big-boy pants on and trying to fix it if it is fixable or to adjust to it if it is not.

Having noted the above, there will be times when it is unfair for parents to expect their son to cope. Some events are so horrible that a son can quite properly be devastated. He might even need professional medical help. However, this is more the exception than the rule. A two-week sulk is generally not appropriate when Aunt Agatha fails to deliver at Christmas.

Within this chapter, particular attention will be drawn to coping with failure, coping with bullying and coping with death.

This is not to say that there are no other significant things a boy has to learn to cope with. It is to say that these three topics represent common challenges to our sons. They also represent a selection of issues he can control and events he cannot control. Skills are needed to deal with both these sorts of setbacks. Among these skills are persistence, optimism and adopting a mindset that contributes to happiness.

Before touching on these things, it is worth spending a moment looking at the issue of over-protection, because this is one of the most corrosive influences on the ability of a boy to cope.

Over-protection

As parents, we naturally try to protect our loved ones from life's hard edges. We are there with the antiseptic, the ice cream and the cooling balm of mending words. All this is right and proper. Most parents are genetically hardwired to protect their own. It's what we do. It's what we are designed to do. It's what we must do.

That said, a consequence of this protection might be that we are bubble-wrapping our sons and allowing them to live in a fantasy land of smiles, hot chocolate and downy-pillowed ease. Our love might be making them weak.

*

I experienced an extraordinary episode in my study some years ago when I was visited by some genuine "heavies" whose job it was to intimidate me. They were there at the request of a father who claimed that his young son was being bullied at school. The irony of the situation was not lost on me.

The son in question was one of the most over-protected children I had ever met. To be fair, this over-protection was something I could understand because his father had been brutalized as a youth and had witnessed all manner of atrocities in another land. As a result, there was no way this father was ever going to allow his son to suffer as he had. Therefore, the father would massively overreact to any real or imagined threat suffered by his son.

The result was predictable. The father ended up with a son who was not only precious, he was precocious. When the boy wanted attention, he knew exactly which buttons to push to get his father to storm in and ascribe his low academic grades to psychological abuse and his low popularity to bullying.

This over-protection resulted in the boy not being able to exist in normal society. He learned the victim talk and developed the victim walk. The boy became socially maladjusted, fearful and completely out of his depth whenever he ventured beyond his front door.

Parents must react appropriately to their son's needs but they must also take care that, in meeting his needs in one area of his life, they are not creating problems in another area of his life. It's no good saving a son from a broken leg if he is going to suffer a broken spirit.

Coping with failure

Failure is inevitable. Coping with failure is conditional. It is conditional on resilience. (Some thoughts on resilience have already been shared in Conversations Five and Six.)

Being resilient does not necessarily mean that every problem is solved and that everything ends happily ever after. It means never giving up, never giving in and never thinking that something positive cannot be found even in the most desperate of situations.

A poignant example is that of Captain Robert Scott's tragic attempt to be the first person to reach the South Pole. Even in death, Scott was able to marvel at the courage and character of his team.

Scott was beaten in his quest to be the first to reach the South Pole. Therefore, it was a dejected party who began their return journey. Scott described it as 800 miles of solid dragging.

Exhaustion and frostbite were to plague the five dispirited adventurers: Scott, Wilson, Evans, Oates and Bowers. Navigational blunders and shortages of food further eroded their physical well-being. Oates had black and gangrenous toes, Evans had a frostbitten nose, Scott had a badly bruised shoulder and Wilson a serious strain to his leg tendon.

There were other forms of injury. Evans suffered a mental breakdown. He fell behind the others and was found wild-eyed and kneeling in the snow when the rest of the party went back to help him. He was put on a sled and taken to the campsite, where he died later that night. He was the first of the five to die. Scott's mental and physical states were stronger but even he had to admit that amputation was the best he could hope for.

A way out of their suffering was to be found in the lethal amounts of opium and morphine carried in the medicine chest by Wilson. The party discussed suicide and Scott ordered Wilson to hand each man 30 opium tablets. It was the measure of each man's courage that none chose to use them.

On March 20, 1912, Scott and his party were stopped by a violent storm. Two of their party of five were now dead. The second person to die was Captain Oates. With acute frostbite on his feet, he knew he was slowing down the party and reducing their chances of survival, so, on March 17, he stumbled out of the tent saying, "I am just going outside and may be some time." The rest of the party knew he was walking to his death. It was a gallant act of self-sacrifice.

The remainder of the party, although severely undernourished and frostbitten, had pushed on until the raging blizzard stopped them 18 kilometers short of "One Ton Depot." The Depot was a food drop that, if reached, would probably have saved their lives.

Knowing he was about to die, Scott wrote 12 letters. To the widows and mothers of those in his party, he wrote of his companions' strength and courage and of looking forward to meeting with them "in the hereafter." In relation to the "hereafter," Scott recorded that he had no fear of meeting God and that he believed that God would be merciful.

His most tender letter was to his wife, Kathleen, in which he described his love for her and the heartache of not being able to see her again. He encouraged Kathleen to take his death "sensibly" and to "cherish no sentimental rubbish about remarriage."

Of his son, Scott reflected on the tales he would have been able to tell the boy. He encouraged Kathleen to get his son interested in natural history rather than limiting him to an interest in sport. Scott hoped that his son would not be lazy and that he would spend as much time as possible in the open air. He also suggested that his son be steered toward a belief in God.

To the general public, Scott wrote:

Had we lived, I should have had a tale to tell of the hardihood, endurance, and courage of my companions which would have stirred the heart of every Englishman. These rough notes and our dead bodies must tell the tale . . .

Scott also pleaded, "For God's sake look after our people."[1]

Eight months later, Scott's frozen body and those of his companions were found. Their diaries and personal effects were recovered and then, after prayers, the tent was collapsed on them and they were buried with a pair of crossed skies marking the location.

Scott's story is one that can be used to introduce a boy to the concept of heroic failure. It is also a significant lesson in the legacy failure can leave. A reputation can be forged by the way in which failure is dealt.

AN IDEA

Teach the lessons associated with snakes and ladders

Someone who learned that life is a mixture of ups and downs was the English statesman Winston Churchill. His story is also worth sharing with a boy.

Snakes and Ladders is not unlike life because everyone has their moments when they happily climb the ladder of success and everyone has their moments when their plans are poisoned in some way.

Churchill's progress up the political game board was erratic—at times he was popular, at other times unpopular, sometimes as a Conservative, sometimes as a Liberal. The outbreak of the First World War was predicted with great accuracy by Churchill, but his views were rejected by his military superiors as "amateur" and "silly." Nonetheless, a good throw of the dice gave Churchill the position of First Lord of the Admiralty, and in that position he readied the British Navy for war.

It was not long before Churchill suffered a poisonous bite. His plan to bring the war to an early end by using a naval force in the Dardanelles to neutralize Turkey was literally blown out of the water when the naval group ran into a minefield. His general management of the Turkish theater in the First World War could only be described as a disaster. After 205,000 casualties were reported, the British people removed Churchill from high command and then from Parliament.

Recovery up the game board was slow. However, Churchill was re-elected to Parliament. He was not an impressive Chancellor of the Exchequer, but, after the outbreak of the Second World War on September 3, 1939, British warships signaled to each other "Winston is back." And indeed he was, as First Lord of the Admiralty.

Further elevation up the game board was to see several near-fatal bites. In Britain's darkest hour, Churchill was elected Prime Minister and promised his nation nothing but "blood, sweat and tears." He kept his promise. The British Forces were driven out of Europe and suffered a humiliating retreat via the beaches of Dunkirk. However, victories were to follow—the Battle of Britain, the Americans abandoning their neutrality, and the D-Day landings.

Then there was the joy of a ladder right to the top row. Victory in Europe, and in the Pacific. The Second World War was won. The nation was in raptures. Churchill wept before a standing ovation in Parliament—the game was nearly over. But there was still one more snake—and on the very next square it bit Churchill. Only two months after winning the war in Europe, Churchill was voted out as Prime Minister of Great Britain.

In October 1951, Churchill was elected Prime Minister again, but he was tired and quit the game of politics a few years later. Nonetheless, his life was one of dogged determination to keep going even when fate had dealt him a crippling blow. Small wonder that Churchill has become an example of a man who would never give up.

Some people experience more than their fair share of disappointment in life and believe their game to be one of Snakes and Ladders. However, the ladders are there. We must teach our sons to continue to roll the dice and play the game.

Coping with bullying

Having looked at failure in a general sense, it is appropriate to discuss some of the specific challenges our sons will face when growing up.

Of tragic relevance is the problem of bullying. There would be very few parents who have not had to comfort a child because they have suffered meanness. Either as victim, bystander or perpetrator, most sons will have come across bullying. Research has shown that bullying is a problem for one in six teenagers.[2]

In order for parents to help their son with this issue, it is important that they know what bullying is (including contemporary forms of bullying) and what to do if a son is being bullied.

What is bullying?

Bullying is the deliberate intention to harm someone who does not have the power to stop it. It is a form of harassment and it is immoral because it interferes with the right of a person to feel safe and valued as a member of a community.

Bullying takes many forms. It can be:

- *Face-to-face*, such as fighting, pushing, taunting, insulting, embarrassing, intimidating and invading personal space, AND *behind-the-back*, such as writing threatening or offensive messages, sending distressing emails and writing anonymous hurtful notes.
- *Done individually*, such as a person mocking or teasing someone, AND it can be *done as a group*, by such means as social exclusion or hate-group recruitment.
- *Physical AND psychological*.
- *Sexual harassment*, which involves behaviors such as unwanted sexual touching, inappropriate joking, exposure, making sexual advances or demeaning someone because of their sexual orientation, AND *racial harassment*, which involves behaviors such as social exclusion, teasing, taunting and threats based on another person's race.
- The causing of hurt by *traditional methods*, such as punching, kicking and spreading hurtful rumors, AND the causing of hurt by *contemporary means*, such as cyber bullying, sexting, engaging in identity theft or by trashing someone on social-networking sites.

The key features of bullying are that it causes hurt and distress, is repeated and involves the use of power in an unfair way.

Bullying need not always be done by the older or stronger. "Bullying up" is bullying done by the smaller, the younger and the weaker, who use anonymous means to bully, such as cyber bullying, or overt means to bully, knowing that any retaliation would make the provoked person look like they are the bully.

For behavior to be classified as bullying, it needs to involve repeated actions that are designed to cause hurt. Not having friends or not being popular isn't necessarily a sign that a boy is being bullied. It may simply mean he lacks interpersonal skills. There is a difference between bullying behavior and what can be described as normal interpersonal conflict.

Some contemporary forms of bullying

The world never ceases to find new ways of hurting someone. Traditional forms of bullying such as verbal taunts and physical assault have been augmented by some new forms of bullying.

Cyber bullying

Cyber bullying is the act of causing hurt via modern technologies such as the Internet, social media and mobile communication devices. It is a growing problem in society. Modern technologies empower the individual—even the most unlikely of individuals—with an immense capacity to cause harm. It is also an attractive means of bullying because it can, under certain conditions, be carried out with relative anonymity.

Cyber bullying can be particularly damaging because of the capacity it has to humiliate, hurt and harm a person in front of a huge "audience." A dangerous feature of cyber bullying is that it can be done quickly and easily. On an impulse, a person can create emotional havoc for another and do so before the voice of reason hints at the inappropriateness of the action.

A further problem with cyber bullying is that the bully is often unaware of the extent of the harm they are causing because cyber bullying seldom occurs face-to-face. The feedback is muted by distance so that the bully is protected from understanding the awfulness of their behavior.

Our sons must learn that pressing buttons can lead not only to police pressing charges; cyber bullying has been linked to depression, self-harm and even suicide.

Before parents accept their son's claim that "I'd never get into that sort of stuff!" they would be as well to check that he knows what "that sort of stuff" is.

Running the following examples of cyber bullying by a son

might make him a touch more thoughtful about his behavior in the electronic realm:

- Sending hateful or threatening comments or pictures via instant messaging, cell phone or the Internet and through social-networking sites such as Twitter and Facebook.
- Using modern technologies to engage in the social exclusion of someone and in hate-group recruitment.
- Posting rude, explicit or embarrassing messages or pictures about someone on the Internet.
- Stealing someone's identity in order to harm him or her.
- Putting pressure on a person to send revealing or compromising pictures of themselves.
- Covertly filming, recording or taking a picture of someone and posting the images on the Internet to cause hurt.
- "Outing" and distributing confidential information about someone.
- "Flaming" and multi-messaging to clog up a person's electronic system and to cause them distress.
- Using aliases and pseudonyms in chat rooms and on social-networking sites in order to harass and upset.
- Engaging in cyber stalking and the invasion of privacy.
- Referring to your school in a negative or disparaging way on the Internet.

If the above is going to drain color in a boy's face, the following might put color back into his face.

Sexting

Another contemporary form of bullying is sexting. Sexting is the act of sending sexual images of anyone, including yourself, using modern electronic means. The boy who engages in "I'll show you a picture of my crown jewels if you show me a picture of your tits" could end up being charged with "Using a carriage service for the purpose of distributing child sex images." That's an ugly charge, a very ugly charge.

A boy sending an image of a nude girlfriend to some of his friends can lead to a prison term. It can also result in him being placed on a sex-offender list, which may prohibit him working in an unsupervised manner with children for the rest of his life.

If this conversation sends your son scuttling up to his bedroom to "do a few things on the computer," good. But not perfect. Anything put in the cyber world cannot be guaranteed to ever be completely erased. Sexting can remain as a reputational risk for the rest of a boy's life, so he needs to be persuaded not to do it in the first place.

If a boy is not completely warned off sexting and the like, and decides to put his trust in beefing up his security via the use of pseudonyms and protective passwords, he needs to be warned that law-enforcement agencies trawl the Internet for criminal activity and often have the technology to get around most aliases and "firewalls" a boy uses to hide his online activity. For this reason, he should be scared—very scared.

It is also worth reminding a boy that more and more employers are researching a candidate's Facebook page and character as revealed in their online behavior before offering them a job.

What to do if your son is being bullied

If conversations with your son reveal that he is being bullied, the temptation may be to get hold of the bully, rip their arms off and beat them about the body with the soggy ends as they writhe in agony because you have also doused them in petrol and set them on fire.

Don't do this. Petrol is expensive. And bullying is seldom solved by further bullying. And what I have described is breaking the law.

Revenge can be delicious in the mind, but that is where it should stay.

*

If parents suspect that their son is being bullied, they must talk to him and gently find out the facts. Don't be surprised if a boy, even one who is being bullied, is reluctant to talk about the problem. He may fear that by telling his parents they will only make the bullying worse. He might also fear being labeled a "snitch" and going against the unwritten boy code of keeping silent on these matters.

This concern is understandable but must not stop a boy from being persuaded to talk about being bullied. If he doesn't want to tell his parents, then he must tell a teacher or some other responsible adult. Most teachers are trained in ways to help victims of bullying in a manner that protects the victim. As well as the above, most countries have anti-bullying helplines that offer free counseling services.

If parents suspect that their son is being bullied, they might make some general inquiries about how their son is traveling. Sometimes, it is best to be slightly oblique when probing in this area, because not every boy is going to respond openly to a direct question as to whether they are being bullied. Examples of the sorts of questions that parents could ask are:

- "How was school today?"
- "Who are your best friends these days? Who are your enemies? Why?"
- "I read that more bullying is being done online than face-to-face these days. Do you agree?"
- "Who do you think gets bullied the most at school? Why? Is there anything that should be done about this?"
- "If you spotted any bullying, what would you do about it?"

AN IDEA

Teach your son to do the "rite" thing if he is being bullied

If you find out that your son is being bullied at school, the school must be informed immediately, and a joint response to the problem arrived at.

If your son recognizes that he is being bullied, you must encourage him to do the RITE thing:

R = RECOGNIZE you have the right to feel safe and to operate in an environment free of bullying.

I = INFORM the bullies that you want them to stop. Do this in a polite but firm way.

T = TELL a responsible adult about the bullying.

E = EVALUATE the situation. If it does not improve, seek further help.

BULLY-PROOFING

There is no way to fully bully-proof a boy. That said, a boy who finds himself a target for teasing and verbal putdowns might benefit from the following advice:

- If you are being bullied, remind yourself that it is the bully who has the problem, not you. Try to think through what inadequacies the bully might have that causes them to behave this way. Understanding a bully is a great way to begin to solve the problem.
- When bullied, try not to get angry or show that you are angry. If your anger is obvious, the bully has the satisfaction of knowing that they control your emotions. They don't deserve this right.
- Admit to imperfections. It can send positive messages about you having a realistic understanding of yourself.
- Use inoffensive humor. Bullying can be blunted by a good laugh. The capacity to laugh at yourself can create a bond with a group that might otherwise remain hostile.
- Review your own behaviors and body language. If you look like a victim, you can become a victim. Squared shoulders and a smile can do much to deter a bully.
- Avoid trouble spots. There are always places that are high-risk areas for bullying. Avoid them.
- Develop your "emotional quotient." This includes the ability to

read body language, to sense mood, to be intuitive and empathetic. Such skills not only make you less of a target, they can also enable you to see where a situation may be heading. Early detection of possible bullying can provide options for avoiding it.

- Surround yourself with good friends. Those with strong friendships are usually less of a target for bullies.
- If bullied, try not to retaliate, for this can often inflame the situation.

Some boys seem to attract bullying behavior when at school. This is not to excuse bullying or condone it in any way. It is to suggest that victims can sometimes reduce their chances of being a target if they try the following suggestions:

- Maintain good self-esteem.
- Work on fitting in, get involved and make a rich contribution to the school.
- Model kindness, thoughtfulness and respect.
- Don't catastrophize a small insult out of all proportion.
- Develop an ability to deal with failure and success, threats and fear, rejection and disappointment, and anger and hurt.
- Maintain good physical fitness. It can help with resilience.

Having noted the above, it is vital that a boy who is bullied can recognize that he has been wronged. He must be encouraged to talk about the matter and not suffer in silence.

Finally, as distasteful as it might seem, there are parents out there whose sons are bullies. If not bullies, then some have been bystanders when someone else has been bullied, and done sweet nothing about it.

Learning to cope involves not only coping appropriately if being bullied; it also means coping appropriately if someone else is being bullied.

Coping with death

A son may, or may not, be bullied. However, he *will* die.

Death is a reality of life. A boy is going to have to cope not only with his own death but probably with the death of others, some of whom will be loved ones. Therefore, we need to talk to our sons about death and dying. Conversation Nine dealt with health and those things that could promote death. This chapter deals more with the processes of dying and the tasks associated with death.

Talking about death is unlikely to fill either parent or son with much joy. So, we don't. But death will not be ignored. It will still visit our homes—it's just a matter of when. Sometimes, death's knock will be expected and we open our door with a resignation born of ample warning. At other times, death's arrival is a shock, a rude surprise that plunges a family into grief. And this is the problem. Too many parents leave the discussion about death until it arrives and then they are too traumatized to talk about it. Small wonder many boys are ignorant of death and remain ill-prepared to cope with it.

That said, great care is needed when broaching the topic of death. Handled poorly, a conversation on death can leave an otherwise untroubled boy deeply disturbed. Some consideration also needs to be given to when to talk about death. Interrupting a carefree vacation on the beach with "It's about time I talked to you about death, son," can come across as forced and is likely to put a dampener on the holiday spirit. However, waiting for the death of a loved one to give relevance to a conversation about death is equally fraught with peril, given that a parent's capacity to mentor a son on the topic is probably going to be complicated by grief.

Should parents talk to their son when they themselves are suffering grief? The answer is yes and no. Death is a reality in life and a son must recognize this and learn that he is not unique in being upset by its presence. That said, excessive expressions of grief by parents in front of their son should probably be avoided. It can frighten a boy. Bearing this in mind, though, a son should know that his parents are not immune from the pain of grief lest he feel himself weak because of his failure to emulate their stoicism. Somewhere in between lies the answer. The wet cheek and confessed sense of sadness can be important for a boy to see—particularly in a father. Big boys should cry.

Some sons live a "Four Weddings and a Funeral" existence: they experience more events at which they will smile than events that will make them cry. However, life will cause us all to cry from time to time, and these moments can sometimes be used to broach the topic of death. Having to bury the dog, or a state funeral played across several TV channels: both provide opportunities for parents to talk to their son about death. Parents need not always wait for a personal calamity. The death of an under-watered geranium can also serve as a natural introduction to the topic.

Whatever is said about death, it needs to be said sensitively and in an age-appropriate way. In the preteen years, death must be explored in a rather more gentle and general way.

During the late teen years, conversations about death can become more raw and touch on the inevitability of death and the implication of this on life. The older teen can handle more abstract issues, such as whether death is really the end, and how God, if He exists, could possibly allow people to die.

AN IDEA

Teach your son some of the terms associated with death

At an appropriate time and at an appropriate age, there can be value in teaching your son about the meaning of the following terms associated with death:

■ *Death certificate.* A death certificate is usually filled in by a doctor or other approved authority. It states the date, location and cause of death. A death certificate is usually required before many of the tasks associated with tidying up a dead person's affairs can be undertaken.

- *Eulogy.* A eulogy is a speech written in praise of the dead person. It is usually given by a member of the family or close friend.

- *Interment/burial.* An interment or burial can be a separate service to the funeral service and involves the actual transfer of the body into the grave.

- *Cremation.* This is the burning of a body so most of it vaporizes with the exception of some mineral fragments. Often, these bone-like grains are put into a small container called an urn and given to the family of the deceased. The fragments are usually called "ashes" (even though they do not look like ashes and are a lot heavier). A cremation can be a separate event to the funeral service.

- *Open/closed coffin.* An open coffin is a coffin with the lid off, allowing people to see the deceased. If an open coffin is used, the dead person may be embalmed, which is a process of presenting the body so it looks natural. It is also treated so that it does not start to decompose.

- *Viewing.* A viewing is when friends and family gather before a funeral service to see the body. The event usually takes place in a funeral parlor. It allows people to say their farewells to the deceased.

- *Wake.* A wake can be another term for a viewing. Sometimes, a wake occurs after the funeral service rather than before, and can take the form of a social gathering.

- *Will.* A will is written instructions that say who gets the assets when a person dies. It is a legal document that appoints someone to make sure the directions are carried out and the estate is wound up properly.

- *Executor.* An executor is the person who is asked to carry out the instructions laid out in a person's will.

- *Intestate.* This occurs when a person dies without leaving a proper will. If this happens, the dead person's assets are distributed by a government-appointed authority.

- *Power of attorney.* This gives written authority for a person to manage matters on behalf of someone else. There are different types of power of attorney that cover things such as health and finance.
- *Probate.* This is part of the administration associated with dealing with a dead person's belongings or "estate." It sorts out any bills, taxes, expenses or claims against an estate and gets the estate ready for the executor to dispose of properly. Probate is granted when it is proved the person has died, that their will is genuine, that they have the assets they claim and that the assets are going to the intended people.

*

I was woefully ignorant of many of these terms when I had to deal with my parents' death. I suspect I am not alone. We tend not to do death very well in the developed world, and in the vacuum of discussion about the grim reaper rests the horror of his eventual arrival. We fear the unknown.

When I was a boy growing up in Malacca in Malaysia, my brother and I would explore the coastline looking for dead sea snakes, avoiding live ones, climbing coconut trees and panning the blackened sands in order to collect tin. We also misbehaved. In between catapult fights with the local boys, we would sneak into the grounds of great oriental mansions and throw rambutans at the windows to annoy the occupants. However, these adventures reached a whole new height when we entered a large shed in the grounds of a Chinese mansion and found several coffins.

A Chinese coffin is large, heavy, wooden and often painted red. Its presence in the house spooked us into compliance with my parents' wishes not to engage in any further trespass. Evidently, the coffins did not spook the Chinese householders. Clearly, they were comfortable with the idea of a coffin or two in their house. Weird. Or was it?

AN IDEA

Encourage your son to start living his eulogy

Keeping a coffin in the house might not be quite the thing for many of us, but having an appreciation that we are, in effect, writing our eulogy each day is not a bad thought to share with your son.

Someday, someone will probably get up in our funeral and say something about us. Something might even be carved about us on our tombstone.

There was once a Chinese Emperor who asked how he could improve the quality of the people in his empire. He was advised, on the strength of what was written on the gravestones, to kill all the living and to resurrect all the dead.

If a eulogy were to relate to true character, funerals could become brutal affairs. We would hear things like:

- "He was given to raising his own standing by putting others down."
- "He was not greatly troubled by his conscience."
- "Although caring to those he loved, he was indifferent to those he did not."
- "His popularity prevented him from noticing the unpopular."
- "He was a person driven more by impulse than principle."

Fortunately, funerals are seldom a time for truth. In death, our lives are edited. However, in life, they are not. Therefore, the challenge for us is to live lives that enable us to deserve our eulogies.

A reflection on heaven

Most of the funerals I have attended were for those described as "good people." Their eulogies pictured them, one and all, as someone who loved their family, loved their friends and loved life. No one pointed out that this also described prairie dogs and brown rats.

We need to be more serious about trying to understand heaven, irrespective of our religion. Whether or not we believe in heaven, as a concept it can serve us well. It inspires us toward a better state. It humbles us with the threat of accountability.

Whatever our belief, it might be as well for our sons to live as though there was a heaven . . . and a hell.

*

Parents will share their own reflections on death and its implications with their son. Faith-based families will draw comfort from their religion, and so they should.

However, in the end, death, like many things, is a mystery. It is a mystery that can fill a son with questions—and these questions deserve to be answered.

Equipped for grief

Coping with failure, bullying and death, and any other of life's challenges, is not easy. Our sons need guidance on how to respond to situations that cause grief. Some reflections on resilience have already been shared. However, there are three other topics that parents can profitably talk about with their son in order to equip him with the skills needed to deal with the trials in his life. These are: persistence, optimism and happiness.

Persistence

Some significant people have shared thoughts about persistence. Numbered among them are a few US Presidents. Calvin Coolidge said:

> *Nothing in this world can take the place of persistence.*
> *Talent will not; nothing is more common than unsuccessful people with talent.*
> *Genius will not; unrewarded genius is almost a proverb.*
> *Education will not; the world is full of educated derelicts.*
> *Persistence and determination alone are omnipotent.*

The words of Theodore Roosevelt are also apposite:

> *It is not the critic who counts; not the man who points out how the strong man stumbles, or where the doer of deeds could have done them better.*
> *The credit belongs to the man who is actually in the arena, whose face is marred by dust and sweat and blood . . . who at the best knows in the end the triumph of high achievement, and who at the worst, if he fails, at least fails while daring greatly, so that his place shall never be with those cold and timid souls who neither know victory nor defeat.*

Great stuff—and worth sharing with your son.

AN IDEA

Teach your son about the Hillary Step

A story also worth sharing that touches on the topic of persistence is that of the Hillary Step.

It is not uncommon for someone to be close to realizing a goal only to find a last-minute obstacle. This last-minute frustration that threatens to turn triumph into failure has been called a "Hillary Step." If the Hillary Step is conquered, then success awaits. If the Hillary Step is not conquered, failure awaits. Most people have Hillary Steps to conquer throughout their lives.

The term comes from John Hunt's British expedition to the Himalayas in 1953. The goal was to put someone on the unclimbed summit of Mount Everest. This was a massive exercise involving some 350 Nepalese porters and dozens of designated climbers transporting equipment to nine campsites at ever-increasing altitudes.

The process of ferrying equipment meant that, in effect, the two that finally did climb Mount Everest for the first time, Sherpa Tenzing Norgay and New Zealand beekeeper Edmund Hillary, climbed the mountain three times. The pair set off on their final assault of the summit on May 29, 1953 from Camp IX, which was at 8,505 meters. The summit was at 8,850 meters. Although this does not sound a great difference, Norgay and Hillary were living in what is known as the "Death Zone." In this zone, the body takes in only 30 percent of the oxygen enjoyed at sea level. The heart pounds, hallucinations are common and the risks of hypothermia, exhaustion and internal bleeding are very real. Added to this are the dangers of blizzards, unstable ice and the hazards associated with falling over edges and down rock faces.

Norgay and Hillary were exhausted as they neared the summit. When it was just 100 meters above them, they were confronted with a 12-meter wall of rock. It seemed impossible to climb this obstacle and they both felt the temptation to turn back. However, Norgay and Hillary did not allow the rock face to defeat them. They worked their way up it, and, at 11:30 a.m., the two mountaineers reached the summit and became the first to stand on top of the highest mountain in the world. The rock wall near the top of Everest is still known as the Hillary Step.

*

Every boy has his mountain to climb. It could be overcoming a smoking habit; it could be dealing with the failure to make a team;

it could be recovering from a quarrel with a girlfriend. Whatever the mountain, there is a strong likelihood that there will be a Hillary Step, a frustrating last-minute obstacle that threatens success.

We need to tell our sons that, when they are confronted by a Hillary Step, they must remember that very few worthwhile things are ever achieved without sacrifice or danger. For Norgay and Hillary, there was the real risk of falling off the rock face and plunging 3,000 meters onto the Kangshung Glacier. There was also a dangerous ice cornice overhanging the rock face with a massive crack in it that suggested it could fall at any time. Far from seeing the crack as a threat, Norgay and Hillary used it as a route on their way to the top. Our sons need to learn to use a bad situation as a means to progress to a good situation.

Optimism

The phone rang in the Kremlin and woke the Russian President. "Sorry to wake you, Mr. President, it's Paddy Murphy from Ireland here. I just thought it best to tell you that me an' the rest of the lads from the Shamrock Inn have decided to declare war on you."

"Well, that's very interesting, but do you realize I have an army of one million infantry?" replied the Russian President and put the phone down.

The next morning, the President was again awakened by a phone call from Paddy. "The war's still on, Mr. President. We've been joined by the darts team from Kilkenny, and O'Reilly is lending us his tractor."

"Paddy," replied the President wearily, "my army not only has one million infantry, it also has 400,000 tanks, making two million troops in all."

"Begorrah," said Paddy. "I'll be getting back to you," and he put the phone down.

Sure enough, Paddy rang the next morning. "Mr. President, the war is still on, for we've got Patrick O'Neill's shotgun and my young Seamus has a great eye with his air pistol."

The President replied, "Paddy, be sensible. Not only have I my infantry and tanks, I have 300,000 artillery units, making three million troops all up."

"By all that is good, that's a large number," said Paddy. "I'll be getting back to you."

The next morning, Paddy rang again. "Mr. President, I've had a chat with the wife and the war's off."

"That's being sensible," said the Russian President. "What finally made you change your mind, Paddy?"

"Well," replied Paddy, "we worked out that, even with Mrs. O'Shaughnessy's potato pies, there is no way in the world we would be able to feed three million prisoners."

*

Okay—no more, I promise. But humor is not a bad way to blunt the pain of a difficult situation. The capacity to laugh, even when confronted with a serious problem, can help cope with the problem. Dr. Patch Adams of the Gesundheit! Institute knew this when he introduced clowning as part of the medical treatment given to his patients.[3]

A capacity to generate a happy frame of mind can go a long way to helping a boy to cope. After all, the mind is an extraordinary thing. If damaged, it can sometimes repair itself. It is the seat of our physical function, character and emotions. If we can control the mind, we can control the body. If we can be optimistic in our thoughts, we can be optimistic in our actions.

An interesting story is told of a man who accidentally locked himself in a refrigerated railway wagon. Realizing he would freeze to death, he scratched out a note of farewell on the wooden floor before dying. When his body was recovered some time later, police were confused, because the refrigeration unit had broken and the temperature inside the wagon was similar to that outside. The man should never have died, but his brain had seen death as inevitable and so death resulted.

We need to pay more attention to the mind and to remaining as positive as we can without losing contact with reality. Our sons need to do mental aerobics as well as physical aerobics. They need to watch their mental diet as well as their physical diet.

Parents can help by modeling resilience and optimistic behavior. Our sons tend to adopt our coping methods. If we remain hopeful and positive, they will.

WHEN YOU THINK YOU'RE A WINNER

If you think you're a loser, you've lost.
When you think you're a winner, you've won.
So never go and say that you can't.
If you do, it's certain you're done.
Don't say you've lost,
Because, you'll find
To win requires the ultimate cost
Of a positive state of mind.

Confidence in oneself
Means you're able to rise
Up and go and get yourself
The means to win the prize.
Achievements do not always go
To the fittest or strongest one.
For the person who usually wins,
Believes it can be done.

(Adapted from an old poem of unknown origin)

AN IDEA

Tell the story of Aron Ralston

To help illustrate the importance of never giving up, you could share with your son the story of Aron Ralston.

For a story of true grit, you don't have to go much further than Aron Ralston's adventure in the Blue John Canyon, in Wayne County, Utah. The Canyonlands National Park is a wild and rugged place, which is why Aron was there. He loved wild places. Aron had given up his work as a mechanical engineer in Phoenix, Arizona, and moved to Aspen, Colorado. Why? Because he wanted to climb mountains. By 2002, Aron had climbed all 59 of Colorado's "fourteeners"—peaks over 14,000 feet high. What's more, he did it in winter and he did it solo.

On April 26, 2003, Aron was in Blue John Canyon negotiating a canyon when he dislodged a 190-pound boulder that trapped his arm against the rock. Not having told anyone where he was going, Aron recognized that, given that his efforts to free himself had been futile—he had no tools to cut himself free—he would die, and it would probably be a slow death.

For five days, Aron sipped his remaining water (about 10 ounces) and ate the last of his food (two cookies). Thereafter, he became delirious and dehydrated. On the fifth day, he was reduced to drinking his own urine.

Aron videotaped his last goodbyes and carved his name, birth date and death date in the rock. He was ready to die.

Then an idea came to him. If he levered his arms against the boulder, he could break the radius and ulna bones in his trapped arm, and then, using a small knife—an instrument that came free when he had bought a $15 flashlight—he could cut off his arm and be free.

It took an hour for Aron to amputate his arm. But, his troubles were not over. He had to climb out of the canyon. Then, using ropes, he had to rappel down a 66-foot cliff and walk many miles to his car. He didn't make it.

Aron was still about 8 miles from his vehicle when he came across Eric and Monique Meijer and their son, who were on vacation from the Netherlands. They were stunned to see this one-armed fugitive from death. After giving him food and water, they immediately contacted rescuers.

This remarkable story ended with Aron making a full recovery and his arm being recovered, cremated, and its ashes given to him. Aron still climbs mountains but also works as a motivational speaker. His book *Between a Rock and a Hard Place* has become a bestseller. Small wonder.

Happiness

When I ask parents what they most want for their son when they enroll him at my school, one of the common responses I get is that the parents want their son to be happy.

This is no surprise. A happy boy is a boy who is able to learn. A mind that is using its energy to process unhappiness is a mind that is not free to learn.

If a boy is having problems with happiness, there can be virtue in having a chat with him about the sorts of things that can be done to promote happiness, including the following:

- *Take control.* Do not let yourself drift through life being buffeted by the whim of whatever breezes are blowing at the time. Set yourself realistic goals and go for them.
- *Take care of your health.* Put the right sorts of fuel into your body . . . neither too much nor too little. Practice good hygiene. Get the right amount of sleep and the right amount of exercise.
- *Look after your "stage presentation."* Even if you don't feel fantastic, act as if you do. It is amazing how often the act can turn to reality. Ensure the character you are playing has a straight back, a quick smile and a ready comment of warm appreciation.
- *Take an optimistic view of life.* Learn to recognize that bad things usually pass and the pain will generally lessen. Try not to overreact, and try to shut down any negative thoughts. Recognize that there are millions in the world who are starving, being abused and who are losing family and friends to senseless violence. Put your problems into perspective.
- *Take note of the positive and happy people around you and choose to spend time with them.* Avoid those who are negative and cause you

to feel unhappy. A tail-wagging dog can be better company than a tongue-wagging person.

- *Focus on what you are good at.* To be reminded of your strengths can be a very encouraging experience. Look at those old letters, cards and school reports (if they are positive). Write out a list of those things you think you can do well and stick it on the mirror.
- *Take the initiative.* Do something about your gripes. Go for a jog. Switch off the computer and go outside to look at the garden. Put on some great music and get into a place where you can process the day and think of ways to improve for tomorrow.
- *Take expert advice.* If sadness persists, see a doctor. There are things that can be done to help.
- *Remember, bad times usually pass.* Life has its ladders as well as its snakes.

SUMMARY

The most important things to keep in mind during this conversation are:

- Boys must recognize that bad stuff occurs, unfairness is rife and disappointment happens. How they cope with these situations is what can define them.
- We must be able to cope with imperfection in ourselves and in others.
- It is not always fair to expect a boy to cope with a horrendous situation. At times, professional medical or pastoral help will be needed.
- The inclination for parents to protect their son is a good thing, but over-protection can be a corrosive influence.
- Everyone will fail at some things. Therefore, we all need to learn coping skills.

■ Our sons will probably experience bullying in some way. There-fore, they will need to learn how to cope with bullying, either as a victim, bystander or perpetrator.

■ There are good and bad ways to respond to bullying. A proper response to bullying can reduce its presence in the life of a boy.

■ There are new forms of bullying, such as cyber bullying and sexting, that our sons need to understand.

■ The consequences of any form of bullying, including bullying by electronic means, can be serious.

■ If a son is being bullied, encourage him to adopt the "RITE" approach:

  ▪ **R**ecognize that he has rights.
  ▪ **I**nform the bully that he wants them to stop.
  ▪ **T**ell a responsible adult.
  ▪ **E**valuate the situation.

■ Our sons need to accept the reality of death in their life. The topic of death and dying is a sensitive one that needs to be handled carefully and in an age-appropriate manner.

■ Recognizing his mortality can be a sobering experience for a boy and one that might help him value his days.

■ In order to cope with life's setbacks, a boy must learn the virtue of persistence. Little of value is ever achieved without effort.

■ "Hillary Steps" (last-minute setbacks) are not uncommon in life. A boy needs to be prepared for such setbacks.

■ Optimism is another virtue that should be encouraged. A positive frame of mind can make a huge difference in how well a boy copes with setbacks.

■ Optimistic thinking can result in positive action.

■ A happy son is one who is better able to cope with life's chal-lenges.

■ There are several ways greater happiness can be encouraged in a son.

Finally

SOME PARENTS WILL FIND that these words have done little other than confirm that they already have a rich dialogue with their son and that the ten themes discussed are already well covered, with many others beside. Brilliant! Be encouraged.

Other parents will have assessed that, in their own way, they have covered some elements of the ten conversations but not all. These omissions may be entirely proper. For example, a son may not yet be of an age to cope with a Socratic debate on the nature of goodness. However, other omissions may be diagnostic of a task that must now be fulfilled. Great! I wish you well in this venture.

A few parents may now feel inadequate and be tempted to condemn themselves for a pattern of conversation with their son that has been insufficient. Without retreating from the fact that they may well have a remedial task to perform, we must all realize that no parent has perfected the art of conversation with a son, and that the variables determining success in this area are so unique to a family that none should ever sit in the seat of judgment. God bless you for your humility.

However a parent might have judged themselves in terms of the richness of their conversation with their son, it is my hope that, either as a checklist or as a job list, this book might have helped in some way.

Failing all, *Ten Conversations You Must Have With Your Son* will, I hope, have provided some stories and illustrations that have entertained. I believe in story and I believe in illustrations. I use them with my sons, of which I currently have 1,531.

I wish you well as you use the stories and illustrations herein. Many of them will benefit from further embellishment and most will benefit from being customized to the unique circumstances of your family.

*

As parents, we must talk to our sons. We must direct, inform and guide them. We must also love them enough to be silent. A boy needs his own space and he needs time to process things. At these times, a parent, although mute in words, can still converse with their son. The mug of hot chocolate can say "You are loved."

Finally, if pressed on what I would say if I only had one letter to write to my son, after writing some deeply private things I think I would close the letter with something like this.

The final letter to my son

My dear Peter,

In closing my final letter to you, I gently encourage you to do the following:

Find yourself
A mind that entertains new possibilities will generally find its true potential. Discover the limits of your ability and test for giftedness— if you search carefully enough, you will find it. Never be content with good if better is possible, and never be satisfied until you have mapped your abilities thoroughly.

Be yourself

We are social animals and enjoy galloping along in the company of others, but sometimes it is important to separate from the masses—particularly if they are heading toward a cliff. Don't be afraid to be your own person, have your own opinion and live your own life. Dare to conform when others are different, dare to be different when others conform, and have the wisdom to choose which of these options is best. In an age dulled by mindless procession, seek to know the difference between truth and popular opinion.

Connect yourself

As it has been said, no one is an island—for there is always something that must join us to the mainland and to others. Make sure you are connected to a group that you care for and a group that cares for you.

Involve yourself

There are some who rarely involve themselves in doing something. They limit themselves to watching. Do not be a spectator. Get involved and be a player.

Like yourself

Remember that you are a miracle of creation. There will be times when others may not like you. There will be times when you may not even like yourself. But remember, you will always be loved by me.

Share yourself

You are blessed with laughter and smiles. Share them. You have a great capacity to love. Cherish those you live with. You have great knowledge and wisdom—share it with your son.

*

I would then go and find him, give him a hug and invite him to a game of cricket in the nets.

Notes

What?

1 Adapted from: Erikson, E. (1968) *Identity, Youth and Crisis*, Norton, New York.

How?

1 Adapted from Cote, J. and Levine, G. (2002) *Identity Formation, Agency and Culture*, Lawrence Erlbaum Associates, Mahwah, New Jersey, p 22.

2 Pittman, F. (1993) "Fathers and Sons," *Psychology Today*, September 1, 1993, pp 52–54.

3 Biddulph, S. (1997) *Raising Boys,* Finch Publishing, Sydney.

4 Pittman, F., op. cit., p 53.

Conversation One: You are loved

1 Biddulph, S. (1997) *Raising Boys*, Finch Publishing, Sydney.

2 Maslow, A. (1954) *Motivation and Personality*, Harper & Row, New York.

3 Chapman, G. (2004) *The Five Love Languages: How to Express Heartfelt Commitment to Your Mate*, Northfield Press, Chicago.

4 Milliken, B. (1968) *Tough Love*, Spire Books, Old Tappan, New Jersey.

5 Moore, M. (2008) "Dying Mother Left Letters of Advice for Young Sons," *The Telegraph*, October 8.

6 Bangladeshis Abroad: www.bangladeshisabroad.com/blog/2013/09/02/a

-voice-chapter-21-a-letter-from-a-young-dying-mother-to-her-only-son
-pp-325-330/, accessed January 6, 2012.

Conversation Two: Identity

1   Les Parrott, quoted in Bellows, A. *Your Teen's Search for Identity*: psychcen
    tral.com/lib/2007/your-teens-search-for-identity, accessed January 8,
    2012.

2   Fredrickson, B. and Losada, M. (2005) "Positive Affect and the
    Complex Dynamics of Human Flourishing," *American Psychology*, Vol.
    60, No. 7, p 681.

Conversation Three: Values

1   Green, C. (2004) "Letters from Exile: Observations on a Culture in
    Decline," *Oxford Forum*, Oxford.

2   Piaget, J. (1932) *The Moral Judgement of the Child*, The Free Press, New
    York.

3   Lickona, T. (1983) *Raising Good Children*, Bantam Books, New York.

Conversation Four: Leadership

1   Cosgrove, P. (2010) *My Story*, HarperCollins Australia, Sydney.

Conversation Five: Living together

1   Gordon, E. (1965) *Miracle on the River Kwai*, Fontana Books, New York.

2   American Ex-Prisoners of War: www.axpow.org/stories-
    whopacksyourparachute.htm.

3   Visual.ly: www.visual.ly/100-social-networking-statistics-facts-2012.

4   Statistic Brain: www.statisticbrain.com/social-networking-statistics.

5   ibid.

6   Digital Buzz: www.digitalbuzzblog.com/infographic-social-media
    -statistics-for-2013.

7   Internet Safety 101: www.internetsafety101.org/cyberbullyingstatistics
    .htm.

8   ibid.

9   Back Off Bully: rmetro12.skills21schools.org/BOB/.

Conversation Six: Achievement

1   Better Health Channel: www.betterhealth.vic.gov.au.

2   The Royal Children's Hospital Melbourne, Center for Adolescent Health: www.rch.org.au/cah/research/Youth_Suicide_in_Australia.

3   A major researcher in this area is Baroness Susan Greenfield. For example, see Derbyshire, D. (2009) "Social Websites Harm Children's Brains," *Daily Mail*, February 24, London.

4   Greenfield, S. (2003) *Tomorrow's People: How 21st Century Technology is Changing the Way We Think and Feel*, Allen Lane, London.

5   ibid.

6   Flipped Learning Network: www.flippedclassroom.org; www.uq.edu.au /tediteach/flipped-classroom/what-is-fc.html.

7   Khan Academy: www.khanacademy.org.

8   For more information on memory types, go to Mind Expanding Techniques: www.mind-expanding-techniques.net/memory-types.html.

9   For more information, go to The Three-Box Model of Memory: www .cla.calpoly.edu/~cslem/101/7-C.html.

Conversation Seven: Sex

1   For more information, see: Lacombe, A. and Gray, J. (1998) "The Role of Gender in Adolescent Identity and Intimacy Decisions," *Journal of Youth and Adolescence*, 27 (6): 795–801; Cimbalo, R. and Novell, D. (1993) "Sex Differences in Romantic Love Attitudes Among College Students," *Psychological Reports*, 73:15–18; Shulman, S., Levy-Shiff, R., Kedem, P. and Alon, E. (1997) "Intimate Relationships Among Adolescent Romantic Partners and Same Sex Friends: Individual and Systemic Perspectives," *New Directions for Child Development*, Winter, p 78; Moore, S., Kennedy, G., Fulonger, B. and Evers, K. (1999) "Sex, Sex-Roles and Romantic Attitudes: Finding the Balance," *Current Research in Social Psychology*, 4(3):124; Dion, K. K. and Dion, K. L. (1993) "Individualistic and Collectivistic Perspectives on Gender and the Cultural Context of Love and Intimacy," *Journal of Social Issues*, 49(3):53–69; Sprecher, S. and Metts, S. (1989) "Development of the 'Romantic Beliefs Scale' and Examination of the Effects of Gender and Gender Role Orientation," *Journal of Social and Personal Relationships*, 6:387–411; Montgomery, M. and Sorell, G. (1998)

"Love and Dating Experience in Early and Middle Adolescence: Grade and Gender Comparisons," *Journal of Adolescence*, 21:677–689.

2 For more information on teenage sexual behavior, go to Better Health Channel: www.betterhealth.vic.gov.au/bhcv2/bhcarticles.nsf/pages /Teenagers_sexual_behaviour.

3 Some of this material has been drawn from "Am I Ready for Sex?" on the Avert website: www.avert.org/ready-sex.htm.

4 Biddulph, S. (2009) "How Girlhood Was Trashed and What We Can Do to Get It Back" in Tankard Reist, M. (ed) *Getting Real: Challenging the Sexualisation of Girls*, Spinifex Press, Melbourne, p 163.

5 ibid., p 165.

6 Levêque, S. (2009) "Our Culture Is Infected with Porn," *The Guardian*, April 24: www.theguardian.com/commentisfree/2009/apr/24/porn-object -protest-feminism/.

7 Tech Addiction: www.techaddiction.ca/pornography-addiction-statistics .html, accessed February 3, 2013.

8 Doyle and Doyle (2006) *The Problem with Pornography*, Choicez Media: A DVD Resource, p 5. This is a tremendous resource, which has contributed much to the content of this "conversation" about pornography.

9 ibid.

Conversation Eight: Money

1 Credit Card Finder: www.creditcardfinder.com.au/how-old-do-you -have-to-be-to-apply-for-a-credit-card.html.

2 Banks.com.au: www.banks.com.au/tools/glossary/m/minimum-age-of -borrower.

Conversation Nine: Health

1 The Royal Children's Hospital Melbourne, Center for Adolescent Health: www.rch.org.au/cah/research/youth_suicide_in_australia/, accessed February 3, 2013.

2 Monash University Modi: www.modi.monash.edu.au/obesity-facts -figures/obesity-in-australia/, accessed February 3, 2013.

3 There are many websites dealing with "brain food," including Your Brain

Matters: www.yourbrainmatters.org.au, and Live Science: www.live
-science.com/3186-brain-food-eat-smart.html.

4   Maryke Steffens writes on the topic of "Why Exercise?" on the ABC
    Health Well-being website: www.abc.net.au/health/library/stories
    /2007/05/10/1919866.htm.

5   Hawkes, T. (2001) *Boy Oh Boy*, Pearson Education Australia, Sydney, p
    198.

6   ibid., p 195.

7   The relationship between tobacco use and other drug use can be found at
    ThinkQuest: library.thinkquest.org/19796/data/t016.html.

8   Hawkes, T., op. cit., p 202.

Conversation Ten: Coping

1   Quoted in Scott, R. (1913) *Last Expedition*, Vol. 1, Ch. 20.

2   Dr. Ken Rigby has done a lot of work in this area. Go to his website:
    www.kenrigby.net.

3   For more information about Patch Adams, go to his website: www
    .patchadams.org.

References

Agee, J. (1971) *A Death in the Family*. London: Peter Owen.

Allen, R. (2008) *Green Light Classrooms: Teaching Techniques that Accelerate Learning*. Victoria, Australia: Hawker Brownlow.

Bainbridge, D. (2009) *Teenagers—A National History*. London: Portobello Books.

Baumeister, R. (2005) "The Lowdown on High Self-Esteem." *Los Angeles Times*, January 25.

Biddulph, S. (1994) *Complete Secrets of Happy Children*. Sydney: HarperCollins.

———(1997) *Raising Boys*. Sydney: Finch Publishing.

———(2009) "How Girlhood Was Trashed and What We Can Do to Get It Back" in Tankard Reist, M. (ed) *Getting Real: Challenging the Sexualisation of Girls*, Spinifex Press, Melbourne, p 163.

Blankenhorn, D. (1995) *Fatherless America*. New York: Basic Books.

Bly, R. (1996) *The Sibling Society*. Australia: Heinemann.

Bolton, R. (1979) *People Skills: How to Assert Yourself, Listen to Others, and Resolve Conflicts*. Englewood Cliffs, New Jersey: Prentice Hall.

Bowlby, J. (1953) *Childcare and the Growth of Love*. London: Penguin.

Bradley, L. (2013) *The Rough Guide to Men's Health*. London: Penguin.

Bradley, M. (2008) *When Things Get Crazy with Your Teen*. New York: McGraw-Hill.

Calvert, S. (2008) "Children as Consumers: Advertising and Marketing." *Children and Electronic Media,* Vol. 18, No. 1, pp 205–234.

Canfield, J., Hanfield, M. and Kirberger, K. (1999) *Chicken Soup for the Teenage Soul.* London: Vermilion.

Carey, W. et al (1995) *Coping with Children's Temperament.* New York: Basic Books.

Carr-Gregg, M. (2005) *Surviving Adolescents.* Melbourne: Penguin Books.

———(2007) *Real Wired Child.* Melbourne: Penguin Books.

———M. (2012) *Surviving Year 12.* Melbourne: Penguin Books.

Chabon, M. (2009) *Manhood for Amateurs.* London: Fourth Estate.

Chalke, S. (2000) *The Parentalk Guide to Your Child and Sex.* London: Hodder and Stoughton.

Chapman, G. (2004) *The Five Love Languages: How to Express Heartfelt Commitment to Your Mate.* Chicago: Northfield Press.

Chopra, D. (1991) *Perfect Health.* London: Bantam Books.

Cimbalo, R. and Novell, D. (1993) "Sex Differences in Romantic Love Attitudes Among College Students." *Psychological Reports,* 73:15–18.

Cline, F. and Fay, J. (2006) *Parenting with Love and Logic: Teaching Children Responsibility.* Colorado Springs, Colorado: Pinon Press.

Comfort, A. (1974) *The Joy of Sex.* London: Quartet Press.

Cooper, G. (2013) *Be Your Own Nutritionist.* London: Short Books.

Corbett, K. (2009) *Boyhoods: Rethinking Masculinities.* New Haven: Yale University Press.

Cosgrove, P. (2010) *My Story.* Sydney: HarperCollins Australia.

Cote, J. and Levine, G. (2002) *Identity Formation, Agency and Culture.* Mahwah, New Jersey: Lawrence Erlbaum Associates.

Covey, S. (1997) *The 7 Habits of Highly Effective Families.* New York: Free Press.

———(1998) *The 7 Habits of Highly Effective Teens.* New York: Simon & Schuster.

———(2004) *The 7 Habits of Highly Effective People: Powerful Lessons in Personal Change.* New York: Free Press.

Cross, G. (2009) *Men to Boys: The Making of Modern Immaturity.* New York: Columbia University Press.

Derbyshire, D. (2009) "Social Websites Harm Children's Brains." *Daily Mail,* London, February 24.

Dion, K. K. and Dion, K. L. (1993) "Individualistic and Collectivistic Perspectives on Gender and the Cultural Context of Love and Intimacy." *Journal of Social Issues* 49(3):53–69.

Dobson, J. (2001) *Bringing up Boys: Practical Advice and Encouragement for Those Shaping the Next Generation of Men*. Carol Stream, Illinois: Tyndale House.

Dowling, J. (2005) *Young Children's Personal, Social and Emotional Development*. London: Paul Chapman.

Doyle, J. and Doyle, K. (2006) *The Problem with Pornography*. Canberra: Choicez Media: A DVD Resource.

Druckerman, P. (2012) *French Children Don't Throw Food*. London: Doubleday.

Edgette, J. (2012) *The Last Boys Picked*. New York: Berkley Books.

Einhorn, S. (2010) *The Art of Being Kind*. London: Piatkus.

Elium, D. and Elium, J. (1992) *Raising a Son: Parents and the Making of a Healthy Man*. Hillsboro, Oregon: Beyond Words.

Erikson, E. (1968) *Identity, Youth and Crisis*, New York: Norton.

Faber, A. and Mazlish, E. (2001) *How to Talk so Kids Will Listen & Listen so Kids will Talk*. London: Piccadilly Press.

Fane, O. (2013) *The Conversations: 66 Reasons to Start Talking*. London: Square Peg.

Field, T. (2002) "Violence and Touch Deprivation in Adolescents." *Adolescence*, 37, pp 735–749.

Forward, S. (1989) *Toxic Parents*. London: Bantam Books.

Fredrickson, B. and Losada, M. (2005) "Positive Affect and the Complex Dynamics of Human Flourishing." *American Psychology*, Vol. 60, No. 7, p 681.

Freegard, S. (2007) *How to Be a Happy Mum*. Netmums.com. London: Headline Publishing Group.

Gabor, D. (1983) *How to Start a Conversation and Make Friends*. New York: Simon & Schuster.

Galbraith, D. (2013) *My Son, My Son*. London: Vintage, Random House.

Gardner, H. (1983) *Frames of Mind: The Theory of Multiple Intelligences*. New York: Basic Books.

Ginott, H. (2003) *Between Parent and Child*. New York: Three Rivers Press.

Goleman, D. (1995) *Emotional Intelligence*. New York: Bantam.

Gordon, E. (1965) *Miracle on the River Kwai*. New York: Fontana Books.

Gray, J. (1992) *Men Are from Mars, Women Are from Venus*. London: Harper-Collins.

Green, C. (2004) "Letters from Exile: Observations on a Culture in Decline." *Oxford Forum*, Oxford.

Greenfield, P. (2009) "Technology and Informal Education: What is Taught, What is Learned." *Science*, Vol. 323, No. 5910, pp 61–71.

Greenfield, S. (2003) *Tomorrow's People: How 21st Century Technology is Changing the Way We Think and Feel*. London: Allen Lane.

Gurian, M. (1996) *The Wonder of Boys*. New York: Tarcher/Putnam.

Hawkes, T. F. (2001) *Boy Oh Boy*. Sydney: Pearson Education Australia.

———(2005) *Learning Leadership: A Leadership Course for Secondary Students*. Books 1–4. Sydney: The King's School.

———(2011) *Blizzard Lines*. Sydney: The King's School.

Holden, R. (2013) *Loveability*. London: Hay House.

Irvine, W. (2009) *A Guide to the Good Life: The Ancient Art of Stoic Joy*. New York: Oxford University Press.

James, O. (2007) *Affluenza*. London: Vermilion.

———(2010) *How Not to F*** Them Up*. London: Vermilion.

Jay, R. (2008) *The 10 Most Important Things You Can Do for Your Children*. London: Pearson Education.

Joffe, N. and Roberts, J. (2011) *Why Did Nobody Tell Me?* London: Mumsnet, Bloomsbury.

Kammer, J. (1995) *Good Will Toward Men*. New York: St. Martin's Press.

Karpf, A. (2006) *The Human Voice*. London: Bloomsbury.

Kasser, T. (2002) *The High Price of Materialism*. Cambridge, Massachusetts: MIT Press.

Kohn, A. (1999) *Punished by Rewards*. Boston: Houghton Mifflin.

Kottler, J. (2002) *Students Who Drive You Crazy: Succeeding with Resistant, Unmotivated and Otherwise Difficult Young People*. Thousand Oaks, California: Corwin.

Kübler-Ross, E. and Kessley, D. (2005) *On Grief and Grieving*. London: Simon & Schuster.

Lacombe, A. and Gray, J. (1998) "The Role of Gender in Adolescent Identity and Intimacy Decisions." *Journal of Youth and Adolescence*, 27 (6): 795–801.

Latta, N. (2006) *The Politically Incorrect Parenting Book*. New Zealand: Harper-Collins.

———(2009) "Confessions of a Bad Parent." *New Zealand Listener*, July 18, pp 16–22.

Leach, P. (1994) *Children First*. London: Michael Joseph.

Levêque, S. (2009) "Our Culture is Infected with Porn." *The Guardian*, April 24: www.theguardian.com/commentisfree/2009/apr/24/porn-object -protest-feminism/.

Lickona, T. (1983) *Raising Good Children*. New York: Bantam Books.

Lindemann, E. (1979) *Beyond Grief*. New York: Jason Aronson.

Lindenfield, G. (1994) *Confident Teens*. London: Thorsons, HarperCollins.

Louis, R. and Copeland, D. (1998) *How to Succeed with Women*. New York: Prentice Hall.

Mansfield, H. (2006) *Manliness*. New Haven: Yale University Press.

Maslow, A. (1954) *Motivation and Personality*. New York: Harper & Row.

Matten, G. and Goggins, A. (2012) *The Health Delusion*. London: Hay House.

McKay, B. and McKay, K. (2009) *The Art of Manliness: Classic Skills and Manners for the Modern Man*. Cincinnati, Ohio: HOW Books.

Mendoza, A. (2002) *Teenage Rampage: The Worldwide Youth Crime Phenomenon*. London: Virgin.

Messner, M. (1992) *Power at Play: Sports and the Problem of Masculinity*. London: Beacon Press.

Miedzian, M. (1992) *Boys Will Be Boys. Breaking the Link between Masculinity and Violence*. London: Virago.

Milliken, B. (1968) *Tough Love*. Old Tappan, New Jersey: Spire Books.

Mitchell, A. (2012) *The Manic Mum's Guide to Calm Parenting and Cooperative Kids*. London: Hay House.

Moir, A. and Jessel, D. (1989) *Brainsex*. London: Mandarin.

Montgomery, M. and Sorell, G. (1998) "Love and Dating Experience in Early and Middle Adolescence: Grade and Gender Comparisons." *Journal of Adolescence* 21:677–689.

Moore, M. (2008) "Dying Mother Left Letters of Advice for Young Sons." *The Telegraph*, October 8.

Moore, S., Kennedy, G., Fulonger, B. and Evers, K. (1999) "Sex, Sex-Roles and Romantic Attitudes: Finding the Balance." *Current Research in Social Psychology*, 4(3):124.

Morris, S. (1971) *Grief and How to Live with It*. London: Allen & Unwin.

Mortimer, R. and Mortimer, C. (2012) *Dear Lupin*. London: Constable & Robinson.

Mucklejohn, I. (2013) *A Dad for All Seasons*. London: Gibson Square.

Munroe, S. (1998) *Communicating with Your Teenager*. London: Piccadilly Press.

Neufeld, G. and Maté, G. (2006) *Hold onto Your Kids: Why Parents Need to Matter More than Peers*. New York: Ballantine Books.

Newbold, I. (2013) *Parenting with Balls*. London: New Holland Publishers.

Nielsen, L. (2008) "Shared Parenting: Facts and Fiction." Research Brochure, *American Coalition for Fathers and Children*, www.acfc.org.

Nikkay, J. and Furman, L. (2000) *Our Boys Speak: Adolescent Boys Write about Their Inner Lives*. New York: St. Martin's Griffin.

Palmer, S. (2007) *Detoxing Childhood. What Parents Need to Know to Raise Bright, Balanced Children*. London: Orion.

Parsons, R. (1995) *The Sixty-Minute Father*. London: Hodder and Stoughton.

———(2007) *Teenagers*. London: Hodder and Stoughton.

Pease, A. and Pease, B. (2004) *The Definitive Book of Body Language*. London: Orion.

———(2009) *The Mating Game*. London: Orion.

Phillips, A. (1993) *The Trouble with Boys*. London: Pandora.

Piaget, J. (1932) *The Moral Judgement of the Child*. New York: Free Press.

Pickhardt, C. (2007) *The Connected Father: Understanding Your Unique Role and Responsibilities During Your Child's Adolescence*. New York: Palgrave Macmillan.

———(2010) *Keys to Successful Step-Fathering*. New York: Baron's Educational Series, Inc.

Pinker, S. (2002) "Boys Will Always Be Boys." *Sunday Times*, News Review, p 3, September 22. An interview with Steven Pinker by Margarette Driscoll.

Pittman, F. (1993) "Fathers and Sons." *Psychology Today*, September 1, pp 52–54.

Plant, J. (2007) *Prostate Cancer*. London: Virgin.

Pollack, W. (1998) *Real Boys: Rescuing Our Sons from the Myths of Boyhood.* New York: Random House.

Pruett, K. (2000) *Fatherneed: Why Father Care is as Essential as Mother Care for Your Child.* New York: Free Press.

Ralston, A. (2004) *Between a Rock and a Hard Place.* New York: Atria Books.

Rao, A. and Seaton, M. (2009) *The Way of Boys: Raising Healthy Boys in a Challenging and Computer World.* New York: William Morrow.

Robertson, D. (2012) *Build Your Resilience.* London: Hodder Education.

Romanietto, J. and Bornstein, A. (2013) *Man 2.0. Engineering the Alpha.* London: Vermilion.

Rosen, C. (2007) "Virtual Friendship and the New Narcissism." *New Atlantis*, No. 17, pp 15–31.

Sapolsky, R. (2004) *Why Zebras Don't Get Ulcers.* New York: Henry Holt.

Sax, L. (2005) *Why Gender Matters.* New York: Broadway Books.

Schlessinger, L. (2000) *Parenthood by Proxy: Don't Have Them if You Won't Raise Them.* New York: HarperCollins.

Scott Peck, M. (1978) *The Road Less Travelled.* London: Random House.

Seligman, M. (2011) *Flourish: A New Understanding of Happiness and Well-being.* London: Nicholas Brealey.

Shulman, S., Levy-Shiff, R., Kedem, P. and Alon, E. (1997) "Intimate Relationships among Adolescent Romantic Partners and Same Sex Friends: Individual and Systemic Perspectives." *New Directions for Child Development*, Winter, p 78.

Sigman, A. (2007) *Remotely Controlled.* London: Vermilion.

———(2009) *The Spoilt Conversation.* London: Little, Brown Book Group.

Silverstein, O. and Rashbaum, M. (1994) *The Courage to Raise Good Men.* Melbourne: Penguin.

Simmons, J. and Curtis, J. (2009) *Can I Give Them Back Now?* London: Square Peg.

Smith, B. (1995) *Mothers and Sons.* Sydney: Allen and Unwin.

Sommers, C. (2000) *The War Against Boys: How Misguided Feminism Is Harassing Our Young Men.* New York: Simon & Schuster.

Sprecher, S. and Metts, S. (1989) "Development of the 'Romantic Beliefs Scale' and Examination of the Effects of Gender and Gender Role Orientation." *Journal of Social and Personal Relationships*, 6:387–411.

Stearns, P. (2003) *Anxious Parents: A History of Modern Child Rearing in America*. New York: University Press.

Stiffelman, S. (2012) *Parenting without Power Struggles*. London: Simon & Schuster.

Sunderland, M. (2006) *The Science of Parenting*. New York: DK.

Tallis, F. (2005) *Love Sick*. London: Century.

Tannen, D. (1990) *You Just Don't Understand: Women and Men in Conversation*. New York: Ballantine Books.

Tate, M. (2001) *Preparing Children for Success in School and Life*. Thousand Oaks, California: Corwin.

Tatelbaum, J. (1983) *The Courage to Grieve*. London: Vermilion.

Taylor, C. (2010) *Divas & Door Slammers*. London: Vermilion.

Taylor, J. (2012) *Raising Generation Tech*. Chicago: Sourcebooks.

Templar, R. (2008) *The Rules of Parenting*. Harlow, UK: Pearson Education.

Wanderer, Z. (1978) *Letting Go*. New York: Warner Books.

Ware, B. (2011) *The Top Five Regrets of the Dying*. London: Hay House.

Webb, L. (2013) *Resilience: How to Cope When Everything Around You Keeps Changing*. Chichester, West Sussex, UK: Capstone.

Wolf, T. and Franks, S. (2002) *Get Out of My Life but First Take Me and Alex into Town*. London: Profile Books.

Zoellner, M., Ybarbo, A., Moline, K. and Kilmartin, L. (2012) *Sh*tty Mum*. London: Hodder & Stoughton.

Websites

ABC Health Well-being: www.abc.net.au/health/library/stories/2007/05/10/1919866.htm

ABCD Parenting Young Adolescents: www.abcdparenting.org

About.com, Alcoholism: www.alcoholism.about.com

About.com, Death and Dying: www.dying.about.com

About.com, Parenting Teens: www.parentingteens.about.com

Action for Happiness: www.actionforhappiness.org

American Ex-Prisoners of War: www.axpow.org/stories-whopacksyourparachute.htm

American Lung Association: www.lung.org

Avert: www.avert.org/ready-sex.htm

Back Off Bully: rmetro12.skills21schools.org/BOB/

Bangladeshis Abroad: www.bangladeshisabroad.com/blog/2013/09/02/a
-voice-chapter-21-a-letter-from-a-young-dying-mother-to-her-only-son
-pp-325-330/

Better Health Channel: www.betterhealth.vic.gov.au

Bully Blocking: www.bullying.com.au

Bullying No Way!: www.bullyingnoway.com.au

Choicez Media: www.choicez.com.au

Digital Buzz: www.digitalbuzzblog.com/infographic-social-media-statistics
-for-2013/

Do Something: www.dosomething.org

Dr. Phil: www.drphil.com

DrinkWise Australia: www.drinkwise.org.au

Drug Free: www.drugfree.org

Empowering Parents: www.empoweringparents.com

eSmart Schools: www.esmartschools.org.au

Family Planning Queensland: www.fpq.com.au

Family Safe Media: www.familysafemedia.com/pornography_statistics.html

Federal Trade Commission, We Don't Serve Teens: www.dontserveteens.gov

Flipped Learning Network: www.flippedclassroom.org

Funeral Advice: www. funeraladvice.com.au

Internet Safety 101: www.internetsafety101.org/cyberbullyingstatistics.htm

Jonathan Doyle: www.jonathandoyle.co

Ken Rigby: www.kenrigby.net

Khan Academy: www.khanacademy.org

Kids Health from Nemours: www.kidshealth.org

Learning Leadership: www.traininginleadership.com

Live Science: www.livescience.com/3186-brain-food-eat-smart.html

Living Life to the Full: www.llttf.com

Making Cents: www.makingcents.com.au

Mathtrain: www.mathtrain.com

Men's Health: www.menshealth.com

Mental Help.net: www.mentalhelp.net

Mentor International: www.mentorfoundation.org

Mind Expanding Techniques: www.mind-expanding-techniques.net
/memorytypes.html

Mind: www.mind.org.uk

Model of Memory: www.cla.calpoly.edu/~cslem/101/7-C.html

Monash University, Modi: www.modi.monash.edu.au/obesity-facts-figures
/obesity-in-australia/

Money Smart Teaching: www.teaching.moneysmart.gov.au

My Out of Control Teen: myoutofcontrolteen.com

National Financial Education Council: www.financialeducatorscouncil.org

Netdoctor: www.netdoctor.co.uk

NIDA for Teens, The Scene Behind Drug Abuse: www.teens.drugabuse.gov

No Tobacco: www.notobacco.org

One Million Kids: www.onemillionkids.com.au

Parent Further: www.parentfurther.com

Parenting People: www.parentingpeople.co.uk

Parentline: www.parentline.com.au

Patch Adams: www.patchadams.org

Psychcentral: psychcentral.com/lib/2007/your-teens-search-for-identity

Quit Now, Australian Government: www.quitnow.gov.au

Raising Children Network: www.raisingchildren.net.au

Slideshare: www.slideshare.net/malpani/facts-of-life-a-talk-for-boys-on-sex
-education

Statistic Brain: www.statisticbrain.com/social-networking-statistics/

Talk with Your Kids: www.talkwithkids.org/sex.html

Tech Addiction: www.techaddiction.ca/pornography-addiction-statistics
.html

The Alannah and Madeline Foundation: www.amf.org.au

The Barefoot Investor: www.barefootinvestor.com

The Flipped Classroom: www.webanywhere.org/blog/flipped-classroom

The Kids Are All Right: www.thekidsareallright.com.au

The Mind: www.themint.org

The Royal Children's Hospital Melbourne, Center for Adolescent Health:
www.rch.org.au/cah/research/Youth_Suicide_in_Australia

ThinkQuest on tobacco and other drugs: library.thinkquest.org/19796/data
/t016.html

University of Queensland Teaching and Education Development Institute,
About Flipped Classrooms: www.uq.edu.au/tediteach/flipped-classroom
/what-is-fc.html

Visual.ly: www.visual.ly/100–social–networking–statistics–facts–2012

Web MD, Teens: teens.webmd.com/boys

Your Brain Matters: www.yourbrainmatters.org.au

Acknowledgments

Ten Conversations You Must Have With Your Son was enriched by the input of a number of parents who I saw modeling the very conversations described within this book. I found these parents inspiring and I thank them for being my mentors in the writing of this book.

A further impetus to write *Ten Conversations* came from a number of colleagues who encouraged me to translate my novel, *Blizzard Lines*, written for teenagers and young adults, into a book for parents. *Blizzard Lines* touched on some of the conversations described in this book. Set in the frozen wastes of Antarctica, the novel describes the getting of wisdom and the growth of understanding. However, the genre of *Blizzard Lines* did not allow the detail wanted by many parents who wished to transmit ancient wisdom to young minds.

The editing of *Ten Conversations* was faithfully and effectively undertaken by Bernadette Foley. The care shown in the exercise of this task was greatly appreciated.

Much support was also given by my Executive Assistant, Michelle White, whose help with proofing and layout was invaluable.

Final thanks go to my wife, Jane, for her forbearance, love and support during the hours spent writing *Ten Conversations You Must Have With Your Son*. Her wisdom permeates this book.

Tim Hawkes

I acknowledge with gratitude the permission of Pearson Education, Australia, to use extracts of my book *Boy Oh Boy* in *Ten Conversations You Must Have With Your Son*.

Index

Dr. Tim Hawkes, OAM, is the author of several books, including *Boy Oh Boy: How to Raise and Educate a Son*, the *Learning Leadership* series, and *Blizzard Lines*. He has taught in England and Australia for over 35 years and been a headmaster for much of that time.

A highly regarded educational resource, author and social commentator, Dr. Hawkes is in demand as a conference speaker around the world.

Dr. Hawkes is married and has three adult children, including a son.

For more details, go to Hawkes Eye: timhawkes.com